Administering and Managing the U.S. Food System

Administering and Managing the U.S. Food System

Revisiting Food Policy and Politics

Edited by
A. Bryce Hoflund, John C. Jones, and
Michelle C. Pautz

LEXINGTON BOOKS
Lanham • Boulder • New York • London

Published by Lexington Books
An imprint of The Rowman & Littlefield Publishing Group, Inc.
4501 Forbes Boulevard, Suite 200, Lanham, Maryland 20706
www.rowman.com

6 Tinworth Street, London SE11 5AL, United Kingdom

British Library Cataloguing in Publication Information Available

Library of Congress Cataloging-in-Publication Data Available

Names: Hoflund, A. Bryce, 1970- editor. | Jones, John C., 1982- editor. | Pautz,
    Michelle C., editor.
Title: Administering and managing the U.S. food system : revisiting food policy and
    politics / edited by A. Bryce Hoflund, John C. Jones, and Michelle C. Pautz.
Other titles: Administering and managing the United States food system
Description: Lanham : Lexington Books, [2021] | Includes bibliographical
    references and index.
Identifiers: LCCN 2021014831 (print) | LCCN 2021014832 (ebook) |
    ISBN 9781793633330 (Cloth) | ISBN 9781793633347 (ePub) Subjects: LCSH:
Public administration—Study and teaching (Higher)—United States. |
    Food supply—Government policy—United States. | Agriculture and state— United
States. | United States—Politics and government.
Classification: LCC JF1338.A3 A353 2021 (print) | LCC JF1338.A3 (ebook) |
    DDC 363.8/5610973—dc23
LC record available at https://lccn.loc.gov/2021014831
LC ebook record available at https://lccn.loc.gov/2021014832

*This volume is dedicated to the policymakers
and public servants who work tirelessly
to transform our food system.*

Contents

List of Figures and Tables

FIGURES

TABLES

Acknowledgments

This volume represents another collaboration of the three of us as we strive to engage more deeply in food systems and food policies. More specifically, we continue our efforts to help bring those conversations into public administration and to bring public administration into the area of food as we believe policy advocacy and evolution will be most successful when these areas come together. We are deeply indebted to the contributors of this volume as their research and passion help move our society forward around these topics. Their chapters are engaging, and we are grateful to each author for their willingness to partake in this project, especially in the circumstances and pressures we all face in the world today.

Additionally, we would like to acknowledge the guidance and support we received from our editor, Joseph Parry, and the rest of the team at Lexington Books. The comments and suggestions we received from the reviewers did much to improve these pages.

Each of us also wishes to express our gratitude for those individuals around us who have helped make this book possible. Bryce would like to thank John and Michelle for sharing their good humor, ongoing friendship, and unparalleled knowledge in food systems and public administration. I also wish to extend my gratitude to my husband, David Bilek, for his profound belief in my work and his unwavering patience. This book would not have been possible without the support and nurturing of my mother, Candace J. Cray, and my sister, Berkeley E. Hoflund. Finally, I would like to thank Jasper, our beloved Shetland Sheepdog, for his sweet affection. He used his herding skills to keep me on track with everything, including his dinnertime. I am fortunate and grateful beyond words to be surrounded by such wonderful individuals.

John is thankful for Bryce and Michelle's continued friendship and mentorship. I could not ask for better coauthors and partners on our quest to create more intersections for the study of the food system and public administration! I am also thankful to my dog Nym, who entered my life unexpectedly one Friday on the eve of the COVID-19 pandemic. Her unwavering affection has helped keep me sane, more or less, through these hard months of isolation and existential dread.

Michelle is thrilled to be working with Bryce and John once again on bridging public administration and food studies. In particular, I appreciate the willingness of my colleagues to include me in this project as I have learned so much from both of you and from the authors whose fascinating work here is compelling and inspiring. My deepest gratitude extends to my spouse, Steven, for his steadfast support as I embark on this and all my academic endeavors. It is not easy to put up with the kind of academic that I strive to be, yet he does so with ease, patience, and grace. Finally, our three wonderful shih tzus, Sydney, Victoria, and Mackenzie, deserve mention here because of their unconditional love and support, especially in recent months as their nap schedules have been disrupted by my more constant presence at home working. At least they have gotten more snacks.

A. Bryce Hoflund, Omaha, Nebraska
John C. Jones, Richmond, Virginia
Michelle C. Pautz, Dayton, Ohio
February 2021

Section I

INTRODUCTION AND OVERVIEW

Introduction

Setting the Table to Study Food Systems through Public Administration

A. Bryce Hoflund, John C. Jones, and Michelle C. Pautz

Food is central to the daily lives of all humans. Yet, the role that the policies and politics around food plays is increasingly more pronounced in our lives as it affects the environment, our individual and collective health, and how we provide for the needs of our most vulnerable individuals. Food also touches on many of the big questions concerning social and health science and practitioners, including questions related to sustainability, social equity, vulnerable populations, health, and how citizens, the nonprofit and the private sectors, and government agencies at all levels interact to address these issues. In a *Food Politics* blog post on March 20, 2014, Marion Nestle, the Paulette Goddard Professor of Nutrition, Food Studies, and Public Health, *Emerita,* at New York University, highlights the importance of food policy and politics when she states, "What could possibly be more democratic than food? Everyone eats."

These big questions lie at the heart of public administration. In spite of this, public administration scholars have, for the most part, neglected the study of food systems and food policy. The last symposium in *Public Administration Review* that addressed food issues was published in 1976. Since 2015, only a handful of authors appearing in *Public Administration Review* have drawn upon data from local farmers, Growing Food Connections (a federally funded research initiative to strengthen community food systems nationwide), or food policy councils (see Siddiki et al., 2015; Clark & Record, 2017; Clark, 2018), but these authors did not focus on the intersection of food policy and administration per se.

Scholarship on food studies and food systems comes from a wide ranging and diverse disciplinary background and, while this is a huge asset to the field of food studies, it is also problematic to integrate theoretical foundations as language differs and paradigms are incommensurable. Food systems scholars

3

often unintentionally draw upon public administration lenses and theories in their analysis of the food system that have entered the broader academic zeitgeist. We argue that the study of food policy and food systems should be pursued more systematically by public administration scholars and practitioners both for theoretical and practical reasons as public administration can provide a commonly scholarly language from which food scholars from other disciplines can communicate.

With the chapters in this book, we seek to break new ground in public administration and advance the language of public administration to help provide cohesion and a common foundation to propel food studies forward. Public administration is inherently multidisciplinary and well poised to help bring together the diversity of disciplinary perspectives that are essential to food studies. While there are a number of books that examine and discuss food systems issues from a variety of academic and practitioner perspectives, our review of this area demonstrates that there is a lack of volumes that examine issues at the intersection of food and public administration. This book begins to fill that deep and vast void.

Accordingly, the chapters in this book attempt to address the following key questions: What role does politics play in the development, implementation, and evaluation of food policy? What are some of the governance challenges associated with implementing food policy? What are some methods for evaluating food systems, and how effective are they? What role does the regulatory state play in the policy process? What role should it play? Are trends in the production, distribution, and consumption of food changing and, if so, how should states and localities adapt to these changes? What role does emergency management play in responding to crises that affect the food system?

The intended readership of this edited book includes academics and students in many disciplines, such as public administration, public policy, public health, economics, political science, nutrition, dietetics, food studies, and urban studies. Others who might find the book useful or interesting include public policymakers at all levels of government, public administrators who develop, implement, and evaluate food policy, and nonprofit organizations involved in food advocacy. We intended this book to serve as a supplementary, or secondary, text in undergraduate and graduate courses related to public administration, public and nonprofit management, public policy, budgeting, or food systems.

The chapters examine some of the current challenges to food systems through the lens and language of public administration as well as potential solutions to those challenges. Broadly, we hope to advance the idea that the scholarly language and various lenses of public administration, examples of which are presented herein, can serve as the common ground for food scholars from different disciplines seeking to advance their ideas beyond their own discipline. The chapters in this book examine current problems in food studies, systems, and policy as they relate to public administration and how various stakeholders are attempting to address problems in unique ways.

Chapter authors for this book came from a variety of academic disciplines, including history, environmental studies and sciences, community development and applied economics, political science, and sociology, among others. Our editing process required us to thread the needle of linking the topic of the food system through the lens of public administration. Our challenge in editing this book was to push our contributors to step slightly outside of their academic comfort zones to incorporate public administration lenses into their work. At times, this was a difficult process. However, this collective challenge, both ours and our contributors, is endemic of the current moment the subdisciplines, or subdisciplines that food systems studies finds itself. Cultivating a shared academic language that all food system scholars can use to further empower both individual and collective scholarship is very important. We hope that readers view this book as the first step toward that shared language.

We have included chapters that address essential public administration questions related to policy formulation and the role of politics in this process (section II), regulation (section III), budgeting and finance (section IV), and emergency management (section V).

In section II, "Politics and Policy," the chapters examine the role of politics and incentives in the formulation, implementation, and evaluation of food policy. We begin with a chapter by Brent Blevins that provides an overview of the history of federal agricultural activities in the United States, the history and the evolution of the farm bill, how it is written, how the bill becomes law, and the challenges facing policymakers in drafting farm policy, including a discussion of the many political and policy questions which members of Congress must address and their rationale for their decisions.

In chapter 2, Angela Babb examines the mathematics that are used to calculate the Thrifty Food Plan (a component of Supplemental Nutrition Assistance Program [SNAP]), paying particular attention to the political bias, institutional discrimination, and adverse implications for SNAP households. She argues that food policy researchers and practitioners need to investigate the mathematics underlying U.S. food policy and related programming and should pursue democratizing these calculative processes.

Chapter 3, by Kristal Jones, Daniel Tobin, Laurie Ristino, Carina Isbell, and Jake Jacobs, provides an historical overview of the Federal Crop Insurance Program and explores if and how crop insurance affects conservation practices among farmers.

Using the attempted rollback of the Healthy, Hunger-Free Kids Act of 2010 as a case study, in chapter 4, Jennifer Geist Rutledge analyzes the governance challenges associated with food policy by underlining the policy paradigms that affect food policy choices. She asks us to consider the different ways in which food paradigms have constructed food as an object, either as a product to be consumed or a tool to be used, and as such how these differing understandings of food affect policy.

In chapter 5, Amy Rosenthal, uses the public administration theory of coproduction to explore student likelihood to participate in the National School Lunch Program (NSLP) and to select and eat certain foods.

Danielle Smith, Erin Feichtinger, and Jodi Benenson, in chapter 6, maintain that current national approaches to measuring food security typically take a static approach to measuring household food insecurity and argue that these limited measures fail to capture the nuances within food insecurity, such as the different shapes hunger can take on a daily, weekly, and monthly basis, and the way social, political, and community settings may influence food insecurity. They introduce one new tool—the Together Self-Sufficiency Outcomes Matrix (TSSOM)—and demonstrate what details can be uncovered when using a multidimensional measure of food insecurity and how it can connect to policy conversations in Nebraska.

We conclude this section with chapter 7 by Rachel Emas that reminds us to keep the big picture in mind and, more specifically, urges us to examine how public administration, given its applied nature, has a central role to play in the construction of sustainability paradigms focused on equity and participative public decision-making.

In section III, we turn to an examination of the role of regulation in the policy process. We begin with chapter 8 by Xaq Frohlich in which he examines the emergence of a present-day tendency to focus on labels in food politics, characterizing it as "informationism." He uses the example of the history of U.S. Food and Drug Administration's (FDA) regulation of food labels in the second half of the twentieth century, in particular the introduction of nutrition labeling, to illustrate how and why food politics get reframed as a problem of good or bad labeling.

In chapter 9, Michael Haedicke examines the debates that surround the federal organic foods regulatory program in the United States, which is known as the National Organic Program (NOP). The chapter discusses the insights that NOP's history might offer into the growing range of food policy programs that bring together state regulators and civil society advocates for food system reform.

Finally, Nurcan Atalan-Helicke, Andrew J. Schneller, Clarivel Gonzalez, Carolyn Lois, and Helen Mebrate in chapter 10 examine, through qualitative methods, the understudied phenomenon of the seed library movement, incorporating the concerns of farmers, activists, and seed savers in the United States. This piece highlights the challenging yet important nature of establishing and maintaining a seed library for protecting biological diversity, bolstering resilience within our agri-food system, and accessing local and regionally adapted seed, especially in light of the U.S. policy framework which favors the interests of the consolidated seed industry, with federal and state laws protecting the quality of commercial seeds and plant breeders.

Section IV explores the role of budgeting and finance in addressing larger food systems questions, especially those related to the sustainability of short-term grants as well as food production. In chapter 11, Can Chen, A. Bryce Hoflund, and Carol Ebdon apply Douglas and Hartley's (2011) theoretical framework of the fly ball effect and the collaborative governance theory to understand the benefits and challenges to sustaining long-term partnerships in a short-term collaborative network. Following that, Sungho Park and Craig S. Maher synthesize policy analysis and food policy studies and provide a framework that can be used by public officials for a cost-benefit analysis of a large-scale food processing plant project. They further explore the constructed framework using the recent case of Costco's Poultry Plant in Fremont, Nebraska.

In the final section, we include chapters that explore the role emergency management plays in crises that affect the food system and the individuals involved in disasters in section V. Chapter 13 by Sheila Fleischhacker examines the role of the administrative state in the U.S. food system in addressing food insecurity and promoting healthy eating during and after humanitarian emergencies and focuses on meaningful ways for public health and public administration professionals to shape relevant research, practice, and policy in the short- and long-term, particularly for addressing food insecurity. In the final chapter, Emily MacNabb and B. J. Fletcher combine two lines of research, that of disaster research and food insecurity to tell the story of how individuals experienced food insecurity during the COVID-19 pandemic.

We conclude this book with a chapter in which we identify some of the major themes that emerged from the fourteen chapters in this book, discuss what the articles demonstrate about the intersection of food policy and politics and public administration, and pose questions and highlight future areas of research.

REFERENCES

Clark, J. K. 2018. Designing Public Participation: Managing Problem Settings and Social Equity. *Public Administration Review*, 78(3), 362–374.

Clark, J. K. & Record, M. 2017. Local Capitalism and Civic Engagement: The Potential of Locally Facing Firms. *Public Administration Review*, 77(6), 875–887.

Douglas, J. W. & Hartley, R. E. 2011. The Fly Ball Effect: A Theoretical Framework for Understanding the Impacts of Short-Term Seed Grants. *Public Budgeting & Finance, 31*(4), 74–92.

Siddiki, S. N., Carboni, J. L., Koski, C., & Sadiq, A.-A. (2015). How Policy Rules Shape the Structure and Performance of Collaborative Governance Arrangements. *Public Administration Review, 75*(4), 536–547.

Section II

POLITICS AND POLICY

Chapter 1

How the Farm Bill Underpins U.S. Nutrition Policy

Brent Blevins

A multiyear piece of legislation, the farm bill is among the most important pieces of legislation affecting every American's life—even if they are unaware of its existence. More than any other single piece of legislation, the farm bill has the largest impact on American agriculture, affecting food, fiber, and feed production in all fifty states. Though commonly referred to as a "farm" bill, it pertains to much more than the products from farms and ranches. Rather, it began as a bill to assist rural Americans during the Great Depression and has continually grown in its scope. Today, it has direct and indirect impacts on virtually every bit of food eaten by Americans, as well as American-grown and raised agriculture products distributed in other countries. The farm bill's importance stems from the certainty it provides to farmers and ranchers as they make annual decisions about production levels of commodities and livestock, commonly referred to as a "safety net," over the course of the farm bill. Guaranteed federal support helps reduce financial risk for farm and ranch operations, which in turn helps ensure that the United States has an affordable and stable food supply regardless of inclement weather, economic downturns, global pandemics, or trade disruptions—the types of events which have profound negative impacts on food systems in other countries.

To understand modern food policy in the United States, it is necessary to have a basic understanding of a farm bill, including what policy areas are addressed in the legislation, what are some of the challenges in crafting the bill, how a farm bill becomes law, how farm bill programs are implemented into law, and why agricultural groups believe a farm bill is so important to the affordability and stability of the U.S. food system. It is also important to recognize that American agriculture does not operate in a vacuum, but is subject to various international influences, including agriculture production in foreign countries and geopolitical events which, though a world away, can have profound impacts on a farmer in the Great Plains. Lastly, one must recognize that the farm bill, like all pieces of legislation passed by Congress and signed by the president, must be understood through the political considerations which influence its writing, but also understand the farm bill is ultimately implemented by dedicated public servants.

THE HISTORY OF FEDERAL AGRICULTURAL POLICY

An understanding of how modern farm bills have evolved, and the role they play in today's U.S. food system relies on a basic understanding of the history of federal agriculture policy. Federal support of agricultural activities began modestly enough in the early years of the Republic (Dupree 1986, 158). The executive branch of the federal government did not have a dedicated department addressing agricultural policy for nearly the first century of the country's existence, with President Lincoln signing legislation establishing the U.S. Department of Agriculture during the Civil War in 1862, at a time when roughly half of the country's populations lived on farms (USDA.gov n.d.). However, this department did not receive the rank of cabinet status until February 1889.

On the other hand, Congress, in part due to the outsized rural representation in early sessions, placed a greater emphasis on agricultural and rural policy. The House of Representatives created the Committee on Agriculture in 1820 with the Senate following suit in 1825. For more than a hundred years, Congress focused more on providing indirect rather than direct assistance to farm producers. An example of Congressional action included land giveaways to promote settlement and farming activities in the Louisiana Purchase and farther west. In 1862, during the midst of the Civil War, Congress passed the first of the Morrill Land-Grant Acts, which established land grant research universities through the donation of federal land to states. The act stipulated that universities established through the land grant would need to focus on serving underrepresented populations as well as promoting agricultural production and research. Other examples of Congressional legislation included the Hatch Act of 1887 and the Smith-Lever Act, which created cooperative partnerships between the federal and state governments to promote agricultural research in communities.

A shift from indirect to direct assistance to farmers and ranchers occurred during the 1930s. A combination of factors, including the reduced demand for U.S. commodities in post–World War I Europe, the onset of the Great Depression, and the Dust Bowl, produced the need for a more activist and centralized approach to federal agriculture policy. The Dust Bowl, in particular, drove this shift in policy. The Dust Bowl resulted from a lack of what are today termed "conservation practices" as well as a severe drought that resulted in improperly nourished farmland. As a result, excessive topsoil blew away, leaving farmers unable to plant new crops for extended periods. The confluence of these events resulted in Congress passing, and President Franklin D. Roosevelt signing, the Agricultural Adjustment Act of 1933—the first farm bill. The first farm bill, modest in its aims compared to contemporary bills, included provisions to reduce the production of commodities with two purposes in mind: to help farmland in the Great Plains recover after years of overproduction and to increase food prices, which would financially assist farmers across the country.

The 1933 farm bill began a process by which Congress would periodically reexamine agriculture policy. The next revision occurred in 1938 and subsequent revisions came at irregular intervals, with periods between reauthorizations ranging between one and ten years. Farm bills until the early 1970s maintained a focus on commodity supply and management while other topics of importance to rural America, such as electrification and credit programs, were addressed in separate pieces of legislation. Subsequent farm bills, however, began to grow in scope.

The Agriculture and Consumer Protection Act of 1973 was the first farm bill to expand beyond the commodity management into other policy areas. The 1973 farm bill amended and reauthorized the Food Stamp Act of 1964, laying the groundwork for additional nutrition assistance programs to be included in future farm bills. The inclusion of the Food Stamp program reauthorization was driven in part by a recognition by rural members of Congress that future farm bills would need broader support in order to pass as the population of the country became more urbanized, and there would be fewer rural members in the House, where representation is apportioned based on population.

WHAT'S IN THE FARM BILL

The farm bill is an omnibus piece legislation, which means that its scope is comprehensive and often contains many other pieces of legislation. Rather than addressing topics on a piecemeal basis through a variety of bills, Congress attempts to address issues related to agricultural, nutrition, and rural policy through one bill. This allows for the consideration of many policy provisions which either would not merit a separate piece of legislation or would otherwise not be considered as a standalone bill. Consolidating many policy topics and potential pieces of legislation in one bill also saves valuable floor time for House and Senate leadership to spend on other policy areas, such as federal spending, health care, and defense policy.

Recent farm bills have included twelve titles, or sections, many of which have little direct relation to food production, though they are important for the regions of the United States which support food production. Farm lending, forestry, renewable energy, and rural development are among the policy areas which have their own title of the larger bill. Though some of these policy areas are not directly connected to farm production, they are usually still topics of interest to rural populations. These sections are important for helping to build a coalition of support for the farm bill from groups who have no direct stake in on-farm production, such as foresters, rural banks, and electric cooperative operators. The support of these groups can help secure votes from members of Congress who would not otherwise have the incentive to support passage of a farm bill given they might not have many traditional farms in their states.

In addition to directing various areas of policy, the farm bill is also an opportunity for Congress to provide legal authority and direction to USDA. Congress reauthorizes the continued functions of existing programs at USDA and authorizes agencies to carry out new programs, which are detailed in each farm bill. Congress uses the farm bill to place limits on how much money the USDA can spend on various programs. Recent farm bills have lasted for five years and coincided with the federal fiscal year, which begins October 1st of each year and runs through September 30 of the following year. When writing a new farm bill, Congress suspends farm bills written in 1938 and 1949, which are considered "permanent law." Reverting back to this legislation would produce significant ripple effects in food markets, particularly for dairy producers, and serves as a powerful motivator for Congress to allow for the opportunity to review and revise current law based on changing market circumstances, geopolitical considerations, and policy needs.

Though several policy areas are addressed in the farm bill, commodities policy and nutrition policy tend to dominate the debate over the bill. Indeed, the first title of every recent farm bill is the Commodities title. Commodities policy includes USDA programs aimed at specific types of commodities (sugar, wheat, and soybeans) and crop insurance programs, which agricultural producers can purchase to protect against catastrophic losses resulting from natural disasters. Commodities policy, which provides revenue support for farmers who grow certain crops, has been a staple of the farm bill since 1933 and is the subject of intense lobbying by farm groups from all regions of the country. Recent farm bills have focused on creating more USDA commodities programs for producers to choose from in order to provide flexibility based on the unique needs in different regions of the country and different crops. The farm bill also establishes eligibility requirements for participation in these programs. Producers whose income exceeds a certain amount are ineligible to participate, and, correspondingly, a suburban family growing vegetables in their backyard is not eligible to participate, either.

Dairy and sugar are two commodity areas which receive a larger share of attention in the farm bill. From 1949 through 2014, U.S. dairy policy consisted of federal dairy price support to maintain a minimum level of financial support for producers of fluid milk, necessary, advocates argued, due to the perishable nature of milk. Prior to the enactment of the 2014 farm bill, U.S. House Speaker John Boehner referred to the then existing dairy program as "Soviet style" and a program proposed at the time would have engaged in supply management by restricting production in order to keep prices artificially high (Wasson and Berman 2014). The 2014 and 2018 farm bills included insurance-based provisions for dairy producers without some of the government purchase programs that had been in place in previous bills.

Sugar policy is often subject to some of the fiercest debates, pitting sugar growers versus sugar processors who purchase sugar for use in their food products. Current sugar policy includes a system of loans to producers, limits on domestic production, and restrictions on the amount of sugar which can be imported. Supporters of current sugar policy argue that the current program operates efficiently without taxpayer support due to the producers who repay these loans to USDA with interest. Additionally, supporters of existing sugar policy argue that support for domestic sugar growers is necessary in order to avoid subsidized sugar from foreign countries enter the U.S. market, putting domestic producers at a competitive disadvantage. Critics of current U.S. sugar policy allege the current program is too restrictive and does not allow new entrants into sugar production, while supporters point to the strategic importance of maintaining a domestic supply of sugar. Additionally, the program restricts imports of sugar from countries where prices are lower, thus reducing competition. Every recent farm bill debate has included attempts to reform the sugar program, yet most have failed to achieve any significant alterations.

Crop insurance has served as an important support mechanism for producers since its initial inclusion in the 1938 farm bill. Participation in the program was limited in the first decades of the program but has grown significantly in the last forty years. In 1980, the program was reconfigured to be a public-private partnership where private companies provide USDA-backed insurance policies to producers. USDA also regulates the terms between the insurance providers and the plan purchasers. Producers purchase a policy and pay a premium that is partially subsidized by USDA. Producers must then provide evidence of a verifiable loss in order to collect from their plan. The crop insurance program is a frequent target of reform attempts as Congressional critics argue the program is too expensive and provides too much support for producers. On the other hand, crop insurance supporters argue that the program plays an essential role in keeping food prices low for Americans by helping farmers to better manage risk when disaster strikes.

Nutrition policy has been a more recent inclusion in the farm bill and is largely attributable to the advent of new coalition-building strategies in Congress. Despite its past commodity-oriented focus, the farm bill's success in the face of growing debate and criticism rested on rural lawmakers' ability to bring urban lawmakers into the fold. The increasing role of nutrition policy in farm bill development began with the inclusion of a Food Stamp program reauthorization in 1973, which had previously been authorized in separate legislation beginning in 1964. Over time, additional programs were created in order to provide more targeted nutrition assistance to Americans. The level of spending on farm bill nutrition programs compared to traditional farm programs has increased dramatically over time. The Nutrition title of the 2002 farm bill accounted for 52 percent of the entire bill's spending plan, an amount which the Congressional Budget Office anticipated would reach 76 percent with the enactment of the 2018 farm bill (CBO.gov n.d.).

The largest nutrition program is the Supplemental Nutrition Assistance Program (SNAP), which until the 2008 farm bill was known as the Food Stamp program. SNAP is deemed as an appropriated entitlement—a unique status among federal programs ensuring that the program continues to be funded even if its Congressional authorization runs out—such as when Congress is unable to pass a new farm bill before its expiration. Eligibility for the program is laid out in statute and, by virtue of the program being an entitlement, anyone who meets the qualification is automatically able to benefit. Enrollment typically fluctuates with economic circumstances, and there is no limit on the amount the federal government can spend on the program. As an example, SNAP enrollment held steady in late 2019 with about 35 million enrollees (down from a prior high of 47 million in 2013). When the COVID-19 pandemic became widespread across America in the spring of 2020, enrollment jumped fewer than 37 million enrollees in February 2020 to nearly 43 million enrollees by April (USDA.gov n.d.). This rapid jump in enrollment demonstrates the program's intent to quickly respond to dire economic situations such as the high unemployment resulting from businesses closing and stay-at-home orders taking effect.

Congress can amend the eligibility for these programs and has done so incrementally in recent bills. Republicans in Congress have focused legislative efforts on tightening eligibility to ensure that participants are the neediest. The House's initial version of the 2014 farm bill was defeated on the floor in part due to the late addition of amendments restricting eligibility for SNAP, though some smaller reforms were included in the bill later signed by President Barack Obama. Beginning in 2015, then House Agriculture Committee Chairman Mike Conaway initiated a comprehensive review of

SNAP to identify potential loopholes in eligibility as well as to improve the education and training components of SNAP which are designed to help SNAP recipients obtain regular employment in order to cycle off the program. This program review informed development of the nutrition title of the 2018 U.S. House farm bill. However, Democrats on both the House and Senate Agriculture Committees successfully defeated overhauls to program eligibility and instead limited changes to modest reforms in the final version of the farm bill signed by President Donald Trump in December 2018. While Republicans have focused principally on tightening eligibility to those most in need of food assistance, Democrats have often focused their policy choices on maintaining, and in some cases, increasing program eligibility.

SNAP, while the largest program, is only one of several nutrition programs under the farm bill's purview. Beyond SNAP, additional nutrition provisions include those which incentivize the purchase of fresh fruits and vegetables. Participation in these nutrition programs is often the subject of lobbying efforts by food groups and companies who argue their products should be eligible for purchase. Examples of efforts to broaden eligibility in these programs include efforts to include new food groups, such as potatoes, in programs incentivizing healthy eating and trade associations who advocate for canned fruits and vegetables to be included in programs which encourage the consumption of fresh fruits and vegetables.

Another large nutrition program authorized by the farm bill is the Temporary Emergency Food Assistance Program (TEFAP), which allows USDA to purchase commodities such as dairy, sugar, and others and donate them to food banks for distribution to those in need. This program receives support across the spectrum of farm production groups and hunger groups because it allows commodities to go directly to food banks and other hunger programs who can distribute to those in need.

As noted earlier in this chapter, the need for increased conservation practices was a driver in the creation of the farm bill. The 1985 farm bill was the first bill to include a separate title dealing strictly with conservation policy. This title authorizes conservation programs administered by USDA which have several purposes, including idling land in order to maintain the health of the land, "working lands" programs, which provide cost-share assistance to producers to implement and maintain conservation practices which improve soil health, help reduce runoff, and preserve wildlife habitat. These conservation programs play an important role by ensuring that farmland can continue to produce food in an efficient number for an increasing domestic and global population. This title enjoys a broad level of support among a wide range of interest groups, including farm producers, water quality supporters, and wildlife groups.

Other titles address diverse topics such as trade, research, forest management, horticulture research, and renewable fuels.

HOW THE FARM BILL IS WRITTEN

Farm bills are drafted in the House and Senate Agriculture Committees, the authorizing committees with jurisdiction over agriculture and nutrition programs. The text of the bills is developed by committee staff, who work for the chair and ranking members of the committee and whose sole focus is on agricultural policy. These staffers utilize a variety of sources in drafting the bill, including the staff of the Members of the committee who hear directly from the constituents in their district or state, stakeholders, farm economists, think tanks, and academic experts. The draft legislation includes the priorities of these same groups in order to build a base of support for the bill. Farm bills are among the issue areas in Congress which have traditionally drawn bipartisan support. The fault lines for the legislation are often regional, a point which will be clarified later in the chapter.

The committees are made up of members of the House and Senate and the membership is on a proportional basis based on the partisan makeup of the chamber. As an example, if there were fifty-eight Senators elected from a party, that party would also hold approximately 58 percent of the seats on the committee and the same principle applies to the House. The chair and ranking members are responsible for hiring committee staff, professionals whose job is to oversee policy development, craft legislative proposals, and provide legislative branch oversight of USDA. These individuals come from a variety of backgrounds, including attorneys, the executive branch, advocacy groups, and academics. Unlike staffers who work directly for members of Congress, committee staff tends to be a bit older and more experienced in policy development.

The Agriculture committees tend to draw members from states or districts where agriculture is a significant economic driver. These districts and states come from across the country, but in each, Congress tends to be concentrated in the south and Midwest. When elected each term, Representatives and Senators indicate their preference for committee assignments, which often reflect the makeup of their district or state. Members accrue seniority the longer they serve on the committee, resulting in increased influence in farm policy and the ability to chair subcommittees, where much of the bill writing process occurs.

A number of traditional farm, rural, and nutrition groups attempt to ensure their priorities are included in the farm bill process. These groups range from large national organizations to small regional groups with only a handful of members. Regardless of size, these groups use many of the same tactics, including meeting with members and staff to state their priorities and advocate for specific policy outcomes. Many trade associations maintain a physical presence in Washington in order to ensure continued access to Congress and USDA. Other groups will retain a lobbyist to advocate on their behalf. All of these groups maintain relations with other members of Congress, their staff, and other groups before and during the farm bill drafting process.

The executive branch also plays a role in development of the legislation. Each administration, acting through USDA, approaches the task differently. Some administrations have offered detailed legislative proposals for consideration by Congress. Other administrations choose to let Congress develop farm bills without input. Every administration is expected to testify at hearings leading up to the farm bill. Additionally, each administration will provide technical assistance to the drafting of the legislation. Congress will submit drafted legal language to USDA and USDA will provide feedback on how the particular agency under consideration would interpret the language.

HOW THE FARM BILL BECOMES LAW

Congress begins the process of writing a new farm bill a year or two in advance of the expiration of the existing legislation. The committees of jurisdiction begin by holding hearings to allow stakeholders to voice their views about current policy and what new policy they would like to see enacted. In particular, the House Agriculture Committee often engages in field hearings, traveling across the country to hear from stakeholders. In that same vein, USDA officials will testify before committees about their execution of existing programs and answer questions from committee members about their views of the effectiveness of existing programs.

The drafting of any large piece of legislation like the farm bill first requires a determination of how much money can be spent on the bill. The House and Senate committees work with the Congressional Budget Office (CBO) to determine a "baseline"—an amount of money available to spend on existing programs based on current market conditions (Monke 2014). CBO maintains a budget baseline throughout the year and updates it based on market conditions. CBO will project how much money will be appropriated if existing law is extended and will help the committees determine whether policy changes will result in cost increases or savings. This is known as "mandatory" money and is derived from a federally run, Depression-era entity known as the Commodity Credit Corporation, which collects revenue based on taxes and fees paid by food processors. The House and Senate Agriculture Committees are known as "authorizing" committees, which means they cannot directly appropriate money from the U.S. Treasury, but they are able to set a maximum amount for the Appropriations Committees of each chamber to do so. Whether the committees are able to spend more or less can result in challenging policy decisions over how to allocate limited dollars.

When farm bill legislation is drafted and introduced in each house, typically by the chair of the House and Senate Agriculture Committees, the bill is marked up in committee, where members of the committee can offer amendments to the underlying legislation by inserting new provisions, striking provisions, or amending language in the bill. After all amendments are considered, the bill is subject to a vote. If the bill is reported out of committee favorably, meaning it receives a majority of the votes, it heads to the floor of the House and Senate where a similar process occurs among noncommittee members who offer and debate amendments. At this point, the Office of Management and Budget (OMB) will issue a Statement of Administration Policy to Congress which indicates whether OMB would recommend that the president sign or veto the bill as written. Once each house of Congress passes its version of the farm bill, the two bills go to a legislative conference where differences are negotiated by members of the House and Senate, usually on the Agriculture committees, known as a conference committee. Once a compromise version is agreed to and passed by each chamber, the bill goes to the president, who will sign or veto the legislation. Farm bills are almost always signed into law, with the exception of the 2008 farm bill. President George W. Bush vetoed the bill citing the amount of money authorized to be spent in the bill, but his veto was subsequently overturned by significant margins in both houses of Congress and was enacted into law.

Passing a farm bill has grown increasingly challenging over time. This is partly due to factors unique to agriculture policy and partly due to broader trends in lawmaking. Fewer bills have passed recent Congresses in general, in part due to a variety of factors, including the increased use of the filibuster in the Senate, increased polarization in Congress resulting in fewer bipartisan bills that are developed on a consensus basis, and less legislative activity at the committee level.

The initial versions of the 2014 and 2018 farm bills were defeated during their first attempts at passage through the full U.S. House. This is a very uncommon occurrence, as House leadership typically only brings bills with a high likelihood of passage to the floor for consideration.

The farm bill has come under increased scrutiny for the overall cost of the bill as well. The rising costs of nutrition programs, which have consumed a larger share of the bill, have elicited criticism in the face of continuous federal budget deficits since 2001. These annual deficits became a political fight in the early 2010s, which resulted in leaders of the House Agriculture Committee to agree to cut projected spending over a ten-year period by $23 billion, which resulted in less money for farm programs for the 2014 farm bill (Rogers 2011). Deficit groups have targeted the farm bill's support for production agriculture, though it has decreased in recent farm bills, believing that a market-oriented approach is more appropriate. Farm groups push back on these arguments, pointing out that agriculture production is subject to many unique circumstances which make a strictly market-oriented policy impractical and could threaten the affordability and reliability of the country's food system.

Additionally, the farm bill has drawn increased scrutiny from groups due as one of the few "must pass" bills Congress must regularly debate. Conservative groups who advocate for more free-market policies have long lobbied for Congress to reduce government interference in and support for agricultural production by reducing price support and crop insurance programs. Liberal groups have grown more interested in the farm bill due to its role in supporting many nutrition assistance programs which comprise a large part of the social safety net. Conversely, many liberal interest groups have also targeted the farm bill for not going far enough to support small farmers.

As production practices have changed across the country and more groups have stakes in the farm bill, new groups such as urban farmers and organic growers, have taken increased interest in crafting policies to support their industries. These groups have either sought inclusion in existing programs or worked to create new programs. One such recent example of this broadening farm bill audience is the inclusion of provisions in the 2014 and 2018 farm bills allowing for the research and production of hemp. The rise of the nascent hemp-growing industry in the country reflects both new entrants into agriculture as well as the needs of producers, such as tobacco growers, to transition into new crops. Additionally, transition to nascent crops such as hemp might help provide farmers the opportunity to avoid commodities more apt to be subject to trade disputes (Nierenberg 2019).

In addition to scrutiny over spending levels, increased challenges posed by trade considerations have created additional pressure points for recent Congresses when passing the farm bill. The United States is a party to numerous trade agreements and organizations such as the World Trade Organization (WTO), which brings about many obligations for policymakers. Any commodity assistance program must meet specifications laid out in these trade agreements which prohibit governments from providing support to producers that allow the sale of products more cheaply in the international market. An example of this challenge occurred during the drafting of the 2014 farm bill when cotton was dropped as a covered commodity due to a long-standing WTO complaint filed by Brazil alleging the U.S. illegally subsidized cotton production. Though the issue was addressed prior to the passage of the 2018 farm bill, it proved to be a challenge for cotton producers in the intervening years.

Farm bill drafters must also be mindful of international considerations when drafting the legislation. Foreign trade is an important source of revenue for U.S. farmers and ranchers, and unfair competition from foreign competitors can put farmers and ranchers at a disadvantage. A recent example of U.S. producers was in 2016, when the Obama Administration filed a complaint with WTO alleging that China had exceeded its allowable subsidization of its agricultural producers. The United States prevailed in the dispute, which allowed for either the United States to levy retaliatory tariffs or China to reduce its subsidies, thus making U.S. producers more competitive in the international market (Hopewell 2019).

Competing regional interests have always been a challenge in drafting a farm bill, but the differences have been exacerbated in recent years. Commodities grown in different parts of the country are often pitted against each other to secure as much funding support as possible in a shrinking pool of available resources. Different growing seasons, different climates, and different amounts of labor often mean that a single commodity program is not generalizable, thus creating competition. Additionally, the aforementioned competition for limited funding can pit groups against each other. This lack of unity among commodity groups results in a fractured coalition of farm groups who push conflicting agendas and do not speak with a unified voice, which can in turn undermine the overall success of the bill.

FROM LEGISLATION TO POLICY

Even once the farm bill has been written, debated, garnered Congressional approval, and received the president's signature, it has only reached the midpoint in the policy process. Before the legislation can start impacting the lives of everyday Americans, it has to be translated into policy. This primarily happens through the operational procedures of the USDA, which is charged with carrying out the various programs authorized in the bill.

By the time the bill is signed into law, USDA has already been examining bill text and determining what policy provisions will require new rules, what provisions will require revised rules, and what provisions do not require any form of rulemaking. USDA has limited resources to allocate to the rulemaking process and must fit into the Office of Management and Budget's unified rulemaking schedule and therefore must prioritize what rules will come first and which might require the longest time to enact. USDA soon begins issuing draft rules and begins the public comment process. It is quite common for USDA to still be in the process of rulemaking for a prior farm bill by the time Congress begins developing a new farm bill.

As USDA takes steps to implement the farm bill, Congress maintains contact with USDA officials to monitor implementation efforts and to ensure that USDA remains true to Congressional intent. When members of the House and Senate file the final negotiated bill in the House and Senate, it includes a conference report which explains why certain provisions were included and why Congress believes these provisions are necessary. This report is key in helping USDA and the public understands Congressional thinking in drafting the legislation. This report also includes nonlegislative language which directs USDA actions, though the report does not carry the force of law and can be ignored by USDA.

Within USDA, there are a number of agencies who implement the several titles of the farm bill. These agencies and offices are on the frontlines of translating legislation into action. For most Americans who receive farm loans, nutrition assistance, and other programs, visits to these offices to receive support, and better understand policy changes are how the farm bill comes to life. For example, farm producers have direct interaction with USDA through local Farm Service Agency offices which administer commodity support programs and insurance agents who are responsible for explaining and selling crop insurance policies. Other examples of community-based offices are Natural Resource Conservation Service offices which administer conservation programs, and rural development offices which help municipalities apply for loans for water systems. Additionally, nutrition programs are carried out by the states, who have discretion in how they implement these programs.

CONCLUSION

If a person wishes to understand nutrition policy in the United States, they must first have a basic understanding of what is in the farm bill, why it is written, and how it is implemented into law. The farm bill has evolved over time to reflect political, economic, and policy considerations and will continue to do so moving forward. Other pieces of legislation such as the Women, Infants, and Children program, the Food Safety Modernization Act, and the Child Nutrition Act of 1966 have outsized impact on U.S. nutrition policy. However, these laws are, to some extent, all affected by the contents of the farm bill because this bill directly affects agriculture production in the United States.

Future farm bills will face many of the same challenges Congresses have faced previously. Balancing traditional farm programs versus nutrition programs, ensuring the best use of limited dollars, deciding what new areas of policy should be included, and the ubiquitous need to reform existing programs for contemporary circumstances will continue to be challenges, particularly as the domestic and global populations continue to grow.

This chapter shows that the Farm Bill, like any other piece of legislation, requires competent public servants who can implement the intent of legislation in an administrative framework on the federal, state, and local levels. Understanding how the farm bill becomes law is important for public administrators to have a better sense for why certain provisions of the bill become law and the motivation for including them in legislation. Additionally, lawmakers have an incentive for understanding the process by which the bills they write are implemented in the months and years after becoming law. In short, understanding the farm bill process from start to finish is a key point for any policymaker considering questions of nutrition policy in the coming years.

REFERENCES

CBO.gov. "USDA's Mandatory Farm Programs—CBO's April 2018 Baseline." Accessed June 15, 2020. https://www.usda.gov/our-agency/about-usda/history.

Dupree, A. Walter. 1986. Science in the Federal Government. The Johns Hopkins University Press.

Hopewell, Kristin. 2019 "The WTO Just Ruled against China's Agricultural Subsidies. Will This Translate to a Big U.S. Win?" Washington Post, October 4, 2019. https://www.washingtonpost.com/politics/2019/03/04/wto-just-ruled-against -chinas-agricultural-subsidies-will-this-translate-big-us-win/.

Monke, Jim. "Budget Issues That Shaped the 2014 Farm Bill." April 10, 2014. Congressional Research Service. https://www.crs.gov/Reports/R42484.

Nierenberg, Amelia. 2019. "Amid Trade War, Farmers Lean on a New Crop: Hemp." New York Times, October 6, 2019. https://www.nytimes.com/2019/10/06/us/hemp -farming-trade-war.html.

Rogers, David. 2011. "Agriculture Panel Leaders Agree to Seek Cuts." Politico, October 17, 2011. https://www.politico.com/news/stories/1011/66158_Page2.html.

Rybicki, Elizabeth. 2019. "Resolving Legislative Differences in Congress: Conference Committees and Amendments Between the Houses." Congressional Research Service. https://www.crs.gov/Reports/98-696.

USDA.gov "SNAP Data Tables." Accessed January 15, 2021. https://www.fns.usda .gov/pd/supplemental-nutrition-assistance-program-snap.

USDA.gov "USDA Celebrates 150 Years." Accessed May 25, 2020. https://www.usd a.gov/our-agency/about-usda/history.

Wasson, Erick and Berman, Russell. 2014. "Boehner Confident of Victory in Dairy Fight." The Hill, January 9, 2014. https://thehill.com/policy/finance/194949-boe hner-confident-of-victory-in-farm-bill-dairy-fight.

Chapter 2

The Politics of SNAP Mathematics

Angela Babb

"By day two, my energy was very low and I was famished for hours at a time. I had difficulty concentrating at work and I was beginning to worry that I had not rationed my food appropriately for the next days. Due to significant exhaustion, I went to bed several hours earlier than usual and had to slip out of a business event early as I was light-headed from hunger."

(Kady on the Food Stamp Challenge, Hunger
Free Colorado guest blog, December 2012)

Like many public officials and anti-hunger advocates, Kady took the Food Stamp Challenge to better understand life on the Supplemental Nutrition Assistance Program (SNAP), formerly known as the Food Stamp Program. In 2012, the average benefit was $4.56 per day, so Kady spent seven days eating only as much as she could afford with $32 to stretch across the week; she started experiencing hunger by the second day. Seven years later, the average SNAP benefit was lower at $4.40 per person per day during the period of October 2018 to July 2019 (CBPP 2019). Last year Americans spent an average $165–$345 per capita on food every month (Fox 2020). Yet approximately 40 million Americans receiving food assistance through the SNAP program received an average of $125–$132 per month to supplement their food budgets.

Before subtracting eligible income and expenses, the U.S. Department of Agriculture (USDA) determines the maximum amount of food assistance that individuals and households can receive through SNAP. This maximum monthly amount for a family of four is $588 or $676, depending on the ages of children in the household; for a family of two: $383 or $403, again dependent on age; and for a family of one: $194 (USDA FNS 2020). So how are these maximum SNAP benefits determined? Who governs this calculation? And what does this process reveal about the challenges of food insecurity in the United States?

In short, these dollar limits on federal food assistance are calculated by the USDA's Center for Nutrition Policy and Promotion (CNPP). Using a computerized mathematical program, the CNPP ultimately produces the Thrifty Food Plan (TFP), which sets the maximum SNAP benefit amounts. This chapter will review the TFP calculation, data and methods used, and the public administrators of the CNPP performing this calculation. Drawing on archives, interviews with public administrators, and mathematical modeling, this chapter will review both the politics embedded in the calculation and the resulting implications for food security.

This examination of the TFP builds a case for researching the mathematics that underlie food policy and related programming, both for theoretical and practical reasons. One major goal is to demonstrate how food policy researchers and practitioners can do this work, and why it is so important. The chapter ends with thoughts on an alternative algorithm for determining SNAP benefits and a preliminary exploration of the politics and governance challenges associated with building, implementing, and maintaining a more dynamic and democratic calculation of food needs for a culturally heterogeneous population.

THE THRIFTY FOOD PLAN: AN INTRODUCTION

The first TFP was developed in 1975 in response to a lawsuit: Miriam Rodway sued the USDA in 1970 for providing insufficient food stamps to households needing assistance (USDA 1973). At the time, the USDA was calculating an Economy Food Plan on graph paper and argued that the maximum benefit was enough for a healthy diet. They resolved to develop a computerized mathematical program in Fortran that would calculate a diet at the dollar amount of the Economy Food Plan. Betty Peterkin, Judy Chassy, Bruce Gray, and Richard Kerr of the USDA's Agriculture Research Service Consumer and Food Economics Institute calculated this first diet with the help of mathematician Joseph Balintfy from the University of Massachusetts (ARS 1975). They named it the TFP, with the implication that individuals need to be "thrifty" to eat a nutritious diet on the same budget of the contested Economy Food Plan (Babb 2019).

In 1983, the calculation moved to the Consumer Nutrition Division of the USDA's Human Nutrition Information Service and was calculated by economists Richard Kerr, Betty B. Peterkin, Andrea J. Blum, and Linda E. Cleveland (Kerr et al. 1983). It was with this TFP calculation that the USDA decided to discontinue calculating a TFP budget for pregnant and nursing women. A separate report from Cleveland et al. (1983) explains that these diets were too difficult to plan, contending that modification to the current food supply would be necessary to this end.

The USDA's CNPP took on the TFP calculation in 1999. According to Rajen S. Anand, executive director of the CNPP at the time, contributors to the calculation included P. Peter Basiotis, Shanthy Bowman, Mark Lino, Myrtle Hogbin, Shirley Gerrior, Carole Davis, Alyson Escobar, and Carol Kramer-LeBlanc (USDA 1999). This team partnered with the Pennsylvania State University to develop a shopping list and two weekly menus of recipes to complement the TFP.

The CNPP calculated the TFP one last time in 2006, using the budget from the previous TFP as usual. Published in 2007, the most recent TFP report cited four economists with expertise in econometrics, Andrea Calson, P. Peter Basiotis, Mark Lino, Kenneth Hanson, and one nutritionist, WenYen Juan, as the architects of the calculation (Carlson et al. 2007). Basiotis supervised the team, and Carlson led the TFP calculations in GAMS (General Algebraic Modeling System). This 2006 food plan sets the maximum SNAP benefits today.

It has been almost fifteen years since the USDA's Center for Food Policy and Promotion revamped the TFP. Yet, the core algorithm has persisted through each TFP iteration since 1975. The calculation is revised only when substantive changes are made to the data inputs or constraints (see figure 2.1); otherwise,

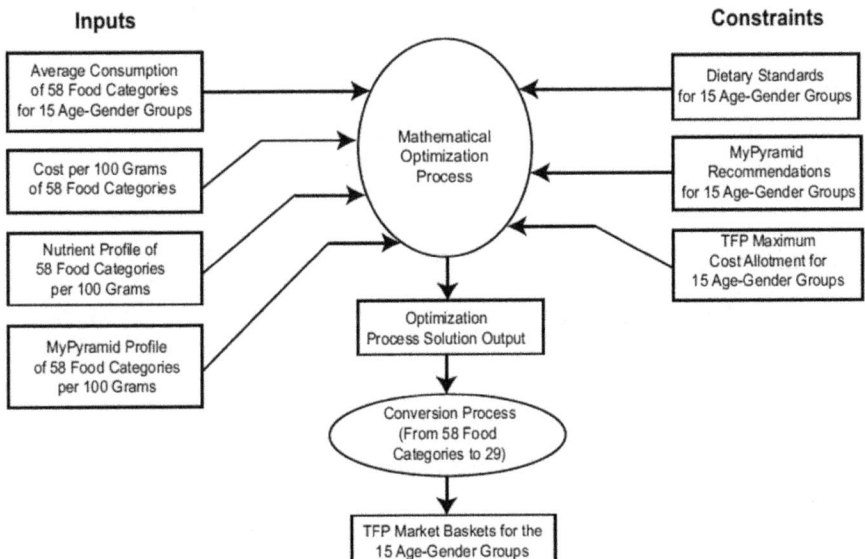

Figure 2.1   Representation of the TFP Mathematical Model. *Source*: Carlson et al. 2007, ES-3.

the commodities that make up the food plan remain static and only the cost of the TFP is updated annually to reflect inflation of the cost of foods therein.

The calculation starts with an objective function that essentially asks for seventeen age-sex groups, *Can new TFP market baskets incorporating current dietary guidance and consumption patterns be developed at the inflation-adjusted cost of the previous TFP?* (Carlson et al. 2007). The solution is then bound by constraints, such as the Recommended Dietary Allowances (RDA) and Upper Limits (UL) associated with particular vitamins and minerals, as well as the recommended daily servings of grains, vegetables, fruits, meat, and dairy, as outlined in the 2005 MyPyramid Guidelines. The solution is also bound by one very important constraint, made explicit in the main research question: cost. For each age-sex group, the daily cost of the TFP is set at the cost of the previous TFP, much like the first TFP was set at the cost of the preceding Economy Food Plan. Ultimately, the CNPP calculates a diet that meets this cost constraint, while trying to meet federal dietary and nutritional recommendations and not straying too far from current consumption behaviors. The calculation is performed in the GAMS, a software program initiated in the late 1970s by Alex Meeraus (ISMP 1976).

The ultimate output from GAMS is fifteen lists of *consumable* foods for fifteen age-sex groups. These are then translated in Statistical Analysis Software (SAS) into fifteen market baskets of *purchasable* foods for the following age-sex groups: children ages 1, 2–3, 4–5, 6–8, 9–11, females ages 12–13, 14–18, 19–50, 51–70, 71+ (see figure 2.2), and males ages 12–13, 14–18, 19–50, 51–70, and 71+.

Finally, the CNPP sums up the cost of these individual food plans for a family of four with one female 19–50, one male 19–50, one child 2–3, and one child 4–5. This becomes the standard allotment used to determine total benefits for families of varying size and ages (see figure 2.3).

The Politics of Calculating Basic Food Needs

"In terms of political pressure . . . there was nothing overt that I saw . . . it didn't mean that it wasn't there, but they pretty much let us do the technical work the way we thought was appropriate . . . and of course the mathematics are mathematics whenever it comes out."

(Member of the 2006 TFP Team, 2016 Interview)

Although he implies that the TFP mathematics are [just] mathematics and thus apolitical, we will next review the ways in which the data, methods, and results of the TFP calculation are absolutely political, and moreover, how they reflect and reinforce discrimination in our political economy of food.

Food category	Females				
	12-13 years	14-18 years	19-50 years	51-70 years	71+ years
Total pounds	**32.18**	**32.77**	**33.51**	**37.13**	**32.64**
			Pounds per week		
Grains					
Whole grain breads, rice, pasta, and pastries (including whole grain flours)	1.67	2.05	1.25	1.68	1.47
Whole grain cereals (including hot cereal mixes)	.15	.12	.38	.07	.07
Popcorn and other whole grain snacks	.02	.00	.00	.00	.00
Non-whole grain breads, cereal, rice, pasta, pies, pastries, snacks, and flours	1.13	1.47	1.14	1.33	.96
	2.96	3.64	2.77	3.08	2.50
Vegetables					
All potato products	1.00	1.68	2.05	1.75	.58
Dark-green vegetables	1.54	1.12	1.29	2.12	5.97
Orange vegetables	.62	.38	1.19	.53	.56
Canned and dry beans, lentils, and peas (legumes)	1.60	1.31	.93	1.32	1.12
Other vegetables	1.42	2.71	1.94	2.72	2.79
	6.18	7.20	7.40	8.44	11.00
Fruits					
Whole fruits	5.28	5.03	5.16	8.02	3.89
Fruit juices	.25	.47	.46	.38	.39
	5.53	5.49	5.62	8.40	4.29
Milk products					
Whole milk, yogurt, and cream	1.84	.47	.20	.21	.18
Lower fat and skim milk and lowfat yogurt	10.55	11.99	11.31	11.32	10.79
All cheese (including cheese soup and sauce)	.00	.10	.03	.00	.02
Milk drinks and milk desserts	.00	.00	.00	.00	.00
	12.40	12.56	11.53	11.53	10.99
Meat and beans					
Beef, pork, veal, lamb, and game	.27	.83	.65	.66	.70
Chicken, turkey, and game birds	.75	.02	2.67	2.57	1.74
Fish and fish products	.63	.29	.43	.45	.25
Bacon, sausages, and luncheon meats (including spreads)	.02	.01	.00	.01	.00
Nuts, nut butters, and seeds	.29	.42	.47	.42	.43
Eggs and egg mixtures	.37	.06	.06	.13	.03
	2.32	1.63	4.28	4.24	3.14
Other foods					
Table fats, oils, and salad dressings	.54	.42	.55	.48	.24
Gravies, sauces, condiments, and spices	.71	.22	.55	.13	.12
Coffee and tea	.00	.00	.02	.02	.02
Soft drinks, sodas, fruit drinks, and ades (including rice beverages)	.00	.12	.00	.06	.00
Sugars, sweets, and candies	.05	.01	.04	.03	.03
Soups (ready-to-serve and condensed)	1.48	1.49	.76	.70	.30
Soups (dry)	.00	.00	.00	.00	.00
Frozen or refrigerated entrées (including pizza, fish sticks, frozen meals)	.00	.01	.00	.00	.00
	2.78	2.26	1.91	1.43	.72

Notes: Food in as-purchased form, which includes uncooked grain products; raw, canned, and frozen vegetables; fruit juice concentrates; and meat with bones.

The numbers are rounded; thus, when summed, they may not equal the respective totals.

Figure 2.2 TFP Market Baskets for Females Age 12 and Older. *Source*: Carlson et al. 2007, ES-8.

Political Bias in the Data

When researching a mathematical calculation underlying food policy, it is first important to investigate the data used in that calculation, as well as the data or variables that are absent in the calculation. This will reveal what politics are already embedded in the building blocks of the calculation in question, as well as what values are included or excluded in the resulting policy

Official USDA Food Plans: Cost of Food at Home at Four Levels,
U.S. Average, July 2020 [1]

Age-gender groups	Weekly cost [2]				Monthly cost [2]			
	Thrifty plan	Low-cost plan	Moderate-cost plan	Liberal plan	Thrifty plan	Low-cost plan	Moderate-cost plan	Liberal plan
Individuals [3]								
Child:								
1 year	$22.90	$30.70	$34.90	$42.10	$99.10	$133.20	$151.00	$182.50
2-3 years	$25.00	$32.10	$38.40	$46.90	$108.20	$139.30	$166.50	$203.10
4-5 years	$26.30	$32.90	$41.20	$49.60	$113.80	$142.60	$178.50	$215.00
6-8 years	$33.60	$47.30	$56.20	$66.00	$145.60	$205.00	$243.70	$286.00
9-11 years	$37.90	$49.70	$65.10	$75.80	$164.10	$215.20	$282.10	$328.50
Male:								
12-13 years	$40.70	$58.00	$72.40	$85.00	$176.20	$251.20	$313.60	$368.40
14-18 years	$41.90	$58.80	$74.50	$86.20	$181.30	$254.80	$322.80	$373.40
19-50 years	$44.90	$58.20	$72.90	$89.40	$194.40	$252.30	$315.90	$387.30
51-70 years	$41.00	$55.00	$68.80	$82.80	$177.50	$238.20	$298.20	$359.00
71+ years	$41.10	$53.90	$67.20	$83.10	$178.00	$233.70	$291.30	$360.20
Female:								
12-13 years	$40.20	$49.60	$60.10	$73.60	$174.30	$214.80	$260.30	$319.10
14-18 years	$39.80	$49.60	$59.40	$73.60	$172.30	$215.10	$257.60	$318.70
19-50 years	$39.70	$50.40	$62.00	$79.00	$172.20	$218.60	$268.50	$342.30
51-70 years	$39.50	$49.20	$61.20	$73.80	$171.30	$213.00	$265.10	$319.90
71+ years	$38.60	$48.50	$60.50	$72.80	$167.10	$210.10	$262.00	$315.40
Families								
Family (Male & Female) of 2: [4]								
19-50 years	$93.00	$119.50	$148.40	$185.20	$403.20	$518.00	$642.90	$802.50
51-70 years	$88.50	$114.50	$143.00	$172.30	$383.70	$496.30	$619.60	$746.80
Family of 4:								
Couple (Male & Female), 19-50 years and children—								
2-3 and 4-5 years	$135.80	$173.70	$214.50	$264.90	$588.50	$752.70	$929.50	$1147.70
6-8 and 9-11 years	$156.10	$205.60	$256.20	$310.20	$676.20	$891.10	$1110.20	$1344.10

[1] The Food Plans represent a nutritious diet at four different cost levels. The nutritional bases of the Food Plans are the 1997-2005 Dietary Reference Intakes, 2005 Dietary Guidelines for Americans, and 2005 MyPyramid food intake recommendations. In addition to cost, differences among plans are in specific foods and quantities of foods. Another basis of the Food Plans is that all meals and snacks are prepared at home. For specific foods and quantities of foods in the Food Plans, see *Thrifty Food Plan, 2006* (2007) and *The Low-Cost, Moderate-Cost, and Liberal Food Plans, 2007* (2007). All four Food Plans are based on 2001-02 data and updated to current dollars by using the Consumer Price Index for specific food items.

[2] All costs are rounded to nearest 10 cents.

[3] The costs given are for individuals in 4-person families. For individuals in other size families, the following adjustments are suggested: 1-person—add 20 percent; 2-person—add 10 percent; 3-person—add 5 percent; 4-person—no adjustment; 5- or 6-person—subtract 5 percent; 7- (or more) person—subtract 10 percent. To calculate overall household food costs, (1) adjust food costs for each person in household and then (2) sum these adjusted food costs.

[4] Ten percent added for family size adjustment.

This file may be accessed at: https://www.fns.usda.gov/cnpp/usda-food-plans-cost-food-reports-monthly-reports.
Issued August 2020.

Figure 2.3　TFP Amounts (Maximum SNAP Benefits) for July 2020. *Source:* USDA FNS 2020.

and related programming. The TFP calculation includes several datasets to be investigated closely (recall figure 2.1):

- Dietary Guidelines for Americans (DGAs)
- MyPyramid Guidelines (replaced by USDA MyPlate)
- Food Prices (A. C. Nielsen)
- Current Consumption (NHANES)

- Food Groups (from over 6,000 foods in NHANES, condensed to 58 food groups for the calculation)

First, let us consider the DGAs. These are guidelines developed every five years by the Dietary Guidelines for Americans Committee (DGAC) and published by the secretary of the USDA and the secretary of the Department of Health and Human Services (HHS). For years, critics have called attention to the conflicts of interest present in the USDA (Schaffer 2002). Most simply, the USDA seeks to both market agricultural commodities and provide dietary guidance, and they have sometimes chosen to support the food industry over the latest science on diet and health (ibid.). According to Herman (2010), members of the DGAC have often had financial ties to major food industry actors, including the following: seven of eleven on the 2000 DGAC, eleven of thirteen on the 2005 DGAC, and at least nine of thirteen on the 2005 DGAC. These members have had financial ties to meat associations, dairy associations, dairy companies, and a sugar association, among other food industry actors and their lobbyists, which influence the final recommendations in their favor.

Similarly, consider the MyPyramid Guidelines (replaced by the USDA MyPlate in 2006) developed by the secretaries of the USDA and the HHS; these guidelines are shaped by the recommendations of the DGAC, and therefore reflect the same political bias (Nestle 2001/2007/2013). Marion Nestle's work in particular illuminates the politics around these guidelines back to the 1990s and the ways in which food industry lobbyists influence public administrators developing federal dietary guidance. Most notably, meat, dairy, and sugar lobbies have weakened dietary guidance advising limited intake of these foods (ibid.). Although meat, dairy, and sugar consumption play major roles toward prevailing chronic diseases (i.e., heart disease, type II diabetes), federal guidelines still recommend significant intake of these foods and thus do not fulfill their main purpose: to prevent chronic diseases (Herman 2010).

Food price data used in the TFP calculation comes from the Nielsen Corporation (Nielsen), formerly known as A. C. Nielsen. This is a global marketing research firm best known for their Nielsen ratings, or measurements of media audiences. The data used for the 2006 TFP calculation are 2001–2002 food prices captured by Nielsen's Homescan program. When trying to acquire updated food price data for developing an alternative calculation, Nielsen quoted approximately $9,000 per food category (personal correspondence). For context, recall that the TFP contains twenty-nine food categories. In addition to the paywall, the price data also reflect bias in the political economy of food. Namely, the U.S. Farm Bill and associated subsidies prioritize certain commodities (i.e., corn, soy, wheat, dairy, and sugar) over "specialty crops" (aka fruits and vegetables) and conventional over organic production (Imhoff 2007). Thus, relative food prices actually contradict the DGAs and MyPyramid guidelines, and cheaper forms of nutrients get prioritized in the TFP calculation (Babb 2019). Moreover, the prices do not necessarily reflect the costs of some culturally important foods, such as Halal, Kosher, organic, humanely raised, or fairly traded foods.

Current consumption data come from the National Health and Nutrition Examination Survey (NHANES). Starting in the early 1960s, NHANES became a permanent program in 1999 under supervision of the National Center for Health Statistics. Conducted biannually with a representative sample of approximately 5,000 individuals across thirty U.S. counties, NHANES consumption data used in the 2006 TFP calculation reflect what the lowest income quartile of the U.S. population was eating in 2001–2002. Some bias exists in the survey instrument itself; particularly, an unduly focus on milk consumption and use of the term "regular milk use" (CDC 2020). This language and focus on milk reflect the bias of white supremacy in a nation where people of color are significantly more likely to experience lactose intolerance (Wiley 2016; DuPuis 2002). Moreover, the data reflect discrimination in the political economy of food access. Given the history of food apartheid in the United States (Bediako 2015), the processes by which Black and Hispanic neighborhoods have been redlined and subject to demarcated devaluation (McClintock 2011), accessing the TFP or any fresh food has become especially difficult in areas commonly referred to as "food deserts" (Walker et al. 2010). Thus, the NHANES consumption data reflects inequitable access to food, yet is problematically used as a proxy for consumer preferences in the 2006 calculation (Babb 2019).

According to the supervisor of the 2006 TFP team: "the most political part is the food groups." Contradicting his statement at the beginning of this section, he claims this is where the political influence is embedded in the calculation. For the 2006 TFP, over 4,000 foods captured in the NHANES for the lowest income quartile of Americans were aggregated into just fifty-eight food groups for the calculation in GAMS, and again into twenty-nine food groups for the final diet plans reported to the public (see figure 2.2). These include four categories of grains, five categories of vegetables, two categories of fruit, four categories of milk products, six categories of meat and beans, and eight categories of other foods. There is just as much variation in milk products as there is in grains, and more variation in milk products than fruit. Interestingly, there are no actual beans listed in the meat and beans group. The list of fifty-eight food categories used in GAMS has further variation in meat and milk groups, including low-cost milk desserts, regular cost milk desserts, regular cost low-fat red meat, regular cost regular fat red meat, low-cost low-fat red meat, and low-cost regular fat red meat. Although milk is not digestible by over 25 percent of Americans, and red meat is linked to prevalent chronic dietary illnesses, these food groups get special attention in the TFP calculation and play a prominent role in the resulting market baskets.

Data that are missing from the TFP calculation reveal the values excluded from this conception of basic food needs, or what is outside the purview of public administrators calculating the TFP. In particular, the labor necessary to provision, prepare, cook, and preserve is not included in the calculation. According to Davis and You (2011), the time it takes to cook may be an even greater challenge than money when it comes to surviving on the TFP budget. Transportation to the grocery store is also excluded, ignoring the barriers to accessing food experienced by many living under food apartheid. The values of organic, humane, and fairly traded foods are excluded, as well as the values around food as social, cultural, spiritual, or anything other than a vehicle for individual nutrition. In this way, food is reduced to an apolitical commodity, while the broader social and ecological contexts necessary to sustaining a human's basic needs are excluded. This reductionism demonstrates how nutrition science data are exceptionally valued in the political arena in which SNAP legislation is negotiated.

Politics of the Methods and Administrators

After reviewing the data used in a calculation underlying food policy, the next step is to investigate how the data are used and by whom. As mentioned previously, some of the data used in the calculation are expensive, and they are combined in the GAMS program, which is also expensive and inaccessible to the general public. The basic version of this program costs $3,200, and each add-in solver costs $1,600 to $12,800 (GAMS 2020). The CNPP used both the MINOS solver and CONOPT solver for the 2006 TFP calculation, totaling at least $9,600 for anyone trying to replicate it. If one is actually able to acquire the data and the program and solvers needed to replicate the calculation, they would still find it impossible without knowing the manual adjustments made by the 2006 TFP team.

Available through a Freedom of Information Act (FOIA) request, a six-page list of programming code is necessary to replicate the 2006 TFP calculation (Babb 2019). The public administrators essentially made a series of adjustments to RDAs, ULs, and consumption thresholds to achieve partial solutions. For instance, RDAs for vitamin E and potassium were decreased sporadically across age-sex groups. Sodium levels were increased from recommended ULs to current consumption levels; for teenage females, the sodium level was adjusted to above already-problematic consumption levels. Intake of vegetables, grains, and meats were also adjusted to varying degrees across age-sex groups. The internal report that lists these adjustments does not include specific justification for most of these changes.

The mathematical translation of individual diet plans into a plan for a "standard" family of two adults (one male and one female) and two young children (ages two to three and four to five) is also problematic. This first assumes a heteronormative conception of U.S. households, excluding the needs of same-sex couples and single-parent households. Moreover, the TFP budget is insufficient for many four-person households of different compositions (DaPonte, Haviland, and Kadane 2004). For instance, a household with one adult and three teenagers would receive the same amount of SNAP benefits as this "standard" household imagined by the CNPP, though they have significantly different nutritional, dietary, and monetary needs.

Another look at the public administrators performing the TFP calculation helps to explain why the calculation continues as such. With every iteration of the TFP and especially with the most recent (and current) calculation, the TFP has been devised by economists and nutritionists, perpetuating a particular perception of food itself and basic human needs. As with most academic disciplines, consumer economics, and nutrition science involve particular training around a set of values that shape theory and practice. With economists, the dominant paradigm in recent history is the neoclassical model, which assumes that individuals have "perfect information" and make rational economic decisions that reflect their preferences (Dau-Schmidt 2001). This aligns with the ideological current of neoliberal governmentality, which views people as individual apolitical rational economic actors whose circumstances are their own fault for making irrational or noneconomic decisions (Guthman and DuPuis 2006).

In the first instance, the TFP calculation was defined during the rise of neoliberal governmentality (Foucault 2010) and as defined, demanded the inclusion (and exclusion) of particular data and expertise. This ideological context as well as the political landscape in which SNAP legislation was negotiated birthed a calculation that assumes each individual has the necessary information as well as the ability and responsibility to access the most economical diet. Combine this with the ideologically compatible field of nutrition science, and the underlying paradigm of nutritionism, which reduces food to simply a source of nutrients (Scrinis 2008), and we continue to get a TFP that defines basic food needs primarily in terms of nutrition and that assumes nutrition is the primary value for individuals choosing what to eat and feed their families. Although food is social, political, cultural, and spiritual (Hayes-Conroy and Hayes-Conroy 2016) and people need food for various reasons other than nutrition (Abbotts and Lavis 2013), and although individuals are not naturally rational economic actors (Urbina and Ruiz-Villaverde 2019), these paradigms of neoclassical economics and nutrition science continue to shape the TFP as these particular public administrators construct and perform the calculation.

IMPLICATIONS FOR POLICY, PEOPLE, AND POVERTY

"Have you ever tried the thrifty food plan diet or the budget?"

"No, not personally."

"Or the food stamp challenge or anything like that?"

"Myself?" (laughter)

"You know of anyone else that has?"

"I think we were talking about competing with my boss . . . like maybe we should follow, everybody follow the food stamp [challenge], but I mean I couldn't tell you because I'm lactose intolerant, too. I mean I would drink soy milk before I could drink dairy product. I don't like cheese (laughter) so I'm . . . I was totally out of the blue. I mean, I don't like beans either. Cause the beans give me some stomach upset."

(Member of the 2006 TFP team, 2016 interview)

The most direct and overt implications affect people in need of nutrition assistance. The 2007 TFP report explains that the market baskets do not meet recommendations for vitamin E, potassium, or sodium for most age-sex groups (Carlson et al. 2007). The authors contend that meeting these RDAs and ULs would require significant changes to consumption patterns and to manufacturing practices of the food industry. Although they do not find solutions that meet these nutritional recommendations, they still conclude that the TFP budget is enough to acquire a nutritious diet.

The TFP budget is also not enough for persons experiencing lactose intolerance (Babb et al. 2019). When fluid milk is excluded from the calculation, the TFP model will not solve at the current cost limit. When the cost constraint is removed from the calculation, a diet without fluid milk that meets the nutritional recommendations costs more than the TFP market baskets for each age-sex group. This indicates that the TFP budget and the resulting SNAP budget is insufficient for approximately 40 percent of the population participating in SNAP (ibid.). Moreover, this disproportionately impacts populations of color with higher rates of lactose intolerance.

Exclusion of food values other than nutrition imply that the TFP and SNAP budgets are not enough for households to purchase organic foods, humanely raised animal products, or fairly traded commodities. The TFP budget is also seemingly insufficient for households seeking to purchase whole grains, which are recommended for persons with type II diabetes, obesity, and cardiovascular disease (Cho et al. 2013). By not including labor or transportation, the TFP is also insufficient for persons traveling out of a food desert to buy groceries and for those persons in gentrified areas with higher costs of living (Gregor 1985). The TFP calculation and resulting SNAP benefit amounts are the same for all forty-eight contiguous U.S. states and has never accounted for the differential purchasing power of food stamps across this economic landscape. More critical analysis is needed to verify and elucidate these implications of the TFP calculation.

Indirect policy implications of the TFP calculation also merit attention. As early as 1992, the TFP calculation has been criticized for its impact on social security benefits (C-SPAN 1992). In a discussion on preserving social security and Medicare, Patricia Ruggles claimed the underlying food index (TFP) misrepresented the poverty rate of the elderly and their social security needs. A senior research associate at the Urban Institute, Ruggles first publicly explained how the 1983 TFP calculation had adverse implications for senior citizens turning sixty-five years of age. Although the caloric needs of the elderly changed drastically at the age of sixty-five under the TFP, the elderly still needed roughly the same amount of food in reality. Thus, they were experiencing a great drop in social security benefits at a time when their need persisted or even increased. With the 2006 TFP calculation, seniors aged seventy-one plus still see a significant drop in calorie and nutritional limits and an associated decrease in SNAP benefits.

Furthermore, Ruggles elucidated how medical expenses had increased particularly for the elderly, and as they were paying more for prescriptions, they were spending less than 33 percent of their income on food. Because food was no longer taking up one-third of household budgets and much more was spent on housing and healthcare, the food stamp calculation in turn was underestimating their need when one-third of their net incomes was subtracted from the maximum food stamp allotment (the TFP). This is another part of the SNAP benefit calculation that needs scrutiny in relation to social security and as it relates to the poverty threshold.

Recall that the TFP is the calculation of a maximum SNAP benefit amount that is then reduced to reach the actual SNAP benefit received by households. In particular, the maximum SNAP benefit for an individual set by the TFP is $194 per month, yet the average SNAP benefit per capita is $125 per month. This is largely the result of the Benefit Reduction Rate (BRR), which is essentially one-third of a household's net income being subtracted from the TFP budget. This BRR is based on research from the 1950s showing households spent approximately one-third of their income on food (Orshansky 1955). This same figure is used in determining the poverty threshold, which is quite literally the cost of a 1963 diet multiplied by three (U.S. Census Bureau 2017).

Although the poverty calculation is ostensibly separate from the TFP, in that the latter is based on updated consumption patterns captured in the 2001–2002 NHANES, the persistent recalculation of SNAP benefits with this underlying assumption (i.e., that households spend one-third of their income on food) does work to reinforce the outdated calculation of the poverty threshold. As long as public administrators continue performing the TFP calculation of basic food needs, assuming the mathematics are apolitical and justify the current TFP budget, they are not doing the work to rethink and recalculate a diet and food budget for setting the poverty threshold. A new valuation of basic food needs together with an updated calculation of household spending would undoubtedly increase the poverty threshold and levels of federal assistance.

A Democratic and Dynamic Alternative

Thus far, this chapter has built the case for researching data and mathematics that underlie U.S. food policy and related programming. This investigation of the TFP demonstrates how food policy researchers and practitioners can do this work, and why it is so important. However, deconstructing the TFP calculation underlying SNAP policy gets us only so far before it's time to develop an alternative. This section presents thoughts on an alternative algorithm for determining maximum SNAP benefits and the anticipated politics and governance challenges associated with creating a more dynamic and democratic calculation of food needs that can inform the SNAP program as well as the poverty threshold. Perhaps it goes without saying that one person, including this chapter's author, cannot formulate a new calculation without the aid of many.

A more democratic calculation of SNAP benefits would begin with broad public input on food needs and values. This will require a multiyear, collaborative, national research initiative. To be democratic, the data and methods used to determine benefits would need to be transparent and more accessible to public administrators outside of the CNPP. A dynamic calculation would be modifiable to reflect geographic variation in food prices and availability and the varied needs of households. Instead of only five public administrators hailing from two academic disciplines, a democratic and dynamic calculation would be performed by state and local SNAP administrators with the input of social scientists (e.g., anthropologists, geographers, sociologists, and critical race scholars) and persons with lived experiences of food insecurity.

This will require the development of new datasets (i.e., food costs, dietary recommendations), rethinking how food groups are defined and aggregated, and the incorporation of more than nutritional values of food. A democratic calculation mandates an accessible program (e.g., Excel, R) for performing the calculation. It will also require abandoning the assumption that consumption patterns reflect consumer preferences, and forgoing the assumption that individuals are rational economic actors with perfect information and laser focus on nutrition at the grocery store.

Developing an alternative TFP that is democratic and more dynamic presents new governance challenges. In particular, it will require more public administrators to be involved in the calculation and for these administrators to be more equitably engaged with the food-insecure publics they serve. This means listening and taking seriously the recommendations of individuals with lived experiences of hunger, poverty, and food insecurity. Much more broadly, this requires public administrators and American society in general to challenge the dominant undercurrent of neoliberal governmentality that shapes how America's poor are expected to eat (Fitchen 1987). The persistent blaming of the poor for their circumstances is what keeps us from truly addressing the root causes of poverty and food insecurity and from reimagining new calculations of food needs and poverty.

Some initial progress has been made toward developing an alternative calculation. Babb et al. (2019b) recently tested three alternative objective functions, finding that they are all superior to the objective function used by the USDA in the official TFP calculation. All three alternative objective functions eliminate the need for arbitrary manual adjustments, provide a better fit to consumption patterns, and are easier to interpret. They also produce less sparse diet plans, meaning more variation and in theory, more well-rounded diets. Still, there is much work to be done to develop an alternative that is democratic and dynamic enough to meet the needs of a heterogeneous population.

CONCLUSION

Since its inception in 1975, the TFP has been calculated by public administrators to set the maximum food stamp budget. In response to each calculation, scholars have shown how the TFP ignores labor time (Davis and You, 2011), geographical variations in food prices (Gregor 1985), and is not generally an accessible diet (Morris 1990; Crockett et al. 1992; Chung and Myers 1999; Hendrickson, Smith, and Eikenberry 2006; Jetter and Cassady 2006; Yaktine and Caswell 2014; Zilliak 2016). The calculation is undemocratic and depoliticizes the food system in which SNAP households are situated, ultimately reproducing a budget inadequate for many SNAP program participants (Babb 2019).

Critical attention to the TFP calculation illuminates how mathematics underlying U.S. food policy can be deconstructed to better understand institutional discrimination and society's major challenges. By uncovering the political bias of the TFP calculation and public administrators performing the calculation, institutional discrimination is laid bare for the public to confront and hopefully to change. In this particular example, and likely in other food policy mathematics, the profit-seeking influence of the food industry combines with the ideologies of nutritionism, neoclassical economics, and neoliberal governmentality in a federal calculation that uniquely impacts the American population, arguably perpetuating the conditions of poverty and food insecurity that the SNAP program is intended to mitigate.

Mathematics are political—data, methods, and people are all shaped by political bias—and this chapter illuminates one example in food policy and the associated role of public administrators. It is urgent now as we confront the major societal issues of white supremacy, patriarchy, and climate change that we reimagine our food system. Given that the definition of poverty and levels of food assistance are based on the TFP, it is paramount that we interrogate and reimagine this powerful calculation, and that we never assume the mathematics underlying food policy or the public administrators performing the mathematics are apolitical.

Democratizing this calculation comes with a host of governance challenges for public administrators, yet failing to embrace and confront these challenges will only perpetuate a discriminatory calculation that reinforces inequity, poverty, and food insecurity. The current SNAP budget is simply not enough for millions of households trying to provision adequate food. Developing an alternative will require more public administrators to get involved in the calculative process and to collaborate with a broad range of social scientists and persons with lived experience of hunger to interrogate the underlying assumptions and their implications, and to develop a new valuation of food that is healthful, sustainable, and culturally appropriate for all Americans.

REFERENCES

Abbots, Emma-Jayne, and Anna Lavis. 2013. *Why We Eat, How We Eat: Contemporary Encounters between Foods and Bodies*. Ashgate Publishing, Ltd.

Babb, Angela M. 2019. "America's 'Thrifty Food Plan': Hunger, Mathematics, and the Valuation of Nutrition Assistance." *Annals of the American Association of Geographers*, DOI: 10.1080/24694452.2019.1664889.

Babb, Angela M., Julie Wasserman , Daniel C. Knudsen and Stephen Lalevich, 2019a. "An Examination of Heterogeneous Dietary Needs within the Framework of the Thrifty Food Plan." *Ecology of Food and Nutrition* 58(3): 236–246. DOI: 10.1080/03670244.2019.1598978.

Babb, Angela M., Daniel C. Knudsen and Scott Robeson. 2019b. "A Critique of the Objective Function Utilized in Calculating the Thrifty Food Plan." *PLOS One*. https://doi.org/10.1371/journal.pone.0219895.

Bediako, Tracy. 2015. "Food Apartheid: The Silent Killer in the Black Community." *Atlanta Black Star*. June 16.

C-SPAN. 1992. "Social Security: The Inter-Generational Compact," January 27, 1992.

Carlson A., Lino, M., Juan, W-Y., Hanson, K., and P.P. Basiotis. 2007. *Thrifty Food Plan, 2006.* (CNPP-19). U.S. Department of Agriculture, Center for Nutrition Policy and Promotion.

CBPP. 2019. A Quick Guide to SNAP Eligibility and Benefits. https://www.cbpp.org /research/food-assistance/a-quick-guide-to-snap-eligibility-and-benefits#:~:text =The%20U.S.%20Department%20of%20Agriculture,household%20and%20%24 132%20per%20person.

CDC. 2020, http://www.cdc.gov/nchs/nhanes/about_nhanes.htm

Cho, S.S., L. Qi , G. Fahey, and D.M. Klurfield. 2013. "Consumption of Cereal Fiber, Mixtures of Whole Grains and Bran, and Whole Grains and Risk Reduction in Type 2 Diabetes, Obesity, and Cardiovascular Disease." *The American Journal of Clinical Nutrition.* 98(2): 594–619, https://doi.org/10.3945/ajcn.113.067629.

Cleveland, Linda E., et al. 1983. "Recommended Dietary Allowances as Standards for Family Food Plans." *Journal of Nutrition Education* 15(1): 8–14.

Chung, C., and S. L. Myers. (1999). "Do the Poor Pay More for Food? An Analysis of Grocery Store Availability and Food Price Disparities." *Journal of Consumer Affairs* 33(2), 276–296.

Crockett, E. G., K. L. Clancy, and J. Bowering. 1992. "Comparing the Cost of a Thrifty Food Plan Market Basket in Three Areas of New York State." *Journal of Nutrition Education* 24(1), 71S–78S.

DaPonte, B.O., A. Haviland , and J.B. Kadane. 2004. "To What Degree Does Food Assistance Help Poor Households Acquire Enough Food?" *Journal of Poverty* 8(2): 63–87.

Dau-Schmidt, K. 2001. "The Neoclassical Model." *International Encyclopedia of the Social & Behavioral Sciences*, 8452–8457. https://www.sciencedirect.com/science /article/pii/B0080430767029259.

Davis, G. C., and W. You. 2011. "Not Enough Money or Not Enough Time to Satisfy the Thrifty Food Plan? A Cost Difference Approach for Estimating a Money–Time Threshold. *Food Policy* 36(2), 101–107.

DuPuis, E. Melanie. 2002. *Nature's Perfect Food: How Milk Became America's Drink.* NYU Press.

Foucault, M. 2010. The Birth of Biopolitics: Lectures at the College De France, 1978—1979 (Lectures at the College De France).

Fox Business. 2020. "What Is the Average Grocery Bill for One Person?" https:// www.foxbusiness.com/lifestyle/what-is-the-average-grocery-bill-for-one-person.

GAMS. 2020. https://www.gams.com/sales/pricing_regular/.

Gregor, J. 1985. "A Review of The Thrifty Food Plan and its Use in the Food Stamp Program." *Subcommittee on Domestic Marketing, Consumer Relations, and Nutrition of the Committee on Agriculture US House of Representatives, Federal Register* H162–7.

Guthman, J., and DuPuis, M. 2006. "Embodying Neoliberalism: Economy, Culture, and the Politics of Fat." *Environment and Planning D: Society and Space* 24(3): 427–448.

Hayes-Conroy, Jessica, and Allison Hayes-Conroy. 2014. *Doing Nutrition Differently: Critical Approaches to Diet and Dietary Intervention.* Ashgate Publishing, Ltd.

Hendrickson, D., C. Smith , and N. Eikenberry. 2006. "Fruit and Vegetable Access in Four Low-income Food Deserts Communities in Minnesota." *Agriculture and Human Values* 23(3): 371–383.

Herman, J. 2010. "Saving US Dietary Advice from Conflicts of Interest." *Food & Drug Law Journal* 65: 285.

Hunger Free Colorado. 2012. https://blog.hungerfreecolorado.org/food-assistance -program/snap-challenge-my-week-with-only-4–56-per-day-for-groceries/.

Jetter, K. M., and D. L. Cassady. 2006. "The Availability and Cost of Healthier Food Alternatives." *American Journal of Preventive Medicine* 30(1): 38–44.

Kerr et al. 1983. *USDA 1983 Thrifty Food Plan.* https://fns-prod.azureedge.net/sites/ default/files/usda_food_plans_cost_of_food/TFP2006Report.pdf.

Meeraus, A. 1976. "Toward a General Algebraic Modelling System." *International Symposium on Mathematical Programming.* Budapest, Hungary. p. 185.

Morris, P. M. 1990. *Higher Prices, Fewer Choices: Shopping for Food in Rural America.* https://fns-prod.azureedge.net/sites/default/files/media/file/Costof FoodJul2020.pdf.

Nestle, Marion. 2013. *Food Politics: How the Food Industry Influences Nutrition and Health.* Vol. 3. University of California Press.

Orshansky, M. "Food Consumption and Dietary Levels of Households in the United States: Some Highlights from the Household Food Consumption Survey, Spring 1955." ARS: 62–6.

Rodway v. United States Department of Agriculture, 482F.2d 722 (1973).

Schaffer, Emily J. 2002. "Is the Fox Guarding the Henhouse? Who makes the Rules in American Nutrition Policy?" *Food & Drug Law Journal* 57: 371, 380.

Urbina, D.A. and A. Ruiz-Villaverde. 2019. "A Critical Review of Homo Economicus from Five Approaches." *The American Journal of Economics and Sociology* 78(10): 63–93.

U.S. Census Bureau. 2017. https://www.census.gov/content/dam/Census/library/ visualizations/2017/demo/poverty_measure-how.pdf.

USDA Center for Nutrition Policy and Promotion. 1999. *The Thrifty Food Plan, 1999 Administrative Report.* CNPP-7.

USDA Food and Nutrition Service. 2020. https://www.fns.usda.gov/cnpp/usda-food- plans-cost-food-reports-monthly-reports.

Wiley, Andrea. 2016. *Re-imagining Milk: Cultural and Biological Perspectives.* Routledge: New York.

Yaktine, A. L., and J. A. Caswell. (2014). SNAP Benefits: Can an Adequate Benefit Be Defined? *Advances in Nutrition: An International Review Journal* 5(1): 21–26.

Ziliak, J. P. 2016. *Modernizing SNAP Benefits.* Policy Proposal, 6.

Chapter 3

The Role of Crop Insurance in Shaping Production Trends and Environmental Outcomes in the U.S. Agri-Food System

Kristal Jones, Daniel Tobin, Laurie Ristino,
Carina Isbell, and Jake Jacobs

INTRODUCTION

This chapter explores the relationships between agricultural production and the Federal Crop Insurance Program (FCIP), the largest component of the U.S. farm safety net, which provides risk protection and support for U.S. farmers (Shields 2015). The FCIP is a policy mechanism that was originally authorized in the 1938 Agriculture Adjustment Act, but enrollment in and impacts of the FCIP have expanded with policy changes that have occurred since the 1980s. Initially established as a response to the Great Depression and the Dust Bowl, the FCIP has evolved into a complicated public-private partnership that constitutes nearly 10 percent of 2018 Farm Bill outlays. The FCIP's central role as a risk management tool has ramifications for environmental outcomes and the resilience of the U.S. agri-food system overall. Yet, despite the research attention that the FCIP and its consequences have received, uncertainty still exists regarding how crop insurance participation relates to other agricultural management decisions that impact the environment and productivity over the long term.

This chapter utilizes data from U.S. Census of Agriculture, gathered and reported by the National Agricultural Statistics Service (NASS) of the U.S. Department of Agriculture (USDA), to explore relationships between the FCIP and agricultural management decisions. Specifically, we analyze if and how participation in the FCIP relates to conservation practices and input intensification as proxies for environmental outcomes. To frame this analysis, we first provide a brief overview of the history of crop insurance, the policy mechanisms used to adapt the program over the course of the twentieth and early twenty-first centuries, and recent literature regarding the effects of FCIP programs on agricultural production strategies and their environmental outcomes. Next, we present the methods used to conduct our analysis, followed by the findings and discussion of how our results illuminate the influence of the FCIP on agricultural management practices and ultimately environmental outcomes, as well as potential policy implications.

BACKGROUND

History, Policy, Adoption

Agriculture as an economic sector is uniquely vulnerable to both weather and to volatility in global commodities markets. In response to these vulnerabilities, the federal government has adopted different policies to help farmers manage their unique production risks since the Great Depression era (Shields 2015). The current FCIP is the latest policy variant in what is commonly known as the "farm safety net," which has experienced several fundamental changes since its creation in 1939. What began as a program to help farmers recover from the Dust Bowl now constitutes the second-largest title under the U.S. Farm Bill and commands nearly 10 percent of Farm Bill funding (Rosa 2018). Despite its history, the dominance of the FCIP as the primary farm safety net has occurred only since the 1990s, by way of a series of substantial policy changes seeking to incentivize higher levels of participation among farmers in the program (Coble and Barnett 2013).

Before the 1990s, crop insurance at its height only achieved 25 percent coverage of eligible areas and was considered a failing program (Glauber 2013). In contrast, today an estimated 85 percent of all major crops are insured under the program (Shields 2015), with participation increasing by 77 percent between 2000 and 2013 alone (Weber, Key, and O'Donoghue 2016). The FCIP owes its dominance in U.S. agri-food policy today to decisions made by policymakers in the 1980s which sought to decrease the role of ad hoc disaster assistance, a one-time payment given to farmers after a disaster that was widely unpopular due to its expense as well as concern that the policy encouraged agricultural expansion into high-risk areas (Schoengold, Ding, and Headlee 2015; Glauber 2013). The Federal Crop Insurance Act of 1980 (FCIA) more prominently engaged the private sector in the structure and function of the FCIP, transforming the program into a public-private partnership. Specifically, the legislation authorized the federal government, through the USDA's Risk Management Agency (RMA), to partner with private companies to sell and service FCIP policies.

The FCIA also introduced subsidies both to insurers for their administrative and operating costs and to farmers for policy premium costs (Coble and Barnett 2013).

Initially, the modest premium subsidies outlined in the FCIA, with 30 percent of premiums paid by the federal government for policies that cover 65 percent of possible losses by producers, did little to induce a significant jump in participation in the FCIP (Wright 2014). Consequently, Congress amended the FCIA through the Federal Crop Insurance Reform Act of 1994 and subsequently the Agricultural Risk Protection Act (ARPA) of 2000 to increase the federal government's premium subsidies, especially for higher coverage levels, resulting in today's widespread adoption rates (Babcock and Hart 2005; Weber, Key, and O'Donoghue 2016). The average premium subsidy paid by the federal government was 62 percent of the total cost from 2008 to 2017 (Rosa 2018).

Despite Congress's attempt to address the publicly unpopular disaster and direct payment policies by shifting to crop insurance, the efficacy and cost-effectiveness of the FCIP is a topic of continued inquiry. One critique is whether crop insurance premium subsidies simply bolster farm income rather than address acute, unexpected losses (Coble and Barnett 2013; Wright 2014). Commenters across the political spectrum have also criticized the fact that the bulk of FCIP payouts are skewed toward farms making $500,000 or more a year (McFadden and Hoppe 2017). Although most farmers generally agree that government programs such as the FCIP are essential tools for risk management and maintain faith in the FCIP's ability to protect them against risk (Sherrick et al. 2004; Arbuckle et al. 2014; Gardezi and Arbuckle 2019), participation rates in the FCIP vary regionally. Specifically, states with large farms and a high degree of commodity production, including corn, soy, and wheat, reap the greatest benefits (Lusk 2016). In contrast, producers and states focused on specialty crop production (which constitute only 17 percent of total crop insurance liability), such as vegetable and fruit producers in the Western and Northeastern U.S., are less likely to utilize the program (Lusk 2016; Rosa and Johnson 2019).

Crop Insurance and Agricultural Production Practices

Among the most critical debates related to the FCIP are the effects of crop insurance on environmental quality. Particularly, since the 1990s, various commentators have questioned whether crop insurance incentivizes cropland expansion into fragile areas and/or promotes other risky planting and management practices (high levels of intensified irrigation water use, fertilizer and chemical application, etc.) that can negatively affect soil health, water quality, and biodiversity (Goodwin and Smith 2003; Mishra et al. 2005;

O'Connor 2013; Schoengold, Ding, and Headlee 2015; Deryugina and Konar 2017). Some argue that crop insurance acts as a disincentive to utilize best conservation practices, and also may lead to "moral hazard," a situation in which farmers deliberately take on more risky production strategies in order to increase expected returns from indemnity payments (Schoengold, Ding, and Headlee 2015).

Public concerns about the environmental implications of crop insurance intensified after the 1996 Farm Bill decoupled eligibility for premium subsidies from Conservation Compliance guidelines, which set minimum conservation requirements for coverage on highly erodible cropland and wetlands (O'Connor 2013; Claassen et al. 2017). Focusing on the steps farmers must take to protect highly erodible land and wetlands, Conservation Compliance and crop insurance premium subsidies were relinked under the 2014 Farm Bill, but uncertainty still exists whether this change is enough to incentivize adequate conservation stewardship (Claassen et al. 2017).

The potential environmental impacts of crop insurance are extensive. According to National Crop Insurance Services (2020), more than 370 million acres of farmland were enrolled through the FCIP in 2019. The majority of corn and soy, the United States' largest commodity crops, are covered under the FCIP at 87 percent and 88 percent of total acreage, respectively (USDA ERS 2018). Notably, of the eleven major U.S. crops, corn and soy account for more than half of all pesticides used (USDA ERS 2019), with herbicides accounting for the largest portion of overall pesticide use (Osteen and Fernandez-Cornejo 2016). Since 1960, total commercial fertilizer use has also grown rapidly, particularly nitrogen fertilizer, which increases yields but can also significantly disrupt the nitrogen cycle with attendant serious environmental consequences (Fields 2004; USDA ERS 2019). Corn, cotton, soybeans, and wheat account for 60 percent of fertilizer used in the United States, with corn accounting for 40 percent of total fertilizer use alone (Daberkow and Huang 2006).

The growth of the FCIP has resulted in a system in which many producers are highly reliant on crop insurance as their primary short-term risk management strategy (Mase, Gramig, and Prokopy 2017). Consequently, it has been speculated that subsidized crop insurance could become a disincentive to adopt other long-term risk management methods such as diversifying crop production or adopting conservation and low-input production practices (Yu and Sumner 2018). Additionally, conservation beyond the basic requirements of Conservation Compliance is still currently supplemental to crop insurance, rather than integral to a diversified risk management strategy (Beckie et al. 2019). That is, crop insurance and conservation policies are not currently designed to work together to achieve sustainable risk management. As such, many studies in the last few decades have sought to examine the relationship between the FCIP and conservation, with many finding that, at least to some degree, the FCIP results in negative environmental outcomes (Horowitz and Lichtenberg 1993; Deal 2004; Miao, Hennessy, and Feng 2014; Claassen, Langpap, and Wu 2017).

Still, gaps and inconsistencies among these studies indicate further investigation into the relationship among the FCIP, conservation decisions, and environmental outcomes are warranted. For example, while crop insurance adoption has been associated with acreage expansion in areas that receive the highest indemnities, specifically Central, Northern, and Southern Plain areas (Young, Vandeveer, and Schnepf 2001), some studies do not find strong support for this trend (Claassen, Langpap, and Wu 2017). In terms of the effect of crop insurance on soil erosion, the findings appear to be context-specific. Soil erosion outcomes are highly dependent on crop type, with insured corn resulting in greater soil erosion and insured wheat resulting in decreased soil erosion (Deal 2004). Similarly, another study that focused on parts of the Plains found that adverse environmental impacts such as wind erosion and total nitrogen loss greatly differ depending on region (Walters et al. 2012). Finally, evidence of crop insurance's impact on chemical usage ranges from crop insurance being beneficial (decreasing usage) (Smith and Goodwin, 1996; Mishra et al. 2005) to detrimental (increasing usage) (Horowitz and Lichtenberg 1993; Plastina 2019). What the divergence in the literature indicates is that the effects of the FCIP on environmental outcomes and conservation practices are still generally poorly understood, which perhaps contributes to the federal government's slow progress in both aligning the FCIP with conservation policies to improve environmental outcomes, and taking a more holistic approach to risk assessment to include planting and conservation practices, soil type, and other risk factors.

METHODS

Research Objectives

We draw on existing data to explore relationships between participation in the FCIP, other federal conservation programs, and agricultural management practices. This study is guided by three objectives: (i) Determine if and how federal agricultural payments, with emphasis on crop insurance, associate with farmers' management strategies (conservation-oriented or input-intensive); (ii) Explore if and how these relationships vary across time (2007–2017); and (iii) Provide a regional description of where agricultural payments and types of practices are most prominent.

Data Sources

We analyzed data from the past three national Censuses of Agriculture (USDA 2007, 2012, 2017a), gathered by USDA NASS. Data are gathered from individual producers, who are asked to complete detailed questionnaires about their operations, demographics, production practices and outcomes, and engagement with a variety of federal policies and programs. Data are then aggregated and estimated at the county, state, watershed, regional, and national levels. For this analysis, we focused at the county level, as the finest resolution for which most of the production practices data are available. All data were downloaded from the NASS QuickStats portal in summer 2020.

To explore variation in relationships between different types of production and federal agricultural policies and programs, we identified several variables that represent two distinct categories of production practices: conservation-oriented practices, which primarily consist of farming practices related to soil health and erosion management, and input-intensive practices, generally represented by the application of external synthetic inputs. For insight into the effects of federal payments and subsidies, we considered two categories that the USDA NASS (2017b) measures: conservation payments and other federal payments. Though the latter includes additional types of payments aside from insurance, crop insurance payments constitute the majority of dollars in this category. Incorporating both conservation and other federal payments into our analysis acknowledges that there may be other federal payment programs (e.g., conservation payments) that help explain the prominence of particular production strategies in specific geographic areas. All but two of the conservation-oriented practice variables are available at the county level only for the most recent Census of Agriculture (2017). Thus, while we consider relationships between federal payments and input-intensive agriculture across all three censuses, consideration of conservation-oriented agriculture is included only in 2017. In addition, we also include several covariates to better account for the effect of different types of payments on production practices. Table 3.1 provides details about each data item directly acquired from NASS, and how each was used to calculate the final set of variables used in the analysis presented in this chapter.

Data Analysis

Data analysis consisted of simple linear regression models, testing a set of predictor variables and covariates for their relationships with each of several dependent variables that represent two types of agricultural practices: conservation-oriented and input-intensive practices. County is the unit of analysis for models, and all data were scaled to per acre, per dollar, or per operation to allow for comparisons across counties. After calculating all final variables (as

Table 3.1   Census of Agriculture Variables Used in Multivariate Regression

Variable name (units)	Numerator	Denominator
Independent variables		
Federal conservation payments	Conservation payments[b]	Agricultural acres[a]
Other federal payments	Government payments[b]	Agricultural acres[a]
Acres insured	Acres insured	Agricultural acres[a]
Covariates		
Average size of operation	Agricultural acres[a]	Total operations
Net income	Net farm income	Agricultural acres[a]
Average age principal producer	n.a.	n.a.
Off-farm labor	Principal producers off-farm >200 days	Total principal producers
Conservation-oriented production practices		
Conservation tillage	Area under conservation tillage	Acres with tillage reported
No tillage	Area under no till	Acres with tillage reported
Organic fertilizer use	Area with organic fertilizer use	Acres with fertilization reported
Manure fertilizer use	Area with manure fertilizer use	Acres with fertilization reported
Cover crop use	Area under cover crops	Cropland area
Agroforestry use	Operations using agroforestry	Total operations
Input-intensive production practices		
Cropland expansion	Cropland area in 2017– in 2007	Cropland area in 2007
Fertilizer use	Acres with fertilization reported	Agricultural acres[a]
Herbicide use	Acres with herbicide reported	Agricultural acres[a]
Insecticide use	Acres with insecticide reported	Agricultural acres[a]

Source: All data were downloaded at the county resolution from NASS (USDA 2007; 2012; 2017a).
Note: [a] Sum of Cropland, Pastureland, Woodland and Other Ag land (exclusive categories)
[b] See Section 5 (page 18) of the 2017 Census of Agriculture Report Form Guide (USDA NASS 2017b) for details about which payments are included in each category.

listed in table 3.1), dependent variables were tested for skewness and kurtosis, and extreme outlier values converted to missing data, to ensure skewness of +/– 1 and kurtosis of +/– 3. Distributions of independent variables were also considered and a few extreme outliers were converted to missing data.

Linear regression models were specified as a set of independent variables regressed on each of several dependent variables. Each model was refined using both R^2 and adjusted R^2 to ensure that the inclusion of additional explanatory variables improved model fit in a specific and significant way. Regression diagnostic plots were used to explore whether the assumptions of linear regression were met by the models, and in a few models, extreme outlier cases were removed to improve overall model fit and diagnostics. Each model was also checked for multicollinearity among predictors using a variance inflation factor (VIF) test, and all VIF values across all models were below 2. Results are presented in tables 3.2 and 3.3 using unstandardized regression coefficients and *p* values. All data cleaning and analysis were conducted using RStudio (R Core Team 2018).

Limitations

As with any analysis relying on secondary data, the findings are limited to the data available. As noted earlier, while indicators for input-intensive agriculture exist across all three censuses, relevant data for conservation-oriented practices were only available for 2017, limiting comparisons between the two over time. Although crop insurance payments constitute the majority of payments reported by NASS in the other federal payments category, we acknowledge that insurance payments do not account for the entirety of that variable's effect on production practices. Relevant data over longer periods of time (pre-2007) were also limited in their availability, preventing the ability to track trends as changes in policy occurred over the last eighty years.

RESULTS

Our analysis begins by focusing on the relationships between government payments and production practices in 2017, the year that the available data allow for the inclusion of both conservation-oriented and input-intensive practices. As displayed in table 3.2, a strong correlation exists between each of the input-intensive indicators and nonconservation federal payments ("other payments"), a proxy for crop insurance payments. Similarly, higher proportions of acres treated with fertilizer, herbicide, and pesticide in a county have strong and statistically significant relationships with the proportion of agricultural acres covered by crop insurance. Crop insurance and percentage of insured acres constitute the most explanatory power in the three models predicting herbicide use ($R^2 = 0.93$), fertilizer use ($R^2 = 0.81$), and insecticide use ($R^2 = 0.62$).

   As shown in table 3.2, higher proportions of insured agricultural acres in a county have statistically significantly lower rates of all conservation-oriented practices other than conservation tillage, a common strategy to reduce soil erosion that is included in Conservation Compliance. Counties with higher conservation payments (measured in dollars per acre) have statistically significantly higher proportions of acres under both conservation tillage and no-tillage practices. Furthermore, conservation payments are three times as

Table 3.2 Multivariate Regression Results for Relationships between Production Practices (Conservation-oriented and Input-intensive) and Federal Programs in 2017

| | Independent Variables | | | | | | | |
Dependent variables	Average Operation Size (acres)	Net Ag Income ($/acre)	Federal Conservation Payments ($/acre)	Other Federal Payments ($/acre)	Acres Insured (Percent of total acres)	Average Age of Producer (Years)	Off-farm Labor (Percent of Producers)	R^2
Conservation-oriented practices								
Conservation till (% tilled acres)		−0.004*	0.461***	0.144***	0.207***		−0.203***	0.20
No till (% tilled acres)	0.002**	0.007*	0.469**		−0.149***		0.541***	0.04
Organic fertilizer (% fertilized acres)	−0.001*	0.001***	−0.023**	−0.011***	−0.017***	−0.035*	−0.006	0.22
Manure fertilizer (% fertilized acres)	−0.002***	0.018***	0.055	−0.119***	−0.175***	−0.781***	−0.161***	0.35
Cover crops (% cropland acres)	−0.001***	0.001**	0.013	0.044***	−0.011***	−0.079*		0.10
Agroforestry (% operations)	−0.001***	0.0001	−0.017*	0.010***	−0.016***	−0.020	−0.039***	0.18
Input-intensive practices								
Cropland expansion (% change 2007–2017)	−0.001		0.398***	0.096*	0.215***		−0.070	0.15
Fertilizer (% ag acres)	−0.008***	0.019***		0.205***	0.663***		−0.065	0.81
Herbicide (% ag acres)	−0.004***	0.008***		0.225***	0.914***	−0.604***	−0.082*	0.93
Insecticide (% ag acres)	−0.003***	0.009***		0.402***	0.291***	0.300***		0.62

Source: Data from USDA (2017a). See Table 3.1 for variable details. Sample size varies from 1641 to 2393.
Note: * $p<0.10$, ** $p<0.05$, *** $p<0.01$

Table 3.3 Multivariate Regression Results for Relationships between Input-Intensive Production Practices and Federal Programs, 2007–2017

	Independent Variables						
Dependent Variables	*Average Operation Size (acres)*	*Net Ag Income ($/acre)*	*Federal Conservation Payments ($/acre)*	*Other Federal Payments ($/acre)*	*Acres Insured (% of Total Acres)*	*Average Age of Producer (Years)*	R^2
Fertilizer use							
2017 (n = 2350)	−0.008***	0.019***		0.205***	0.663***		0.81
2012 (n = 2263)	−0.006***	0.032***	−0.428**	0.533***	0.601***		0.84
2007 (n = 2582)	−0.008***	0.032***	−0.321***	0.285***	0.740***		0.81
Herbicide use							
2017 (n = 2393)	−0.004***	0.008***		0.225***	0.914***	−0.604***	0.93
2012 (n = 2333)	−0.003***	0.015***	−0.083	0.159***	0.971***	−0.471***	0.93
2007 (n = 2656)	−0.004***	0.014***	−0.154*	0.109***	0.912***	−0.922***	0.89
Insecticide use							
2017 (n = 2147)	−0.003***	0.009***		0.402***	0.291***	0.300***	0.62
2012 (n = 2317)	−0.001***	0.018***	−0.557***	0.764***	0.267***	0.563***	0.72
2007 (n = 2514)	−0.001***	0.017***	−0.219***	0.692***	0.182***	0.070	0.74

Source: Data from USDA (2007; 2012; 2017a). Table 3.1 has variables details. Sample size varies from 2147 to 2656.
Note: * $p<0.10$, ** $p<0.05$, ***$p<0.01$

strongly correlated with conservation tillage as compared to nonconservation payments. The overall predictive power, however, of these conservation-oriented models is much lower than the input-intensive models, with the model looking at use of manure fertilizer having the highest explanatory power (R^2 = 0.35).

When comparing across all models, the effect of crop insurance is consistent: crop insurance is negatively associated with conservation-oriented practices and positively associated with input-intensive practices. The only other variables that are as consistently significant across models are average operation size and net agriculture income, but their effects are quite low. Other variables emerged as strong predictors in individual models (e.g., off-farm labor on no tillage and average age of principal operator on manure fertilizer use), but those variables were not uniformly significant across all models.

The available data also allowed for temporal analysis across three waves of agricultural census data (2007, 2012, and 2017) on the effects of the same independent variables as in the models in table 3.2 (except for the off-farm labor variable) and the indicators of input-intensive practices. As shown in table 3.3, the relationships between the independent variables and the three dependent variables (fertilizer use, herbicide use, and insecticide use) hold consistent across the decade, with each model once again explaining a large proportion of the overall variance. Since 2007, crop insurance and the proportion of acres insured have strong associations with more intensive use of inputs, while the trend for conservation payments is that they are negatively correlated with these practices. Although the average age of principal producer shows statistically significant relationships with herbicide and insecticide use, we do not believe that these are empirically meaningful. The standard deviation of the age variable is between 2.0 and 2.3 for each year, highlighting the lack of variation in age of producers in the United States (the mean age was 58.7 years old in 2017).

Although subnational statistical analysis is beyond the scope of this study, spatial representations of some of the key variables in our analysis highlight large regional variation among all of the variables (USDA 2017a). Looking at the spatial distribution provides a more complex picture of the coincidence of both conservation and input-intensive incentives and practices, particularly in Midwestern states and states along the southern Mississippi River.

DISCUSSION

The FCIP is a prominent portion of the Farm Bill, and its effects on management practices and the resulting environmental outcomes still require clarity, despite the research attention it has already garnered (Horowitz and

Lichtenberg 1993; Young, Vandeveer, and Schnepf 2001; Deal 2004; Miao, Hennessy, and Feng 2014; Claassen et al. 2017). The results in this chapter provide further evidence that, at the national level, the type of federal payment that farmers receive is significantly related to the type of management practices they implement. Though perhaps not surprising that what farmers receive payments for relates to how they manage their production, the degree of relationship indicated by our analysis foregrounds the importance of understanding the structural effects of agricultural policy on production practices. Our analysis using data from 2017 provides substantial evidence that crop insurance payments are highly correlated with input-intensive practices and mostly operate in opposition to conservation-oriented practices, whereas conservation payments encourage at least some conservation-oriented practices.

Together, these findings add credence to previous studies documenting the connections between crop insurance and higher usage of chemicals (Horowitz and Lichtenberg 1993; Plastina 2019), which have broader environmental implications given the well-established linkages between synthetic inputs and environmental degradation (Brondizio et al. 2019). Our findings suggest that Plastina's (2019) conclusion that crop insurance encourages more application of fertilizer may hold across other management practices generally detrimental to the environment at higher levels, such as pesticide and insecticide use.

The divergent relationship between conservation tillage and crop insurance (table 3.2) further suggests that the structure of subsidies is tightly tied to farmer behavior. Conservation tillage was the only conservation practice positively associated with crop insurance, which can perhaps be explained by the relinking of Conservation Compliance and eligibility for crop insurance premium subsidies that occurred in the 2014 Farm Bill. While Claassen et al. (2017) caution that even this recoupling may not be sufficient to adequately incentivize conservation practices, our analysis, drawn from the first available data since the 2014 Farm Bill, identifies an association between crop insurance and conservation tillage, a practice consistent with meeting the requirements of Conservation Compliance (Claassen et al. 2017). Although data were not available to allow us to trace the trends in conservation tillage before and after the 2014 Farm Bill, the preliminary findings from our analysis provide the basis for future research to test the hypothesis that the Conservation Compliance requirements have encouraged producers to adopt more environmentally sustainable practices, a strand of inquiry that holds important implications for the ability of federal policy to incentivize particular behaviors deemed desirable. Moreover, the high correlation between input-intensive practices and crop insurance also provides the basis for critical future research to test whether crop insurance policy can be altered to disincentivize those behaviors deemed harmful.

IMPLICATIONS AND RECOMMENDATIONS

The broader lens of this book, with a focus on the role of public administration in food policy and food systems outcomes, highlights the need to understand how policies and administration of those policies can incentivize or discourage behaviors and outcomes important for social well-being and environmental sustainability. The findings presented in this chapter suggest that the FCIP, and the policies that underpin it, requires a new set of goals, incentives, and implementation approaches that prioritize conservation and production practices with an eye toward long-term resilience of the agri-food system. The good news is that a track record already exists for embedding conservation goals into the FCIP through relinking Conservation Compliance with crop insurance eligibility. We thus call for more comprehensive integration, such that the FCIP is wholly contributing to, as opposed to operating against, sustainable land management practices. Based on the findings of this chapter, we conclude that the FCIP is critical to affecting farmers' behavior and so must be constructed in such a way that protects farmers' short-term and long-term risk and benefits society.

Although our analysis focused at the national level, looking at the spatial distribution of the prevalence of different payments and production practices suggests variation across and within regions (USDA 2017a). Subnational and subregional studies would thus constitute an important research focus in the future to capture more nuance regarding the degree to which farmers engage with federal subsidy schemes and how that engagement leads to different outcomes for land management, environmental sustainability, and ultimately, resilience in the agri-food system. These types of analyses would be particularly worthy, given that previous studies have found that the environmental effects of crop insurance vary both by region and crop type (Deal 2004; Walters et al. 2012). Differences across geography also provides important opportunity for more nuanced and targeted policymaking to incentivize the environmental sustainability of agriculture. Policy mechanisms to encourage conservation-oriented behavior that reduce risk may need to differ between places where there is high coincidence of both crop insurance and conservation payments (i.e., the Midwest) as opposed to regions, for example, where federal payments are far less common (i.e., the Northeast).

This chapter offers substantial evidence that the current configuration of crop insurance is strongly associated with input-intensive production practices. Given that the existing water, soil, and pest challenges confronting agriculture are expected to intensify (Gowda et al. 2018), maintaining subsidy mechanisms central to agricultural policy that appear to promote input-intensive practices that are likely to exacerbate environmental degradation seems imprudent. While conservation payments operate in parallel to crop insurance and do associate with conservation-oriented practices, our analysis suggests that conservation payments do not have as powerful an effect on production practices as crop insurance payments, based on their explanatory powers (table 3.2). Perhaps even more importantly, crop insurance appears to work at odds with the goals of conservation payments, given the negative association between crop insurance and conservation practices but for conservation tillage. There is, therefore, reason to pay attention to the concern raised by Yu and Sumner (2018) that crop insurance may disincentivize farmers to pursue long-term risk management strategies.

As Beckie et al. (2019) point out, opportunity exists to further integrate the FCIP with best conservation practices beyond conservation tillage. We concur with Plastina (2019) and many others that incentives are key to motivate farmers' behavior and must be oriented toward conservation practices that offer risk reduction and other long-term cobenefits. In this chapter, we have shown that the current configuration of FCIP, the primary farm safety net, strongly relates to agricultural production that relies more heavily on synthetic inputs. This trend, however, is not intractable; rather, it reflects a failure of the structure and implementation of the policy. Since its inception nearly a century ago, the FCIP has undergone several significant changes, demonstrating that it is a policy mechanism able to adjust to changing priorities and needs on the ground.

REFERENCES

Arbuckle, J. G., J. Hobbs, A. Loy, L. W. Morton, L. S. Prokopy, and J. Tyndall. 2014. "Understanding Corn Belt Farmer Perspectives on Climate Change to Inform Engagement Strategies for Adaptation and Mitigation." *Journal of Soil and Water Conservation* 69 (6): 505–516. https://doi.org/10.2489/jswc.69.6.505.

Babcock, Bruce A, and Chad E. Hart. 2005. "Influence of the Premium Subsidy on Farmers' Crop Insurance Coverage Decisions." *CARD Working Papers*. 375.

Beckie, Hugh J., Stuart J. Smyth, Micheal D. K. Owen, and Savannah Gleim. 2019. "Rewarding Best Pest Management Practices via Reduced Crop Insurance Premiums." *International Journal of Agronomy* 2019 (January): 1–11. https://doi .org/10.1155/2019/9390501.

Brondizio, Eduardo S., J. Settele, S. Díaz, and H. T. Ngo. 2019. "Global Assessment Report on Biodiversity and Ecosystem Services of the Intergovernmental Science-Policy Platform on Biodiversity and Ecosystem Services." *IPBES Secretariat: Bonn, Germany*.

Claassen, Roger L., Maria Bowman, Vince Breneman, Tara Wade, Ryan Williams, Jacob Fooks, LeRoy Hansen, Rich Iovanna, and Chuck Loesch. 2017. "Conservation Compliance: How Farmer Incentives Are Changing in the Crop Insurance Era." 261814. *USDA-ERS*.

Claassen, Roger, Christian Langpap, and JunJie Wu. 2017. "Impacts of Federal Crop Insurance on Land Use and Environmental Quality." *American Journal of Agricultural Economics* 99 (3): 592–613. https://doi.org/10.1093/ajae/aaw075.

Coble, K. H., and B. J. Barnett. 2013. "Why Do We Subsidize Crop Insurance?" *American Journal of Agricultural Economics* 95 (2): 498–504. https://doi.org/10.1093/ajae/aas093.

Daberkow, Stan, and Wen Huang. 2006. "Nutrient management." In K. Weibe and N. Gollehon (eds.), *Agricultural Resources and Environmental Indicators* (Chapter 15). New York: Nova Science Publishers, Inc.

Deal, John L. 2014. "The Empirical Relationship Between Federally Subsidized Crop Insurance and Soil Erosion." PhD diss. North Carolina State University.

Deryugina, Tatyana, and Megan Konar. 2017. "Impacts of Crop Insurance on Water Withdrawals for Irrigation." *Advances in Water Resources* 110: 437–444.

Fields, Scott. 2004. "Global Nitrogen: Cycling out of Control." *Environmental Health Perspectives* 112 (10): 556–563. https://doi.org/10.1289/ehp.112-a556.

Gardezi, Maaz, and J. Gordon Arbuckle. 2019. "Spatially Representing Vulnerability to Extreme Rain Events Using Midwestern Farmers' Objective and Perceived Attributes of Adaptive Capacity." *Risk Analysis* 39 (1): 17–34. https://doi.org/10.1111/risa.12943.

Glauber, J.W. 2013. "The Growth of the Federal Crop Insurance Program, 1990–2011." *American Journal of Agricultural Economics* 95 (2): 482–488. https://doi.org/10.1093/ajae/aas091.

Goodwin, Barry K., and Vincent H. Smith. 2003. "An Ex Post Evaluation of the Conservation Reserve, Federal Crop Insurance, and Other Government Programs: Program Participation and Soil Erosion." *Journal of Agricultural and Resource Economics*: 201–206.

Gowda, Prasanna H., Jean Steiner, Carolyn Olson, Mark Boggess, Tracey Farrigan, and Michael A. Grusak. 2018. "Chapter 10: Agriculture and Rural Communities. Impacts, Risks, and Adaptation in the United States: The Fourth National Climate Assessment, Volume II." U.S. Global Change Research Program. https://doi.org/10.7930/NCA4.2018.CH10.

Horowitz, John K., and Erik Lichtenberg. 1993. "Insurance, Moral Hazard, and Chemical Use in Agriculture." *American Journal of Agricultural Economics* 75 (4): 926–935. https://doi.org/10.2307/1243980.

Lusk, Jayson L. 2016. "Distributional Effects of Crop Insurance Subsidies." *Applied Economic Perspectives and Policy* 39 (1): 1–15. https://doi.org/10.1093/aepp/ppw002.

Mase, Amber Saylor, Benjamin M. Gramig, and Linda Stalker Prokopy. 2017. "Climate Change Beliefs, Risk Perceptions, and Adaptation Behavior among Midwestern U.S. Crop Farmers." *Climate Risk Management* 15: 8–17. https://doi.org/10.1016/j.crm.2016.11.004.

McFadden, Jonathan and Robert A. Hoppe. 2017. "The Evolving Distribution of Payments from Commodity, Conservation, and Federal Crop Insurance Programs." *USDA-ERS Economic Information Bulletin* 184.

Miao, Ruiqing, David A. Hennessy, and Hongli Feng. 2014. "Sodbusting, Crop Insurance, and Sunk Conversion Costs." *Land Economics* 90 (4): 601–622. https://doi.org/10.3368/le.90.4.601.

Mishra, Ashok K., R. Wesley Nimon, and Hisham S. El-Osta. 2005. "Is Moral Hazard Good for the Environment? Revenue Insurance and Chemical Input Use." *Journal of Environmental Management* 74 (1): 11–20. https://doi.org/10.1016/j.jenvman.2004.08.003.

National Crop Insurance Services. (2020). "Facts and Figures." Cropinsurance.org. Accessed August 12, 2020. https://cropinsuranceinamerica.org/about-crop-insurance/facts-figures/.

O'Connor, Claire. 2013. "Soil Matters: How the Federal Crop Insurance Program Should Be Reformed to Encourage Low-Risk Farming Methods with High-Reward Environmental Outcomes." Paper presented *at the Agricultural & Applied Economics Association's 2013 Crop Insurance and the Farm Bill Symposium.* Louisville, KY, October 8–9, 2013.

Osteen, Craig D., and Jorge Fernandez-Cornejo. 2016. "Herbicide Use Trends: A Backgrounder." *Choices* 31 (4): 1–7.

Plastina, Alejandro. 2019. "The Missing Piece in the Nutrient Reduction Puzzle: Economic Incentives." *Ag Decision Maker* 24 (2): 1–4.

R Core Team. 2018. "R version 3.5. 1 (Feather Spray): A Language and Environment for Statistical Computing." *R Foundation for Statistical Computing, Vienna, Austria.* www.r-project.org.

Rosa, Isabel. 2018. "Farm Bill Primer: Federal Crop Insurance." *In focus.* Washington, DC: Congressional Research Service.

Rosa, Isabel, and Renée Johnson. 2019. "Federal Crop Insurance: Specialty Crops." R45459. Washington, DC: Congressional Research Service.

Schoengold, Karina, Ya Ding, and Russell Headlee. 2015. "The Impact of ad hoc Disaster and Crop Insurance Programs on the Use of Risk-Reducing Conservation Tillage Practices." *American Journal of Agricultural Economics* 97 (3): 897–919. https://doi.org/10.1093/ajae/aau073.

Sherrick, Bruce J., Peter J. Barry, Paul N. Ellinger, and Gary D. Schnitkey. 2004. "Factors Influencing Farmers' Crop Insurance Decisions." *American Journal of Agricultural Economics* 86 (1): 103–114. https://doi.org/10.1111/j.0092–5853.2004.00565.x.

Shields, Dennis. 2015. "Federal Crop Insurance: Background" R40532. Washington, DC: Congressional Research Service.

Smith, Vincent H., and Barry K. Goodwin. 1996. "Crop Insurance, Moral Hazard, and Agricultural Chemical Use." *American Journal of Agricultural Economics* 78 (2): 428–438. https://doi.org/10.2307/1243714.

USDA NASS. 2012. *2012 Census of Agriculture.* National Agricultural Statistics Service. Complete data available at www.nass.usda.gov/AgCensus.

USDA NASS. 2007. *2007 Census of Agriculture.* National Agricultural Statistics Service. Complete data available at www.nass.usda.gov/AgCensus.

USDA NASS. 2017a. *2017 Census of Agriculture.* National Agricultural Statistics Service. Complete data available at www.nass.usda.gov/AgCensus.

USDA NASS. 2017b. "2017 Census of Agriculture report form guide." https://www.nass.usda.gov/AgCensus/Report_Form_and_Instructions/2017_Report_Form/2017_Census_of_Agriculture_Report_Form_Guide.pdf.

USDA ERS. 2018. "Insured acres for selected commodities, 1989–2018." Last updated February 11, 2019. https://www.ers.usda.gov/data-products/chart-gallery/gallery/chart-detail/?chartId=91179.

USDA ERS. 2019. "All Fertilizer Use and Price Tables in a Single Workbook." Last updated October 30, 2019. https://www.ers.usda.gov/data-products/fertilizer-use-and-price.

Walters, Cory, Richard Shumway, Hayley Chouinard, and Philip Wandschneider. 2012. "Crop Insurance, Land Allocation, and the Environment." *Journal of Agricultural and Resource Economics* 37 (2): 301–320.

Weber, Jeremy G., Nigel Key, and Erik O'Donoghue. 2016. "Does Federal Crop Insurance Make Environmental Externalities from Agriculture Worse?" *Journal of the Association of Environmental and Resource Economists* 3 (3): 707–742. https://doi.org/10.1086/687549.

Wright, Brian. 2014. "Multiple Peril Crop Insurance." *Choices* 29 (3): 1–5.

Young, C. Edwin, Monte L. Vandeveer, and Randall D. Schnepf. 2001. "Production and Price Impacts of U.S. Crop Insurance Programs." *American Journal of Agricultural Economics* 83 (5): 1196–1203.

Yu, Jisang, and Daniel A. Sumner. 2018. "Effects of Subsidized Crop Insurance on Crop Choices." *Agricultural Economics* 49 (4): 533–545. https://doi.org/10.1111/agec.12434.

Chapter 4

Hating Healthy Meals

Policy Rollbacks and School Meals

Jennifer Geist Rutledge

The Healthy, Hunger-Free Kids Act (HHFKA) passed in 2010 by the U.S. Congress was a funding reauthorization bill for the federal school meal and other child nutrition programs. The bill included a number of changes to the meal programs, most significant of which is that the USDA is now required to establish and use science-based nutrition standards, based on recommendations from the Institute of Medicine. One of the other significant changes to the program was the creation of the Community Eligibility Provision which allows schools to provide free lunches to all students if a certain percentage of their students already qualify for free or reduced-price meals. In short, the bill improved nutritional standards and increased access to the meal programs.

The bill was met with immediate outcry from Republicans who critiqued the nanny state nature of the bill. Further, when the new nutritional standards were established in 2012, students complained about the smaller portion sizes and supposedly less tasty food, while Republican lawmakers complained about plate waste, as the students refused to eat healthier food (Yee 2012; Philpott 2019). However, as the new nutritional standards were implemented much of the criticism died down, particularly as the School Nutrition Association embraced the reforms and local school districts began implementing the Community Eligibility Provision resulting in increased access to meals. Research from the USDA and academics alike showed that the problems with plate waste were not as severe as initially reported, that meal access, particularly for students of color had increased, and showed significant improved dietary outcomes for children who ate at school (Kogan 2019). For instance, by 2014, 90 percent of schools were meeting the standards (Evich). Further, a USDA study released in April 2019, which was the first comprehensive examination of school meals following the implementation of the HHFKA, demonstrated that the Healthy Eating Index rose roughly 20 points (on a scale out of 100) for both breakfasts and lunches, and that there was greater participation (Reiley 2019). The revisions were working to achieve the particular policy goals of improved nutrition and increased access.

However, Trump's election gave Republicans an opening to rollback this policy and revisions were first announced in 2017, going into effect in 2019. These initial policy rollbacks focused on allowing sugary, fatty milk back into the meals, and less-restrictive sodium and whole grain requirements. The administration was immediately hit by a lawsuit filed by six state attorneys general arguing that the policy rollbacks did not follow proper administrative procedures, but the weakened standards have still gone into effect. In addition, the School Nutrition Association has reversed its former stance and no longer supports the new nutritional standards. Finally, the Trump administration is working to restrict access to food stamps, which in turn would restrict access to free school meals under the Community Eligibility Provision program. What explains the weakening of a policy that was clearly working to improve the health of schoolchildren?

A straightforward answer is suggested by journalists who point to the connections between the School Nutrition Association and food corporations that provide the majority of their budget, as well as the firing of the SNA's longtime lobbyist, who was well connected to the USDA, in favor of a lobbying firm that also represents the NRA and has ties to many congressional Republicans (Overby 2014; Confessore 2014; Evich 2014; Bittman 2015). The entrenched interests of the agro-food industry are strong, and yet, players in the agro-food industry spoke in favor of the changes during the hearings leading up to the 2010 Act (Rutledge 2017. Further, the food industry has the resources to easily pivot and create new "healthy" meals that meet the requirements and, the sunk costs of creating new products that meet the standards suggests that it can actually be counter-productive to profits to have regulatory flip-flopping (Simon 2014). I argue that the attempted rollback of the nutritional standards is less about a materialist understanding of interests and lobbying, and instead can be understood as a process of contestation between two different understandings of what food is. On the one hand, food, and especially food through the school lunch program, has been structured as an industrial privatized good that is designed to get as many calories into people as possible while also making a profit for food corporations. In this construction, food is seen as a product, and this construction is arguably an artifact of neoliberal economic policies. On the other hand, food is being structured by public health advocates as the solution to a variety of health problems, most prominently obesity. In this construction, food is seen as a tool. The threat to the HHFKA can be understood as a moment of contestation over what food is, and food governance and policy can only be understood by analyzing the ideas at play.

By using the implementation and rollback of the HHFKA of 2010 as a case study, this chapter deals directly with the politics of food policy and particularly looks at some of the governance challenges associated with food policy. Theoretically, this piece integrates recent work on ideational analysis in public policy to bear on food policy. Using primary sources such as news reports, congressional testimony, agency reports from the USDA and School Nutrition Association, and the lawsuits filed in U.S. District Court regarding the revised nutritional standards, this chapter traces the weakening of the HHFKA and examines the way in which child food insecurity, health concerns such as obesity, and agro-food corporations are intertwined in the development and implementation of the national school meals programs. This piece deals directly with the complicated politics of governing food policy and presents a case study of how ideas can be used in causal analysis by examining policy implementation and rollback of the revised nutritional standards in the meals programs.

IDEATIONAL ANALYSIS IN POLICY STUDIES

This piece focuses on the role of ideas in the policy process and the relationship between ideas and interests, which builds on a line of inquiry first explicated by Max Weber and brought more fully into the fold of policy studies by Hugh Heclo with his distinction between puzzling and powering (1974). Despite this pedigree ideational analysis was slow to come to policy studies, which has traditionally been dominated by historical institutionalists who focused on material and rationalist explanations for policy change. In a 1995 *Polity* Forum on institutionalism, the authors shift uneasily between positions that see ideas as secondary to institutions (Skocpol; Fiorina) to others that see institutions and ideas as intermeshed (Skowronek; Orren; Smith). In the second argument, most clearly explicated by Smith, ideas are seen as necessary but not sufficient, leading to a focus on the mutually constitutive nature of institutions and ideas, as ideas must "be thought about in terms of their institutional locations, just as institutions always have to be thought about in terms of the ideas embedded in them and constitutive of them" (Smith 1995, 139). This argument is further extended by Kloppenberg who cautions that to analyze institutions in a historically, temporally grounded manner requires an examination of how "ideas and institutions develop in relation to each other in particular situations, because neither ideas nor institutions exist in the absence of the other" (1995, 126). Since then scholars have delved deeply into the relationship between ideas and institutions, focusing on the effect ideas have on policy through institutions (Hass 1992; Adler and Haas 1992; Hall 1989; Sikkink 1991; Goldstein 1988; Yee 1996). This literature clearly concludes that ideas matter to the policy process and further that ideas and institutions interact and "even become interdependent to shape human behavior and institutions" (Béland 2019, 4). As such, it becomes important to understand not only that ideas matter to the policy process but how they matter (Mehta 2011).

Ideas matter to the policy process in several important ways. At their core, ideas are causal factors; in the simplest formulation "ideas help us think about ways to address problems and challenges we face, and therefore are the cause of our actions" (Béland and Cox 2011, 4). Relatedly, ideas also help us make sense of policy problems and provide policy solutions (Kingdon 1984; Mehta 2011); the strength or salience of an idea explains which problems end up on the policy agenda and which ideas are chosen as solutions to that problem and enacted in policy. In this way then, ideas can become institutions; in fact, we can understand policy institutions as embedded ideas (Béland and Cox 2011). Thus, ideas act as causal factors in the creation of institutions, which in turn then "reinforce and reproduce those ideas" (Béland and Cox 2011, 9). Similarly, ideas create interests that have been constructed out of "normative and subjective/intersubjective conceptions of self-good" (Mehta 2011, 79). These interests then work, like institutions, to reinforce the ideas from which they were constructed. Ultimately, ideas are important to the policy process because they are the building blocks that structure our understanding of policy problems and solutions and that construct self-reinforcing interests and institutions.

This last point suggests a certain static quality to institutions and interests, that they will remain the same as the ideas embedded in them are strengthened by the institution and interests themselves and yet, "ideas are constantly in flux, being reconsidered and refined as actors communicate and debate with one another" (Béland and Cox 2010, 4), which suggests a certain malleability to institutions and policy as ideas can change or be challenged over time. Thus, examining the ideas embedded in interests and institutions as they change or are challenged can allow us to understand policy change. While policy change can be driven by material interests, those interests were created by certain ideas and assumptions that policy actors carry about the world; these ideas and assumptions are often informed by paradigms. A policy paradigm has been defined as "a framework of ideas and standards that specifies not only the goals of policy and kinds of instruments that can be used to attain them, but also the very nature of the problems they are meant to be addressing" (Hall 1993, 279).

Food policy has clearly operated under a productionist paradigm that focuses on increasing the amount of food through intensive monoculture farming (Lang and Heasman 2004) and the attendant production of industrialized cheap food products for consumption (Gaddis 2019). This paradigm is tied to the dominant economic paradigm of neoliberalism (Friedmann 2015) with the result that other aspects that are affected by food, such as both human and ecological health, are ignored in favor of increasing economic returns. In the realm of agriculture, this paradigm is being challenged by an agroecological approach to growing food (Gaudreau 2015), while in the realm of food consumption a public health nutrition paradigm is emerging that prioritizes the role of food in health (Ridgway et al. 2019). Each of these paradigms seeks to solve different problems and thus creates different solutions. In the case of the productionist paradigm, the problem was both hunger and the well-being of farmers, while in the public health paradigm the problem is poor health, and particularly obesity. Kingdon (1984) established that problem definition tends to determine the particular solutions. In this case, the paradigms define the problems differently: on the one hand, the productionist paradigm defines the problem as hunger and farm efficiency; on the other hand, the public health nutrition paradigm defines the problem as obesity.

These differing problem definitions lead to different solutions: one the one hand, the production of cheap, industrialized food, while on the other hand, the solution is to reduce reliance on these same cheap, industrialized foods. The conflict between these two paradigms is playing out in the contestation over the nutrition rules for the school meals programs. To understand the attempted rollbacks of the revised nutritional rules it is not enough to simply know that food corporations have vested, material interests in the meals programs, but to go further and understand the ideas that drive those interests. This is in part because a simple institutional answer cannot explain this case of policy change or policy rollback, but more importantly because we cannot understand public policies themselves unless we integrate ideational analysis into institutional analysis (Béland 2019). The fights over the school meal program represents a contestation over two different understandings of what food is, and what food can be. It is imperative to understand these competing paradigms to understand food policy in the United States and the school meals program provides a useful lens to examine this moment of paradigmatic tension. The story of the passage of the HHFKA, followed by the attempted rollbacks, is a story of two food paradigms in tension with one another and as such provides a lens with which to analyze ideational contestation and the future of food policy and governance.

HEALTHY, HUNGER-FREE KIDS ACT

The passage of the HHFKA of 2010 updated the nutritional standards for school meals for the first time since 1995, primarily by giving the USDA the authority to set standards for all foods sold in schools. Following recommendations from the Institute for Medicine, the USDA created their new standards which mandated increased servings of fruits and vegetables, more whole grains, less sodium, the elimination of trans-fats, and a requirement to offer only low-fat or no-fat milk. Further, these standards set new calorie minimum and maximums, whereas previously there had only been minimums. These new standards were a triumph for food and nutrition advocates, while a challenge to the potato and dairy industries, as well as the processed food industries that so many schools had come to rely on as providers for their meals. The creation of the HHFKA was the result of years of lobbying by child nutrition advocates, including the School Nutrition Association which is the organization that represents school lunch workers. The campaign was aided immeasurably by Michelle Obama's focus on obesity during her tenure as first lady and public attention to the issue of obesity forced food corporations to support the bill (Rutledge 2017; Confessore 2014). The bill passed by unanimous voice vote in the Senate and with largely Democratic support in the House.

While Republicans, particularly those in the House, had always opposed the bill due to its supposed nanny state nature, major food corporations such as Mars Snackfood, the American Beverage Association, ConAgra Foods, the American Frozen Food Institute, the Potato Industry Child Nutrition Working Group, the National Dairy Council, and the Schwan Food Company were all on record supporting the new Act (United State Senate 2009). Similarly, the School Nutrition Association had worked closely with the Obama administration and Michelle Obama to pass the law. However, by 2011, representatives from the state branches of the School Nutrition Association were critiquing the new law as an unfunded mandate (U.S. Senate 2012). By 2013, the School Nutrition Association was in a full-scale war against the new law, while food corporations were actively lobbying against the new standards (Confessore 2014; Bittman 2015; Overby 2014; Stillerman 2015; Evich 2014; Gaddis 2019). In 2014, House legislation included a measure that created a waiver process for schools allowing them to opt-out of the new standards if they were having trouble complying or operating at a financial loss due to the new rules. The idea of a waiver was heavily promoted by the School Nutrition Association based on concerns that the new standards were driving away the students that paid full price, making it impossible for the cafeterias to remain financially viable. Food corporations also lobbied to ease the new standards. These pieces, combined with Republican dislike of regulations and the Obama administration, worked together to create a ripe background for a policy rollback. During the committee meeting for this waiver, Republicans admitted that their goal was to kill of the new standards entirely (Overby 2014; Hamburger 2014).

The SNA's opposition to the new standards continued through 2015 as the next appropriations act was up for debate, despite evidence showing that

90 percent of schools had successfully met the standards within the first two years of the new rules and that plate waste was not any greater than before the standards went into effect (Stillerman 2015). The 2015 appropriations act was a compromise between the administration and the SNA lobbyists; the outlines of the HHFKA stayed in place, but with some easing of the requirements such as extended time for the sodium reductions and more flexibility with the whole grain requirements. This compromise was seen with alarm by nutrition advocates who worried that it was just a first step in rolling back the standards (Bittman 2015).

More alarming for nutrition advocates was the election of President Trump who, while saying nothing about school meals on the campaign trail, came into office with a seeming vendetta against any policy passed by the Obama administration as well as a "skepticism of government regulation" (Dewey 2016). Indeed, six days after starting as secretary of Agriculture Sonny Perdue announced rollbacks to the HHFKA standards. Specifically, he announced rollbacks in the whole grain and sodium requirements, as well as the instructions to begin serving 1 percent flavored milk instead of nonfat (USDA 2017). Perdue stressed the idea of returning local control to the schools, arguing that schools should have the freedom to make decisions about regional foods, particularly those often made with white flour (Severson 2017).

An interim rule was passed in 2017 delaying the sodium reduction requirement and allowing waivers for the whole grain requirement to continue. Then, in 2018, the USDA issued a final rule that continued the sodium reduction delay and eliminated the final sodium reduction target as well as gutting the whole grain requirement entirely. By April 2019, two lawsuits had been filed in U.S. district courts alleging that the process of making these new rules violated the Administrative Procedures Act. One suit was filed by New York, California, Illinois, Minnesota, New Mexico, Vermont, and D.C. in the Southern District of New York, and a second one filed by Center for Science in the Public Interest and Healthy School Food Maryland in the District of Maryland. In April 2020, the Maryland court ruled against the USDA on the basis that the difference between the Interim Final Rule and Final Rule was so great as to have violated the Administrative Procedures Act. Importantly, the justice rejected the other arguments, stating that while nutritional standards should conform to nutritional science, the USDA could also consider "student taste preferences, operational flexibility, and product innovation" (U.S. District Court for the District of Maryland 2020). The Obama standards remain in place, but only because of procedural irregularities from the Trump administration. The fact that the case was decided on technical irregularities rather than arguments about public health and nutrition suggests that the court decision upheld the paradigm of industrialized, privatized food. While the paradigm of industrialized food is prominent throughout the United States, and in fact transnationally (Gaudreau 2015), it is instructive to understand the way in which this paradigm became embedded in school feeding policy, and the implications that has for policy change.

INDUSTRIAL FOOD AND HUNGRY CHILDREN

Following the agrarian crisis in the 1930s for U.S. farmers, the U.S. reorganized their farm sector with an emphasis on supply management policy (Winders 2009). This reorganization, understood as a mercantilist-industrial food regime had substantial implications for exports and world development, upending traditional trade patterns and reducing national self-sufficiency in agricultural goods (Friedmann 2005). Further, the U.S. commodity programs created pressures for the U.S. agricultural industry to become ever more industrialized at the same time as the food industries were constructing a desire for processed foods (McMichael 2009). By the mid-twentieth century, the United States was dependent on an industrialized, privatized food regime for its meals run by "Big Food" (Gaddis 2019). These Big Food corporations presciently saw the school lunch program as the next frontier in expanding their markets.

The National School Lunch Program was created with the express purpose of supporting U.S. agriculture and national security (U.S. House of Representatives 1946). The program was designed to take advantage of surplus products produced under the perverse incentive structures of supply management policy, resulting in both shifting supplies, which could not only make yearly meal planning difficult but also meant that school meal programs became a kind of dumping ground for whichever agricultural product most successfully lobbied for support (Levine 2008). Further, the meal programs were ham-strung by a funding formula that demanded municipal and state aid in order to gain federal aid, which exacerbated inequality (Gaddis 2019). While meal programs have access to commodity foods, federal reimbursements, and a lunch fee that is regulated by the government, at the same time, they are expected to act as independent businesses, paying for "employee salaries and benefits, as well as overhead costs like utilities, site maintenance, pest control and garbage collection" (Siegel 2019, 101). These requirements have traditionally left schools with very little money to spend on the food itself.

Initially, the school lunch program was forbidden from working with private contractors, but the pressure to feed children on underfunded budgets, combined with pressure from food corporations to expand their markets helped convince the USDA to lift the restrictions in 1970. Further, the American public had begun embracing the convenience foods created by food corporations in the 1950s and 1960s, paving the way for the acceptance of these new foods in the lunchroom (Gaddis 2019). Since that time, agro-food corporations have infiltrated every part of the school food ecosystem, providing bulk convenience foods, which have cut labor costs (and jobs) and reduced food quality, and yet increased the amount of money spent by school districts on processing foods (Gaddis 2019; Siegel 2019). Despite claims that school meals are run as a private/public partnership, in practicality the school lunchroom was privatized and this privatization resulted in food that was largely regarded as highly processed, industrialized, and, ultimately, unhealthy.

The health results of the privatized, industrialized school meals were inescapable—an incredible rise in childhood obesity, to the point where it is predicted that 60 percent of children today will be obese by the time they are thirty-five (Siegel 2019). To be clear, school meals are not the only cause of the obesity crisis, roughly "60 percent of the country's diet currently comes from highly processed foods, and . . . almost all American kids—regardless of their weight—are missing out in a big way on whole plant foods (Siegel 2019, 125). Child obesity started to increase in the mid-1980s, and there is now good evidence that obesity is the result not only of unhealthy diets but also of the built environment in which children live (such as a reliance on car transportation or lack of access to grocery stores), chemicals in the environment, and genetics (Guthman 2009; Ludwig and Pollack 2009). Beginning in the 1990s, obesity became defined as a public health issue, and school meals were increasingly constructed as a target for improving children's health (Mokdad et al. 1999; Hill and Peter 1998; Schazenbach 2009; Milliment et al. 2010; Eagle et al. 2010). Thus, Congressional action on the school meals program in 2010 reflected the construction of obesity as a public health problem (Rutledge 2017). The solution was to serve healthier foods, which was a direct challenge to an industrialized food system that focused on highly processed, nutritionally poor, cheap food.

Serving healthier foods would seem to be in the best interest of both children, and ultimately, the country. And yet, these changes were attacked from the minute they were announced and the attacks have solidified under the Trump administration. The Trump administration's attacks on the healthier meal standards could be explained by a historical institutionalist analysis that analyzes this puzzle by looking at the shift in electoral power brought by the Trump election and the lobbying power of agro-food corporation. However, this analysis obscures an understanding of where those interests come from and how actors' beliefs and assumptions affect policy change (Hall 1993), which would help us understand the animus that exists toward these changes. There are real interests at work here, but those interests were created by certain ideas about government responsibility, agricultural policy, and hunger. Those ideas created the school lunch program in such a way that abdicated much of the responsibility for the meals to private industry which in turn has led to the rise of highly processed, cheap foods in school meals. What we are seeing now, through the implementation of the HHFKA, is a challenge to this model, which is a challenge certainly not only to these interests but also to the fundamental ideas that created these interests in the first place. The HHFKA represented the institutionalization of a certain set of ideas about the relationship between health and nutrition, which was a challenge to a competing set of ideas about the relationship between food production, consumption, and profits.

The school lunch program, an institution in its own right at this point, was created out of the idea of agricultural exceptionalism, the idea that farmers deserved particular support from the government (Skogstad 1998); at the same time, there was a dominant idea that the federal government should not take responsibility for families (U.S. House of Representatives 1946). Thus, the particular shape of the school lunch program was created by these twin and dueling ideas, about who deserved government support and who would be "a politically and morally acceptable outlet for the 'surplus' foods" (Gaddis 2019, 48). These ideas became institutionalized in the school meal programs and, in turn created farmers who were dependent on school meals as an outlet for their products, while at the same time the school meal became more dependent on those products. Similarly, the dominance of ideas about convenience and the efficiency of private industry paved the way for the acceptance of agro-food corporations into the meal programs (Gaddis 2019). As privatized, industrial food became a regular part of the meals, it created more and more demand for these kinds of foods and a larger food industry catering specifically to school meals and children (Siegel 2019). In both instances, the ideas and the interests became mutually imbricated, making change to the school meals policy both so difficult and such an ideological and interest-based affront, thus engendering the resistance to healthier meals.

CONCLUSION

Food studies have received attention from a variety of disciplines, such as sociology, anthropology, agricultural economics, consumer studies, and history, to list just a few, while it has been relatively ignored by political science and policy studies. And yet, so much of food access or consumption is governed by policy choices. The theoretical insights of policy studies are uniquely positioned to help scholars understand the issues around food, while also benefiting from the inter-disciplinary commitments of other food scholars. In the case of the passage and then attempted rollbacks of the HHFKA theories of policy change can help us understand this case, and, in particular, point to ways to understand why a policy rollback was attempted in the face of policy change that was achieving its stated goals. In this case, institutional explanations of policy change cannot explain the vehemence with which the Trump administration has attacked the HHFKA. Large food corporations had already invested resources into following the new regulations and both schools and food corporations were easily meeting the new standards. When standard institutional explanations cannot wholly explain a phenomenon, we should add ideational explanations to our analysis: analyzing ideas and interests in conjunction can explain policy change, due to the way in which ideas become interests, which in turn "constrain and empower actors in various settings" (Béland 2019, 5). An ideational analysis illuminates important factors in policy change and, in this case, important factors in food governance.

The institution of the school meals program as we know it today was created by ideas about farming, families, convenience, and economics, and reflects the dominant, productionist paradigm. Certainly part of the explanation for the Trump administration's attempted rollback of the updated nutritional standards reflects regulatory capture by the food industry (the rollbacks have been a particular boon to the dairy industry for instance), but regulatory capture could only occur after certain ideas about agriculture and food had become embedded in institutions. More fundamentally, the attempted rollbacks reflect the entrenchment of the productionist paradigm and demonstrates the way in which policy change that challenges the dominant paradigm can be hard to achieve, largely because policy paradigms tend to reinforce existing policy arrangements (Béland 2005). The passage of the HHFKA reflected ideas, the public health paradigm, that challenged the productionist paradigm, and this contestation is fundamentally a contestation over ideas about what food is and ought to be. Food governance is riven by this tension, whether food is a product to be consumed or a tool to improve lives. While competing paradigms can exist simultaneously, there is often an ongoing process of negotiation between a dominant and upstart paradigm (Gaudreau 2015). In the case of food governance, we are in the middle of that negotiation process and the reaction of the Trump administration to the public health challenge of the HHFKA reflects how entrenched and "sticky" dominant paradigms are, as well as how much of our food access and consumption is determined by that dominant paradigm. The HHFKA represents a challenge to that paradigm and, perhaps, foreshadows a new and improved food paradigm.

REFERENCES

Adler, Emanuel, and Peter M. Haas. 1992. "Conclusion: Epistemic Communities, World Order, and the Creation of a Reflective Research Program." *International Organization* 46(1): 367–390.

Béland, Daniel. 2005. "Ideas and Social Policy: An Institutionalist Perspective." *Social Policy and Administration* 39(1): 1–18.

———. 2007. "Ideas and Institutional Change in Social Security: Conversion, Layering, and Policy Drift n." *Social Science Quarterly* 88(1): 20–38.

———. 2016. "Kingdon Reconsidered: Ideas, Interests and Institutions in Comparative Policy Analysis." *Journal of Comparative Policy Analysis: Research and Practice* 18(3): 228–242.

———. 2019. *How Ideas and Institutions Shape the Politics of Public Policy.* New York: Cambridge University Press.

Béland, Daniel, and Robert Henry Cox. 2010. *Ideas and Politics in Social Science Research.* New York: Oxford University Press.

Bittman, Mark. 2015. "Opinion | Feeding Kids Well." *The New York Times,* Accessed April 22, 2020. https://www.nytimes.com/2015/03/11/opinion/mark-bittman-feed ing-kids-well.html.

Confessore, Nicholas. 2014. "How School Lunch Became the Latest Political Battleground." *The New York Times.* Accessed April 22, 2020. https://www.nyt imes.com/2014/10/12/magazine/how-school-lunch-became-the-latest-political-b attleground.html.

Dewey, Caitlin. 2016. "Trump Doesn't Threaten Only President Obama's Legacy: He Could Ruin Michelle Obama's, too." The Washington Post. Accessed April 24, 2020. https://www.washingtonpost.com/news/wonk/wp/2016/12/14/trump-doesnt -just-threaten-barack-obamas-legacy-he-could-ruin-michelles-too/

Eagle, Taylor F., Roopa Gurm, Caren S. Goldberg, Jean DuRussel-Weston, Eva Kline-Rogers, LaVaughn Palma-Davis, Susan Aaronson, Catherine M. Fitzgerald, Lindsey R. Mitchell, and Bruce Rogers. 2010. "Health Status and Behavior among Middle-School Children in a Midwest Community: What Are the Underpinnings of Childhood Obesity?" *American Heart Journal* 160(6): 1185–1189.

Evich, Helena Bottemiller. 2014. "Behind the School Lunch Fight." *Politico.* Accessed April 22, 2020. http://www.politico.com/story/2014/06/michelle-obama -public-school-lunch-school-nutrition-association-lets-move-107390.html.

Fiorina, Morris. 1995. "Rational Choice and the New (?) Institutionalism." *Polity* 28(1): 107–115.

Friedmann, Harriet. 2015. "Governing Land and Landscapes: Political Ecology of Enclosures and Commons." *Canadian Food Studies* 2(2): 23–31.

Gaddis, Jennifer E. 2019. *The Labor of Lunch: Why We Need Real Food and Real Jobs in American Public Schools.* Berkeley: University of California Press.

Gaudreau, Matthew. 2015. "Paradigm Change and Power in the World Food System—Synthesis Paper." *Canadian Food Studies* 2(2): 32–38.

Goldstein, Judith. 1988. "Ideas, Institutions, and American Trade Policy." *International Organization* 42(1): 179–217.

Guthman, Julie. 2011. *Weighing In: Obesity, Food Justice, and the Limits of Capitalism.* Berkeley: University of California Press.

Haas, Peter M. 1992. "Banning Chlorofluorocarbons: Epistemic Community Efforts to Protect Stratospheric Ozone." *International Organization* 46(1): 187–224.

Hall, Peter A. 1993. "Policy Paradigms, Social Learning, and the State: The Case of Economic Policymaking in Britain." *Comparative Politics* 25(3): 275–296.

———. 1989. *The Political Power of Economic Ideas: Keynesianism Across Nations.* Princeton: Princeton University Press.

Hamburger, Tom. 2014. "First Lady Gets Moving against House Measure to Let School Districts Duck Lunch Mandates." *Washington Post.* Accessed April 22, 2020 https://www.washingtonpost.com/politics/first-lady-gets-moving-against -house-measure-to-let-school-districts-duck-lunch-mandates/2014/05/26/f3da60ae -e507–11e3-afc6-a1dd9407abcf_story.html.

Hay, Colin. 2011. "Ideas and the Construction of Interests." In *Ideas and Politics in Social Science Research*, edited by Daniel Béland and Robert Henry Cox, 65–82. New York: Oxford University Press.

Hill, James O., and John C. Peters. 1998. "Environmental Contributions to the Obesity Epidemic." *Science* 280(5368): 1371–1374.

Kingdon, John W. 1984. *Agendas, Alternatives, and Public Policies.* Boston: Little, Brown.

Kloppenberg, James T. 1995. "Institutionalism, Rational Choice, and Historical Analysis." *Polity* 28 (1): 125–128.

Kogan, Rachel. 2019. "Rollback of Nutrition Standards Not Supported By Evidence." *Health Affairs.* Accessed January 14, 2020. https://www.healthaffairs.org/do/10 .1377/hblog20190312.130704/full/.

Lang, Tim, and Michael Heasman. 2015. *Food Wars: The Global Battle for Mouths, Minds and Markets.* New York: Routledge.

Levine, Susan. 2008. *School Lunch Politics: The Surprising History of America's Favorite Welfare Program.* Princeton: Princeton University Press.

Ludwig, David S., and Harold A. Pollack. 2009. "Obesity and the Economy: From Crisis to Opportunity." *Jama* 301(5): 533–535.

Mehta, Jal. 2010. "The Varied Roles of Ideas in Politics." In *Ideas and Politics in Social Science Research*, edited by Daniel Béland and Robert Henry Cox, 23–46. New York: Oxford University Press.

McMichael, Phillip. 2009. "A Food Regime Genealogy." *Journal of Peasant Studies* 36(10): 139–169.

Millimet, Daniel L., Rusty Tchernis, and Muna Husain. 2010. "School Nutrition Programs and the Incidence of Childhood Obesity." *Journal of Human Resources* 45(3): 640–654.

Mokdad, Ali H., Mary K. Serdula, William H. Dietz, Barbara A. Bowman, James S. Marks, and Jeffrey P. Koplan. 1999. "The Spread of the Obesity Epidemic in the United States, 1991–1998." *Jama* 282(16): 1519–1522.

Ogden, Cynthia L., Margaret D. Carroll, Brian K. Kit, and Katherine M. Flegal. 2014. "Prevalence of Childhood and Adult Obesity in the United States, 2011–2012." *Jama* 311(8): 806–814.

Orren, Karen. 1995. "Ideas and Institutions." *Polity* 28(1): 97–101.

Overby, Peter. 2014. "Lobbyists Loom Behind the Scenes of School Nutrition Fight." NPR.Org. Accessed April 23, 2020. https://www.npr.org/sections/thesal t/2014/06/11/320753007/behind-the-scenes-of-school-nutrition-fight-big-food -money-flows.

Philpott, Tom. 2019. "The Bizarre Trump-Fueled Backlash to Healthy School Lunches." *Mother Jones*. Accessed January 14, 2020. https://www.motherjones.com/food/2019/09/the-bizarre-trump-fueled-backlash-to-healthy-school-lunches/.

Reiley, Laura. 2019. "Why Is the USDA Downplaying Good News about This Obama-Era School Nutrition Program?" *Washington Post*. Accessed May 3, 2020. https://www.washingtonpost.com/business/2019/06/07/why-is-usda-downplaying-good-news-about-this-obama-era-school-nutrition-program/.

Ridgway, Ella, Phillip Baker, Julie Woods, and Mark Lawrence. 2019. "Historical Developments and Paradigm Shifts in Public Health Nutrition Science, Guidance and Policy Actions: A Narrative Review." *Nutrients* 11(3): 531.

Rutledge, Jennifer. 2017. "School Lunch Reform and the Problem with Obesity." In *The Intersection of Food and Public Health: Current Policy Challenges and Solutions*, edited by Bryce Hoflund, A. Bryce, John C. Jones, and Michelle C. Pautz, 259–274. Boca Raton, Florida: CRC Press/Taylor and Francis.

Schanzenbach, Diane Whitmore. 2009. "Do School Lunches Contribute to Childhood Obesity?" *Journal of Human Resources* 44(3): 684–709.

School Nutrition Association. 2014. "School Cafeteria Professionals Call on Congress to Support FY15 Ag Approps Bill." Accessed May 3, 2020. http://schoolnutrition.org/5—news-and-publications/2—press-releases/press-releases/school-cafeteria-professionals-call-on-congress-to-support-fy15-ag-approps-bill/

Severson, Kim. 2017. "Will the Trump Era Transform the School Lunch?—The New York Times." Accessed May 3, 2020. https://www.nytimes.com/2017/09/05/dining/school-lunch-trump-obama.html.

Siegel, Bettina Elias. 2019. *Kid Food: The Challenge of Feeding Children in a Highly Processed World*. New York: Oxford University Press.

Sikkink, Kathryn. 1991. *Ideas and Institutions: Developmentalism in Brazil and Argentina*. Ithaca: Cornell University Press.

Simon, Michele. 2014. "Who Is Pulling the Strings at the School Nutrition Association?" *Aljazeera*. Accessed May 3, 2020. http://america.aljazeera.com/opinions/2014/8/school-lunches-healthfoodmichelleobamaschwan.html.

Skocpol, Theda. 1995. "Why I Am an Historical Institutionalist." *Polity* 28(1): 103–106.

Skowronek, Stephen. 1995. "Order and Change." *Polity* 28(1): 91–96.

Smith, Rogers M. 1995. "Ideas, Institutions, and Strategic Choice." *Polity* 28(1): 135–140.

Stillerman, Karen Perry. 2015. "The School Nutrition Association—Opposing Better Nutrition in Schools Since 2013." Accessed May 3, 2020. https://blog.ucsusa.org/karen-perry-stillerman/the-school-nutrition-association-opposing-better-nutrition-in-schools-since-2013–689.

USDA. 2017. "Ag Secretary Perdue Moves to Make School Meals Great Again." Accessed April 24, 2020. https://www.usda.gov/media/press-releases/2017/05/01/ag-secretary-perdue-moves-make-school-meals-great-again.

US District Court for the District of Maryland. 2020. Center for Science in the Public Interest v Sonny Perdue, Case Number: GJH-19–1004.

United States House of Representatives. 1946. Report No. 2080, May 20 1946.

United States Senate. 2009. Senate Hearing 111–242 "Beyond Federal School Meal Programs: Reforming Nutrition for Kids in Schools" March 31, 2009.

United States Senate. 2012. Senate Hearing, Committee of Appropriations, 112–137.

White, Ann Folino. 2014. *Plowed Under: Food Policy Protests and Performance in New Deal America*. Bloomington: Indiana University Press.

Winders, Bill. 2009. *The Politics of Food Supply: US Agricultural Policy in the World Economy*. New Haven: Yale University Press.

Yee, Albert S. 1996. "The Causal Effects of Ideas on Policies." *International Organization* 50(1): 69–108.

Yee, Vivian. 2012. "No Appetite for Good-for-You School Lunches." *The New York Times*, Accessed May 24, 2020. https://www.nytimes.com/2012/10/06/nyregion/healthier-school-lunches-face-student-rejection.html.

Chapter 5

Taking Students and Staff Seriously

The National School Lunch Program as Coproduction

Amy Rosenthal

INTRODUCTION

From its inception, the National School Lunch Program (NSLP) has had a mandate "to safeguard the health and wellbeing of the Nation's children" (Richard B. Russell National School Lunch Act 1946). But in school year (SY) 2014–2015, only 56 percent U.S. students participated in the NSLP on the average day (Fox and Gearan 2019). Students may bring their own lunches (of unknown nutritional value), leave campus for other eating places, or forego lunch altogether. Even those students who do go through the lunch line may eat only part of their school lunch, and studies show that fruits and vegetables are the items students most often throw away (Byker Shanks, Banna, and Serrano 2017; Fox and Gearan 2019).

If students skip school lunch or avoid the fruits and vegetables meant to offer a significant portion of the meal's nutrients, then the NSLP is not promoting student health in the way that many school food advocates, practitioners, and parents would like. The eleven million U.S. students who live in families with low food security especially miss an opportunity for nutrition they need if they don't eat, or eat much, at school (Coleman-Jensen et al. 2019). The most recent reauthorization of the NSLP lays out goals of "end[ing] childhood hunger" and "reducing childhood obesity and improving the diets of children" (Healthy, Hunger Free Kids Act 2010). If students don't participate in the meal program, neither goal will be achieved. And if they do not select and eat healthy foods, the second will not.

However, few researchers have investigated why students choose to participate in the NSLP or why they select and eat certain foods if they do. And despite its status as the country's second-biggest nutrition program, the NSLP is rarely studied as policy by public policy or administration scholars (exceptions include Schwartz and Wootan (2019), Pautz, Jones, and Hoflund (2018), Rutledge (2018) and Tabak and Moreland-Russell (2015)).

In this chapter, I suggest that public administration theory, namely the idea of coproduction, can help us better understand how the NSLP can achieve its goals of supporting student health and well-being. Coproduction, at its most general, refers to the involvement of a program's clients in the production of the service(s) it offers. Especially for public services whose goal is to somehow change the recipient, such as in education and health, client involvement is an essential element of service provision (Osborne, Radnor, and Nasi 2013; Alford 2016). For example, in the case of school lunch, a student must eat the full school meal in order for the health goals of the NSLP to be achieved.

Recent literature on coproduction suggests conceptualizing public programs as offering a "value proposition" to the client, and only if the client decides to engage is value cocreated (Osborne 2018). In the context of the NSLP, foodservice staff offer a value proposition, that is, the meal, to students. Student participation in the program, and especially their consumption of healthy foods, is the creation of the value of the NSLP. To understand and ultimately influence the success of school meals policy, we must better understand both sides of this value transaction: 1) the value offering, that is, the meal experience that NSLP staff create and 2) how students see and react to it.

I apply this lens of coproduction to data collected through the PreK–12 School Food: Making It Healthier, Making It Regional (MHMR) project,[1] which investigated NSLP operations in six school districts in the Southeast and Midwest United States. Using fifty-two interviews with district- and school-level foodservice staff and seventeen group interviews with students, I compare foodservice staff and student perspectives on the characteristics of the foods that will encourage students to eat at school and particularly to eat healthy foods like fruits and vegetables.

I find that while students and staff see many of the same food characteristics as important, such as attractiveness and freshness, foodservice staff may not recognize some qualities that students value, such as sensory attributes other than taste. And in some cases, even when foodservice staff think they are providing a meal with the characteristics they and students value, students may not experience it as such. For example, in several districts, staff offer what they see as freshly prepared meals, but students do not interpret them that way.

In the language of coproduction, these findings indicate that the value proposition of the NSLP is not always such that its clients are encouraged to use the service, that is, to eat the school meal. The value proposition provided by the staff is either not designed or not executed such that students react as the program staff desire. Students have the final say in whether a healthy meal ends up in their stomachs or the trash can, so without the appropriate action on their part, the ultimate goals of the program, student health and well-being, are not achieved.

To encourage student participation in the NSLP and consumption of healthy foods, staff could adjust the value offering of the school meal to reflect the characteristics that students find important and may be currently lacking. This chapter offers empirical evidence to support such a change by showing reasons why students may not eat at school and offering practical suggestions to make school meals, and fruits and vegetables in particular, more appealing to students. More broadly, these findings suggest the usefulness of studying the NSLP as a public program—notably one that depends on coproduction for its success and so for which we must take seriously the perspectives of both program providers and clients.

THE NSLP AS COPRODUCTION

In public administration literature, coproduction is the idea that individuals and groups beyond the state contribute to the delivery of public services (Nabatchi, Sancino, and Sicilia 2017; Brandsen and Honingh 2018). The term has been used and defined in many ways since its initial introduction in the early 1980s (Dudau, Glennon, and Verschuere 2019; Brandsen and Honingh 2018; Nabatchi, Sancino, and Sicilia 2017). In this chapter, I draw on one of the primary conceptions of coproduction: as "self-help efforts in human service delivery" (Sharp 1980, 113) in which citizens assist in bringing about positive changes in themselves.

Certain public services are designed to change their recipients and as such, "the primary beneficiaries are the clients themselves . . . [they are the] 'raw material,' 'finished product' and 'consumer'" (Whitaker 1980, 240). The role of the service deliverer is to help bring about the changes. But it is ultimately the recipient who must personally transform in order for the desired results to be achieved, and thus they are the coproducer of these results. The classic example of this type of coproduction is education: the government can build schools and teachers can give lessons, but students will not learn without active participation, such as coming to class and doing their homework. The policy goal will not be achieved unless students help transform themselves from uneducated to educated.

The NSLP requires coproduction in a similar way: the service deliverer offers the opportunity to produce value, and the recipient is a necessary coparticipant. To the extent that foodservice staff want to encourage healthy eating by students, they need students to behave in certain ways. If students do not eat at school or do not eat healthy foods, they will not become healthy, well-fed children, and the hunger prevention and health promotion services that the NSLP aims to provide will not occur.

Alford (2016) and Nabatchi and colleagues (2017) offer the frame of public and private value as products of the coproduction process. Alford notes that most coproductive processes will generate both private value, which solely benefits the client, and public value, which he defines as the things that people value beyond their own self-interest such as "protecting children, upholding human rights or assisting the poor" (2016, 680). Alford gives the example of education, which has the public value of social, cultural, and economic benefits to society in addition to private value for the child in terms of improved opportunities.

Similarly, for school lunch, the private value in the short-term would be the child's satiation and enjoyment of the meal. Students may also receive long-term private value from improved health and associated financial and personal benefits. The public value of the NSLP, as suggested by the goals stated in its original and reauthorizing legislation, is in fulfilling a shared commitment to safeguarding children from hunger while also providing societal benefits via increased human capital and decreased health care costs. When students choose to eat the meal, they create value for themselves because they enjoy it or are no longer hungry and value to the public because some measure of child food security has been secured and the student's current or future health has been enhanced. But if the student doesn't eat the meal, then no value, public or private, is created.

The major implication of this coproduction framework is that the consumer and their experience of the service matters greatly to public service delivery outcomes. Osborne and colleagues highlight that all value creation is dependent on the client. The service provider can only offer a "value proposition," which the client may or may not take them up on (Osborne 2018; Dudau, Glennon, and Verschuere 2019; Eriksson 2019; Chandler and Lusch 2015). If the client chooses not to take advantage of the value proposition, then no value is created. Clients are incentivized to participate because they expect to receive private value as a result of using or engaging with the service (van Eijk and Gasco 2018). This value corresponds to their material interests and is comprised of "their satisfaction with the service, the impact of the service experience upon their wellbeing and the extent to which it meets their social, health or economic needs" (Osborne, Radnor, and Strokosch 2016, 643).

As a result, a major task of the service provider is to create in the recipient a desire to coproduce through an appeal, largely, to the client's private value. Although public programs may be provided on a broad basis and justified by public value, ultimately services are "interpreted and made sense of by individual consumers" (Dudau et al. 2019, 1584). To that end, the user's value creation process should be the starting point for analysis, specifically understanding "[the] individual's lived experience and the social context in which value is created" (Trischler and Charles 2019, 14).

Within the context of the NSLP, this means that policymakers as well as on-the-ground service providers should pay attention to how students make sense of the service offered (i.e., the meal), what generates value for them, and what encourages them to coproduce, while taking account of their specific experiences and context. However, little research has investigated the reasons why students do or do not eat lunch at school or the reasons why they select and eat particular foods. Although adults may make assumptions or find their own ways to explain students' behaviors, few studies have actually asked students their perspective on what influences them to participate in the NSLP and why they eat what they do, especially in terms of healthy foods (Byker Shanks, Banna, and Serrano 2017; Guerrero, Olsen, and Wistoft 2006). (Notable exceptions include Zhao et al. (2019), Asada et al. (2017), and Payán et al. (2017).)

Trischler and Charles (2019) suggest that a "microanalysis" of users' "specific needs, motivations, and preferences" (29) can illuminate what encourages service users to coproduce in a way that cocreates private, and ideally public, value. The next section offers such a microanalysis, using empirical evidence from research with students and school foodservice staff.

STAFF AND STUDENT PERSPECTIVES

This section examines the NSLP coproduction process by looking at the alignment (or lack thereof) between the perspectives of school foodservice staff and students on the value offering that is the school lunch. Clients must see a benefit in the program in order to participate in the ways that providers want them to. If the meal program staff offer a service that students do not expect to be positive, they will not take advantage of it. Without clients using the service, the policy does not create any value for the proposed beneficiaries or the broader public. Thus, in order for cocreation of value to take place, the program providers must take into account the factors influencing their clients' coproductive activities and adjust what they provide accordingly or otherwise respond to the clients' concerns.

There are many factors which influence whether students anticipate that taking advantage of the school meal offering will create private value (i.e., enjoyment, satiation, positive social experience) for them and thus whether they participate in the NSLP and which foods they select and eat (Rosenthal 2020). Here I focus on the characteristics of the food provided, although many other factors (such as students' familiarity with foods, the diversity and variety of options provided, and the experience of the cafeteria) also influence students' perceptions of the school meal and whether they choose to eat it.

In this section, I give a brief overview of the research methods used to collect and analyze data in the MHMR project. I then draw on this data to compare staff and student perspectives on the food offered at school, using as examples their perceptions of the sensory attributes of the food and its freshness. Foodservice staff and students agree that the food available at school should be tasty, appealing, and fresh. However, staff may not always be able to execute or communicate these characteristics in a way that students experience positively. In other cases, staff may not recognize or prioritize certain characteristics that are significant to students. As a result, students may not see as much value in the school lunch offering as staff anticipate they will, and thus students do not react by participating and eating as staff would expect.

Methods

The MHMR project, which ran from November 2015 through May 2018, examined meal program operations in six school districts. (See table 5.1 for demographic details of participating districts.) The six districts were all relatively large, in sound financial health, and committed to providing healthy meals to students.

The research team conducted twenty-eight interviews with district-level foodservice staff (e.g., foodservice director, menu planner, and procurement

Table 5.1   Participating School District Demographic Details, SY 2016–2017[a]

State	School District County Classification[b]	Student Enrollment	Students Qualifying for Free or Reduced-Price Lunch (%)	Student Lunch Participation Rate (%)
Florida	Large central metro	186,332	68	60
Georgia	Large fringe metro	180,000	42	68
Iowa	Micropolitan	32,979	74	66
Kentucky	Large central metro	100,063	68	68
South Carolina	Medium metro	17,301	35	68
Virginia	Large fringe metro	89,901	40	62

[a] Most of the project data collection took place in SY 2016–2017, and we asked participating districts to provide demographic information for this year.

[b] Counties designated as "metro" are part of a metropolitan statistical area (MSA). "Micropolitan" refers to a county that is part of a "micropolitan statistical area," similar to an MSA but which contains nonmetropolitan counties and has a smaller nucleus.

Source: County classification is from the 2013 National Center for Health Statistics Urban-Rural Classification Scheme for Counties by Deborah Ingram and Sheila Franco, *Vital and Health Statistics* 2(166). Student enrollment and free or reduced-price lunch qualification rates were calculated using data from the National Center for Education Statistics of the U.S. Department of Education, available at http://www .nces.ed.gov. Lunch participation rates were self-reported by district foodservice staff.

manager) and twenty-four with school-based cafeteria managers (recommended by the district's key informant, a district-level staff member).[2] Interviews with staff covered details on school meal operations (e.g., budgets, staff training, menu planning, and food preparation), the interviewee's experience providing healthy foods in school meals, and their perceptions of other stakeholders' attitudes to healthy foods.

We also held seventeen group interviews with three to eight students each, in elementary, middle, and high schools. In most schools, the student participants were members of a culinary class, agricultural program, or the student council. We did not collect demographic information other than age for the students in the group interview. (See table 5.2 for demographic details of the schools in which we conducted student interviews.) Most of the schools were close to the national average for the percentage of students qualifying for free or reduced-price meals (48%).[3] Fourteen of seventeen schools had a majority of students classified in racial groups other than white.[4]

Student group interviews focused on students' perspectives on the quality and experience of school lunch as well as their understanding of and opinions on healthy foods in particular. The interviews used a modified "draw and write" approach: we began by asking students to draw pictures of a typical school lunch, what they usually eat, a healthy lunch, their favorite school foods, and the cafeteria environment (Nomakhwezi Mayaba and Wood 2015). This methodology allows for greater student agency, as children can use their own language and categories instead of responding to suggestions made by the researcher (Wills 2012; Honkanen, Poikolainen, and Karlsson 2018; Nomakhwezi Mayaba and Wood 2015; Punch 2002).

I analyzed individual and group interviews using a "generic" coding approach, accompanied by writing analytical memos and comparing coded data using matrix data displays (Lichtman 2013; Saldaña 2013; Miles and Huberman 1994). From this analysis, I drew on literature related to consumer perceptions of food quality (Fernqvist and Ekelund 2014) as well as anthropological and sociological explorations of eating behavior (Stok et al. 2017; Furst et al. 1996) to develop models of staff and student perspectives on the influences on student participation, selection, and consumption in the NSLP (Rosenthal 2020).

Sensory Attributes

Students on Sensory Attributes

Consistent with previous literature, the students in this study reported the taste of foods as a key motivator for them to eat or not at school (Krølner et al. 2011; Brug et al. 2008; Ludvigsen and Scott 2009; Contento et al. 2006). Almost every student talked about the taste of the school's food in

Amy Rosenthal

Table 5.2 Demographic Characteristics of Students and Schools Participating in Group Interviews

District	School Level	Number of Students in Interview	Age Range of Students in Interview	Students Qualifying for Free or Reduced-Price Lunch (%)	Student Lunch Participation Rate (%)
Florida	High	6	15–17	53	37
	Middle	5	12–14	52	43
	Elementary	3	6–8	100	98
Georgia	High	4	16–19	76	n/a
	Middle	3	13	26	n/a
	Middle II	6	12–13	88	n/a
	Elementary	8	10–11	30	n/a
Iowa	Middle	8	11–14	78	92
	Elementary	7	8–10	83	n/a
Kentucky	High	7	15–18	32	35
	Middle	7	11–15	47	67
	Elementary	7	8–11	60	71
South Carolina	High	5	16–17	18	76
	Middle	3	11–12	55	69
	Elementary	6	8–11	100	77
Virginia	High	4	16–17	45	63
	Middle	7	11–12	53	82
		Total Students	*Range; Mean; Standard Deviation*	*Mean (%)*	*Mean (%)*
		96	6-19; M = 12.3; SD = 3.3	58	67
	High	26	15–19; M = 16.4; SD = 1.0	45	53
	Middle	39	11–15; M = 12.4; SD = 1.1	57	71
	Elementary	31	6–11; M = 9.4; SD = 1.3	74	82

n/a indicates not available

Source: Free or reduced-price lunch qualification rates were calculated using data from the National Center for Education Statistics of the U.S. Department of Education, available at http://www.nces.ed.gov. Lunch participation rates were self-reported by meal program staff but were not reported for schools in Georgia or for the elementary school in Iowa.

some way, using adjectives from "delicious" to "nasty." Although students did think that "some [foods] have good tastes," students generally described the taste of school lunch negatively.

Students used poor taste or lack of taste to explain why they don't eat lunch at school or don't eat certain foods. For example, a high school student noted that the food being "bland" means students aren't inspired to "go back the next day and get some more." Other high schoolers specifically said that their expectation that certain foods will taste bad means they don't choose those items and that in general they don't eat the food when it doesn't taste good.

Students across school levels frequently expressed concerns about other sensory attributes of cafeteria food as well. Nearly, every group negatively described the appearance of school foods, noting food looking "like plastic," inedible, overcooked, or not appetizing. In describing foods, they do and don't like at school, students often referred to the item's texture. Items might be too hard or soft, too wet or dry, as well as lumpy, bruised, chewy, grainy, slimy, or feeling like plastic or tinfoil in the mouth. Students also noticed when foods were not executed as they would expect in terms of temperature and doneness, commenting on finding foods such as broccoli or chicken nuggets that seemed either burnt or undercooked. Students noted several items that were served too warm, such as salads, or too cold, including juice, cinnamon buns, and peanut butter sandwiches.

Staff on Sensory Attributes

Like students, foodservice staff frequently mentioned how foods taste, and several described taste as what matters most to students. Staff highlighted the appearance of the food and the lunch line almost as frequently as they did taste, often referring to the adage that "you eat with your eyes first." Foodservice staff responsible for creating menus described that they choose types of foods that they expect students will like, and then they find items to purchase or create recipes to provide them. These staff expressed a great deal of concern about choosing brands or creating recipes such that the menu items will taste and look good to students.

However, only a few foodservice staff mentioned the texture of items making a difference to students' liking of them or referred to serving items at the correct temperature. None explicitly mentioned cooking foods to the appropriate doneness as something they or students pay attention to.

Sensory Attributes in Practice

Both staff and students expressed the importance of cafeteria food tasting and looking good, and staff do try to provide lunches they think students will like. But in practice, students often do not experience school lunch as appealing to their senses. The process of menu creation is driven by staff members' palates and their own sense of what will look appealing on the lunch line—which may not align with students' senses. While most districts do some kind of testing of items with students before serving them, the isolated context of a taste test may not suitably reflect the reality of the situation in which a student will eat the item (Koster 2009).

On a regular day in the cafeteria, an item may not turn out like it did when prepared for a special tasting. Cafeteria staff may have forgotten an ingredient or set the oven to the wrong temperature. Foods could have been sitting out between lunch periods and gotten too hard or too dry, too cold or too warm. Cafeteria staff did not frequently mention concern about the temperature and texture of what they serve, and without appropriate attention to execution, items may not be appealing to students when they see or taste them. While a menu planner may have carefully selected a pizza brand that they think has the best flavor, students may only experience a pizza that is too greasy or too cold.

Similarly, while staff noted that the appearance of the serving line and the items available are important, they may not always be able to make everything look as they might like and as students will find appealing. Cafeteria staff may not notice whether a film has formed on the macaroni and cheese or may not have time to keep it looking appealing as hundreds of students come through the lunch line. A sandwich that looks fine on a plate when observed by the menu planner may not be as attractive when wrapped in plastic in the cafeteria.

As a result, even something that district-level staff liked and that met with student approval in a taste test may not end up being something that students select and eat. Issues in execution could arise every time an item is served, and over time, students learn not to select this item because they know they will not enjoy it. And even if a student has only a few, or even one, negative experiences of an item, it can shape their expectations. A lack of consistency in how products are prepared may make students reticent to choose them because they cannot trust the quality they will receive. Overall, if students do not trust that the foods served at school will be appealing for them to eat, they may choose not to use the program at all.

Freshness

Students on Freshness

The students in this study also frequently judged school foods based on how they thought foods had been prepared or processed. The idea of freshness came up repeatedly in student discussions. All students described fresh foods positively, such as suggesting that the best way to improve the cafeteria would be "just fresher food." They particularly wanted fresh fruits and vegetables, contrasting them with those that had been canned or frozen. For example, students in two different schools said they disliked the vegetables that they can tell were frozen because they turn out watery or tasting bad.

Students found it self-explanatory that high-quality food would be freshly made in their cafeteria by the cafeteria staff; as a middle schooler put it, the cafeteria staff "should start making fresh food." Another middle school student thought it would be "better" if the foodservice workers "made the pizza, like, in the back with fresh cheese and pepperoni . . . They put it in the oven and take it out." Students also explicitly expressed a distaste for foods that had been made elsewhere and reheated.

Staff on Freshness

School foodservice staff agreed that freshness is a desirable attribute of the school meal. In every district, the foodservice leadership made comments about their desire to use "fresh stuff," "go fresh," or "try to keep it as fresh as possible." All the districts prioritized serving produce that had not been canned or frozen. A few staff members made direct connections between freshness and enhanced student appeal, suggesting that fresh foods, especially fruits and vegetables, would taste better to students, and thus they would then be more likely to eat them.

All of the districts in this study were also attempting to do more cooking or preparation of items in their cafeterias to avoid serving reheated, premade convenience foods. Depending on the district infrastructure and capacity, this could mean cooking from scratch in each cafeteria (e.g., turning raw ground beef into homemade tomato sauce or baking specialty breads); combining premade ingredients for entrees (e.g., topping a premade pizza dough with cheese or putting together fresh sandwiches); or using a centralized production facility to make full meals or components of meals (e.g., macaroni and cheese or sauces). However, while many staff saw these types of preparation as indicative of a quality school food program, they did not necessarily suggest that students would be more likely to participate in the program or eat foods that had been prepared this way. In one district, student participation had gone down as they put more scratch-cooked entrees on the menu, and a staff member explained that they provide such items not because students want them but "to say that we have them" to parents.

Freshness in Practice

Student comments indicated that even if staff see themselves as providing fresh foods, students often do not experience what they are served as fresh. Students in only two schools described any of the food in their cafeteria as "fresh." They reported that fruits and vegetables, even if they had not been canned or frozen, might seem old, stale, or "about to be moldy." In other districts, even where staff cooked food in the school cafeteria, students did not recognize items as freshly prepared. In the district doing the most scratch cooking, a middle school student offered a suggestion to the cafeteria staff to "make your own stuff. You guys are the lunch ladies, you're supposed to be making food." Although food may be made in the cafeteria, students' experience of it may not align with what they expect of fresh food.

This lack of recognition becomes an even greater issue in districts that use a central kitchen model. Foodservice staff saw central facilities as a way of providing scratch-cooked food more efficiently. However, as one district leader recognized, those outside of the meal program staff may not see these foods as scratch cooking: "I don't know if people understand that we really do do a lot of scratch cooking . . . Because it's here [at the central facility], and it's not at their school, then they don't smell it, and see it."

Indeed, students may not see food from a central kitchen any differently from other prepackaged items. Student groups in two different districts vividly described seeing staff members open bags of macaroni and cheese or taco meat, and they referred to what they had seen as "jail food" and "disgusting." These students did not recognize, let alone value, that these foods had been specially prepared at the centralized facility with great attention by staff to what they thought students would enjoy and benefit from. They only saw the end result of food coming from a bag—both viscerally unappealing and an indication that the food had been poorly prepared.

Overall, it seems that although they do believe that freshness is important, some staff may not fully recognize the value that students place on freshness and the impact it has on their decisions about eating at school. In some cases, staff may value freshness, but the relatively high cost of purchasing, preparing, and storing fresh foods may prevent schools from serving them, especially produce. Further, even when staff are able to purchase and prepare what they see as fresh, elements of their execution of meals may mean that students do not get the visual cues or the sensory experience that aligns with their expectations for fresh or freshly prepared foods. As a result, while adults may see their value offering as a fresh meal, students may not interpret or experience it in this way and will not be moved to participate in the NSLP or eat the "fresh" items that adults want them to.

IMPLICATIONS OF THE COPRODUCTION LENS

The findings above indicate that while much of what foodservice staff would like to provide in the meal program (tasty, fresh, attractive foods) should appeal to students, often students do not perceive school food this way. Though foodservice staff work hard to offer a meal that students will enjoy, they may not recognize that some characteristics they want to provide, like freshness, are not translating to the student experience. Further, adults may not prioritize some of the specific qualities that matter to students, such as the temperature and texture of items.

If students do not find value in the meal service, through the characteristics of the food or other elements of the lunch experience, they may choose to avoid certain foods or not participate at all. When this happens, the public value of the NSLP is not created. The program's value is in the prevention of student hunger and the promotion of student health—so if students don't eat or don't eat healthy foods, there is no public value created. Nor is there private value created: if students do not participate, they cannot benefit from the meal, and their families do not benefit from the subsidy intended for them.

Thus, student perceptions of the meal service are a major factor in the success of the NSLP as a program, through their contribution to students' coproduction behaviors. On the other side of the coproduction process, the school meal program must offer a service that students want to take advantage of. If foodservice staff do not understand students' perceptions of the service offered, the steps they take to encourage students to create value through using the service may not have the desired effect. Staff and student perceptions of the value offering—what it should be and what it actually is—must align for cocreation of value and the desired program outcomes to result.

The findings above suggest that foodservice staff should focus on executing items to maximize their sensory attributes, making sure they are properly cooked and served with the appearance, temperature, and texture that students will find appropriate. Making items as appealing as possible, within the constraints of the NSLP regulations and structures, is important to positively impacting students' experience of school lunch and ensuing likelihood to use the program.

In order to do so, staff need feedback from students, both about characteristics of the school meal that students value and about whether the meals have met student standards. Based on the responses of those in this study, many students would be willing to provide more input about the food served at school. Literature on coproduction hypothesizes that involving users in design of services is a key way to improve their quality, make them more efficient, and achieve other benefits such as enhancing democracy (Sharp 1980; Moynihan and Thomas 2013; Bevir, Needham, and Waring 2019; Brandsen, Steen, and Verschuere 2018; Voorberg, Bekkers, and Tummers 2015). Institutionalizing mechanisms for students to provide feedback might also help students feel a greater sense of ownership of the program and interest in participating. Involving students more in the design of the meal program could be, at its most robust, an opportunity to develop their sense of themselves as citizens and their ability to participate in civic discourse.

To make the process of engaging students worthwhile, it is crucial that adults not only listen to students but take their suggestions seriously and implement them where possible. However, both collecting and acting on student feedback might go beyond the resources currently available to many school district meal programs. Meal programs operate under tight budgets and without much extra time or labor to develop new ways of interacting with clients and to change practices based on what they learn. While some improvements could no doubt be made within the current context, institutionalizing the ability of NSLP providers to fully recognize and respond to their clients' needs would require legislators and administrators to increase guidance and funding for school foodservice programs.

Ideally, involvement of students in NSLP decision-making processes would expand to program administration and legislation as well, such that students could provide input on processes of NSLP policymaking beyond the school or even school district. Coproduction literature suggests that explicitly involving clients and service providers in the design of policies and regulations could be a way to achieve better alignment among these actors and to create social programs that truly generate both public and private value (Nabatchi, Sancino, and Sicilia 2017; Voorberg, Bekkers, and Tummers 2015).

APPLICATIONS

Applications for the NSLP

Applying a lens of coproduction to the findings of the MHMR study offers a valuable way to understand why the NSLP may or may not produce the healthy, hunger-free kids that policymakers, practitioners, and parents want it to. When we see school lunch as a value offering that students may or may not take advantage of, students become clients of a social program, agents whose experiences we must understand in order to encourage the behaviors that will create positive program outcomes. A coproduction lens also highlights the foodservice staff whose perspectives and ensuing decisions create the value offering of the meal. And in turn, taking students and staff seriously as contributors to the success of the NSLP suggests how we should engage with them, in research as well as in practice.

Student and staff perceptions of what is desirable in the school meal and whether meals meet those standards must better align in order for students to respond positively to the NSLP. Providing meals that will encourage students to eat healthfully at school will require greater efforts by program providers to solicit and learn from firsthand student perspectives about the characteristics of the food that matter to them, how to improve those, and whether changes are effective. And while the food itself is of major importance, other factors (e.g., customer service, the built environment of the cafeteria) also influence how students see and respond to the value offering of the school meal. Not only school foodservice staff but also administrators and policymakers must be attentive to the broad range of elements of the school meal as they try to design and implement policies that will encourage students' participation and consumption in the NSLP. A key component is insuring that school food providers are able to purchase, prepare, and serve food in ways that will appeal to students—which may require increases in the Federal reimbursement rate for school meals as well as other financial and technical support.

Academics and other researchers also can play a role in improving school meal policies and practices, through both the content and approach of their work—namely by including students and foodservice staff as subjects and informants. Researchers can expand our understanding of school food programs by asking questions about worker and student perspectives on various aspects of the NSLP. In doing so, they should prioritize methods that collect information from participants directly about their own experience and triangulate by observing students' and workers' behavior to see how it aligns with what they report.

Applications Beyond School Food

More broadly, the findings generated by using a coproduction framework to understand the NSLP suggests the potential of applying a coproduction lens to other food- and health-related public programs, especially those that seek certain behaviors from beneficiaries. For example, the clients of the Special Supplemental Nutrition Program for Women, Infants and Children (WIC) are caregivers with low incomes who receive food benefits and are supposed to change how they feed their children to align with mainstream nutritional advice (Hand 2014). Exploration into perceptions of WIC services and the alignment of client and provider perspectives on offerings may suggest ways the WIC program could be adapted such that more clients respond as desired to this program.

Further theoretical and empirical analysis covering different types of programs would advance understanding of coproduction as well as provide useful information to improve provision of these services. Studies should explore clients' responses to different value offerings, especially for services which rely on eliciting specific client behaviors to be successful. Similarly, more research on the potential of program clients as codesigners of program practices, legislation, and regulation could help facilitate client engagement and ensuing benefits to program delivery and beyond.

Studying coproduction requires analysis of the service itself, in context, and *how* outcomes are created as users do or do not take up a value offering. Focusing on the experience of program recipients is a fundamental shift from trying to improve program outcomes by adjusting wording of policy text, creating new regulations, or improving fidelity to program rules. Understanding social services as coproduction means prioritizing the client experience, the provider experience, and their interaction as a site of both research inquiry and intervention.

Food programs are particularly apt for this kind of attention, given both the collective desire to change what people eat and the agency that individuals retain over those decisions. The students in this study had strong ideas about what they wanted to eat and how that aligned with school offerings. Public administration theory can help us understand the role of such beliefs in whether programs are successful or not and more important, how programs can adapt to better achieve their goals.

CONCLUSION

In this study, analyzing the NSLP as a case of coproduction generated empirical evidence about clients' and providers' perspectives on the program, which suggested ways to make students more likely to use the program as intended and thus for the NSLP to meet its goal of supporting student health and well-being. In addition to its practical applicability, the use of coproduction theory suggests a potentially fruitful way to approach public programs both in theory and practice. The application of coproduction to the NSLP highlights an often-overlooked element of public administration: the contribution of on-the-ground program actors to whether programs achieve their goals. When we recognize the NSLP or other social services as programs that depend on coproduction for their success, we see we must take seriously the contributions of both program providers and clients.

Attempts to better understand and engage stakeholders of public programs are especially relevant for food-related programs. Developing and implementing public policy related to food requires collaboration with many stakeholders, from producers and policymakers to cooks and customers. However, too often consumers (especially children) and food-service workers are left out of the discussion. In this particular case, we see how the tools of public administration can help those interested in the outcomes of the school food system to articulate the mechanisms affecting what is provided and who eats it. Public administration not only offers a language with which to identify stakeholders and make sense of how they interact but also suggests solutions—namely, that the incorporation of these stakeholders into the development and implementation of the programs affecting them can bring food policies closer to achieving our collective goals for the public good.

NOTES

1. The MHMR project was funded by the Robert Wood Johnson Foundation and conducted by School Food Focus and FoodCorps.

2. The study was approved by the Rutgers University Institutional Review Board. All quotations from interviews are presented anonymously.

3. Based on my calculations using data from the National Center for Education Statistics of the U.S. Department of Education, available at http://www.nces .ed.gov.

4. Based on data from data from the National Center for Education Statistics of the U.S. Department of Education, available at http://www.nces.ed.gov.

REFERENCES

Alford, John. 2016. "Coproduction, Interdependence and Publicness: Extending Public Service-Dominant Logic." *Public Management Review* 18 (5): 673–91. doi :10.1080/14719037.2015.1111659.

Asada, Yuka, Alejandro Hughes, Margaret Read, Marlene Schwartz, and Jamie Chriqui. 2017. "High School Students' Recommendations to Improve School Food Environments: Insights From A Critical Stakeholder Group." *Journal of School Health* 87 (11): 842–49.

Bevir, Mark, Catherine Needham, and Justin Waring. 2019. "Inside Coproduction: Ruling, Resistance, and Practice." *Social Policy & Administration* 53 (1): 1–6. doi:10.1111/spol.12483.

Brandsen, Taco, and Marlies Honingh. 2018. "Definitions of Coproduction and Co-Creation." In *Coproduction and Co-Creation: Engaging Citizens in Public Services*, edited by Taco Brandsen, Trui Steen, and Bram Verschuere, 9–17. New York: Routledge.

Brandsen, Taco, Trui Steen, and Bram Verschuere. 2018. "How to Encourage Co-Creation and Coproduction: Some Recommendations." In *Coproduction and Co-Creation: Engaging Citizens in Public Services*, edited by Taco Brandsen, Trui Steen, and Bram Verschuere, 299–302. New York: Routledge.

Brug, Johannes, Nannah I. Tak, Saskia J. Te Velde, Elling Bere, and Ilse De Bourdeaudhuij. 2008. "Taste Preferences, Liking and Other Factors Related to Fruit and Vegetable Intakes among Schoolchildren: Results from Observational

Studies." *British Journal of Nutrition* 29 (Suppl. 1): 7–14. doi:10.1017/S0007114508892458.

Byker Shanks, Carmen, Jinan Banna, and Elena L. Serrano. 2017. "Food Waste in the National School Lunch Program 1978–2015: A Systematic Review." *Journal of the Academy of Nutrition and Dietetics* 117 (11): 1792–1807. doi:10.1016/j.jand.2017.06.008.

Chandler, Jennifer D., and Robert F. Lusch. 2015. "Service Systems: A Broadened Framework and Research Agenda on Value Propositions, Engagement, and Service Experience." *Journal of Service Research* 18 (1): 6–22. doi:10.1177/1094670514537709.

Coleman-Jensen, Alisha, Matthew P. Rabbitt, Christian A. Gregory, and Anita Singh. 2019. "Household Food Security in the United States in 2018." *U.S. Household Food Security: Statistics and Analysis for 2014*. doi:10.2139/ssrn.2504067.

Contento, Isobel R., Sunyna S. Williams, John L. Michela, and Amie B. Franklin. 2006. "Understanding the Food Choice Process of Adolescents in the Context of Family and Friends." *Journal of Adolescent Health* 38 (5): 575–82. doi:10.1016/j.jadohealth.2005.05.025.

Dudau, Adina, Russ Glennon, and Bram Verschuere. 2019. "Following the Yellow Brick Road? (Dis)Enchantment with Co-Design, Coproduction and Value Co-Creation in Public Services." *Public Management Review* 21 (11): 1577–94. doi:10.1080/14719037.2019.1653604.

Eijk, Carola van, and Mila Gasco. 2018. "Unravlleing the Coproducers: Who Are They and What Motivations Do They Have?" In *Coproduction and Co-Creation: Engaging Citizens in Public Services*, edited by Taco Brandsen, Trui Steen, and Bram Verschuere, 63–76. New York: Routledge.

Eriksson, Erik M. 2019. "Representative Coproduction: Broadening the Scope of the Public Service Logic." *Public Management Review* 21 (2): 291–314. doi:10.1080/14719037.2018.1487575.

Fernqvist, Fredrik, and Lena Ekelund. 2014. "Credence and the Effect on Consumer Liking of Food—A Review." *Food Quality and Preference* 32: 340–53. doi:10.1016/j.foodqual.2013.10.005.

Fox, Mary Kay, and Elizabeth Gearan. 2019. "School Nutrition and Meal Cost Study: Summary of Findings." Alexandria, VA: U.S. Department of Agriculture, Food and Nutrition Service. https://fns-prod.azureedge.net/sites/default/files/resource-files/SNMCS_Summary-Findings.pdf. Accessed February 6, 2020.

Furst, Tanis, Margaret Connors, Carole A. Bisogni, Jeffery Sobal, and Laura Winter Falk. 1996. "Food Choice: A Conceptual Model of the Process." *Appetite* 26 (3): 247–65. doi:10.1006/appe.1996.0019.

Guerrero, Kayla, Annemarie Olsen, and Karen Wistoft. 2006. "What Role Does Taste Play in School Meal Studies? A Narrative Review of the Literature." *Journal of Child Nutrition & Management* 42 (1).

Hand, Laura C. 2014. "Negotiating Healthy Self-Government: A Grounded Theory Study of Interactions in Arizona's WIC Program." Doctoral thesis, Arizona State University.

Healthy, Hunger-Free Kids Act of 2010. 2010. P.L. 111–296, 124 Stat. 3183.

Honkanen, Kati, Jaana Poikolainen, and Liisa Karlsson. 2018. "Children and Young People as Co-Researchers–Researching Subjective Well-Being in Residential Area with Visual and Verbal Methods." *Children's Geographies* 16 (2): 184–95. doi:10 .1080/14733285.2017.1344769.

Koster, E. P. 2009. "Diversity in the Determinants of Food Choice: A Psychological Perspective." *Food Quality and Preference* 20: 70–82. doi:10.1016/j. foodqual.2007.11.002.

Krølner, Rikke, Mette Rasmussen, Johannes Brug, Knut-Inge Klepp, Marianne Wind, and Pernille Due. 2011. "Determinants of Fruit and Vegetable Consumption among Children and Adolescents: A Review of the Literature. Part II: Qualitative Studies." *International Journal of Behavioral Nutrition and Physical Activity* 8 (1): 112. doi:10.1186/1479-5868-8-112.

Lichtman, Marilyn. 2013. "Making Meaning From Your Data." In *Qualitative Research in Education*, 241–68. SAGE Publications, Inc. doi:10.4135/9781849208574.

Ludvigsen, Anna, and Sara Scott. 2009. "Real Kids Don't Eat Quiche." *Food, Culture & Society* 12 (4): 417–36. doi:10.2752/175174409x456728.

Miles, Matthew B., and Michael Huberman. 1994. *Qualitative Data Analysis: An Expanded Sourcebook*. Thousand Oaks, CA: SAGE.

Moynihan, Donald P., and John Clayton Thomas. 2013. "Citizen, Customer, Partner." *Public Administration Review* 73 (6): 786–96. doi:10.1111/puar.12109.786.

Nabatchi, Tina, Alessandro Sancino, and Mariafrancesca Sicilia. 2017. "Varieties of Participation in Public Services: The Who, When, and What of Coproduction." *Public Administration Review* 77 (5): 766–76. doi:10.1111/puar.12765.

Nomakhwezi Mayaba, Nokhanyo, and Lesley Wood. 2015. "Using Drawings and Collages as Data Generation Methods With Children." *International Journal of Qualitative Methods*. doi:10.1177/1609406915621407.

Osborne, Stephen P. 2018. "From Public Service-Dominant Logic to Public Service Logic: Are Public Service Organizations Capable of Coproduction and Value Co-Creation?" *Public Management Review* 20 (2): 225–31. doi:10.1080/1471903 7.2017.1350461.

Osborne, Stephen P., Zoe Radnor, and Greta Nasi. 2013. "A New Theory for Public Service Management? Toward a (Public) Service-Dominant Approach." *American Review of Public Administration* 43 (2): 135–58. doi:10.1177/0275074012466935.

Osborne, Stephen P, Zoe Radnor, and Kirsty Strokosch. 2016. "Coproduction and the Co-Creation of Value in Public Services: A Suitable Case for Treatment?" *Public Management Review* 18 (5): 639–53. doi:10.1080/14719037.2015.1111927.

Pautz, Michelle C., John C. Jones, and A. Bryce Hoflund. 2018. "On the Front Lines in School Cafeterias: The Trials and Tribulations of Food Service Directors." In *The Intersection of Food and Public Health: Current Policy Challenges and Solutions*, edited by A. Bryce Hoflund, John C. Jones, and Michelle C. Pautz, 121–32. Abington: Routledge.

Payán, Denise D., David C. Sloane, Jacqueline Illum, Tahirah Farris, and Lavonna B. Lewis. 2017. "Perceived Barriers and Facilitators to Healthy Eating and School Lunch Meals among Adolescents: A Qualitative Study." *American Journal of Health Behavior* 41 (5): 661–69. doi:10.5993/AJHB.41.5.15.

Punch, Samantha. 2002. "Research with Children: The Same or Different from Research with Adults?" *Childhood* 9 (3): 321–41. doi:10.1177/0907568202009003045.

Richard B. Russell National School Lunch Act. 1946. 42 U.S.C. § 1751.

Rosenthal, Amy. 2020. "'It Should Be Healthy but It Should Be Good': Perspectives of Students and Staff on the National School Lunch Program." Doctoral thesis, Rutgers University.

Rutledge, Jennifer Geist. 2018. "School Lunch Reform and the Problem with Obesity." In *The Intersection of Food and Public Health: Current Policy Challenges and Solutions*, edited by A. Bryce Hoflund, John C. Jones, and Michelle C. Pautz. Abingdon: Routledge.

Saldaña, Johnny. 2013. *The Coding Manual for Qualitative Researchers*. Second. Los Angeles: SAGE Publications, Ltd. doi:10.1017/CBO9781107415324.004.

Schwartz, Colin, and Margo G. Wootan. 2019. "How a Public Health Goal Became a National Law: The Healthy, Hunger-Free Kids Act of 2010." *Nutrition Today* 54 (2): 67–77. doi:10.1097/NT.0000000000000318.

Sharp, Elaine. 1980. "Toward a New Understanding of Urban Services and Citizen Participtaion: The Coprodution Concept." *Midwest Review of Public Administration* 14 (2): 105–18.

Stok, F. Marijn, Stefan Hoffmann, Dorothee Volkert, Heiner Boeing, Regina Ensenauer, Marta Stelmach-Mardas, Eva Kiesswetter, et al. 2017. "The DONE Framework: Creation, Evaluation, and Updating of an Interdisciplinary, Dynamic Framework 2.0 of Determinants of Nutrition and Eating." *PLoS One* 12 (2): 1–24. doi:10.1371/journal.pone.0171077.

Tabak, Rachel G., and Sarah Moreland-Russell. 2015. "Food Service Perspectives on National School Lunch Program Implementation." *Health Behavior Policy Review* 22 (5). doi:10.14485/HBPR.2.5.4.

Trischler, Jakob, and Michael Charles. 2019. "The Application of a Service Ecosystems Lens to Public Policy Analysis and Design: Exploring the Frontiers." *Journal of Public Policy and Marketing* 38 (1): 19–35. doi:10.1177/0743915618818566.

Voorberg, W. H., V. J. J. M. Bekkers, and L. G. Tummers. 2015. "A Systematic Review of Co-Creation and Coproduction: Embarking on the Social Innovation Journey." *Public Management Review* 17 (9). Routledge: 1333–57. doi:10.1080/1 4719037.2014.930505.

Whitaker, Gordon P. 1980. "Coproduction: Citizen Participation in Service Delivery." *Public Administration Review* 40 (3): 240–46. doi:10.2307/975377.

Wills, Wendy J. 2012. "Using Spoken and Written Qualitative Methods to Explore Children's and Young People's Food and Eating Practices." *Sociological Research Online* 17 (3). doi:10.5153/sro.2670.

Zhao, Chenchen, Chloe Panizza, Kira Fox, Carol J. Boushey, Carmen Byker Shanks, Selena Ahmed, Susan Chen, et al. 2019. "Plate Waste in School Lunch: Barriers, Motivators, and Perspectives of SNAP-Eligible Early Adolescents in the US." *Journal of Nutrition Education and Behavior* 51 (8). doi:10.1016/j. jneb.2019.05.590.

Chapter 6

Using a Multidimensional Food Insecurity Framework to Inform Public Policy

Danielle Smith, Erin Feichtinger, and Jodi Benenson

INTRODUCTION

The 690 million people worldwide (FAO et al. 2020) and 37 million (Coleman-Jensen et al. 2019) people in the United States who are food insecure, coupled with the health, economic, educational, social, and other consequences of such deprivation, make the issue of food insecurity indisputable. The U.S. Department of Agriculture (USDA) defines food insecurity as "a household-level economic and social condition of limited or uncertain access to adequate food" (U.S. Department of Agriculture 2019). Thus, while people from food secure homes have enough food at all times for an active, healthy, life, food insecurity occurs when households do not have money for food or run out of food.

Each discipline brings with it its own language to define, operationalize, and measure food insecurity. In recent years, there has been increased interest in the field of public administration around whether the approaches used to measure food insecurity are sufficient for understanding its implications for public policymaking. For example, the Community Food Security Measurement (CFSM) developed by the USDA measures food security annually, using a static measure of household food insecurity. However, this limited measure fails to capture the nuances within food insecurity, such as the different shapes hunger can take on a daily, weekly, and monthly basis, and the way social, political, and community settings may influence food insecurity. Recent scholarship around social determinants of health suggests that food insecurity does not exist in isolation, but intersects and overlaps with other issues such as under- or unemployment, low wages, social isolation, and lack of affordable housing (Roncarolo et al. 2013). Measures of food insecurity that capture the multiple conditions that affect a wide range of health, functioning, and quality-of-life outcomes and risks could provide opportunities to not only understand the causes and consequences of food insecurity, but can lead to the development of targeted policy interventions that both reduce chronic reliance on emergency food services and the causes of food insecurity.

To address these challenges, states and cities across the United States have begun to put together a series of tools to take a holistic approach to measuring food insecurity and self-sufficiency. While the notion of self-sufficiency has received criticism because it ascribes the responsibility of welfare to the individual, we consider the ways that findings from these tools can support effective public policy. This chapter uses a new tool—the Together Self-Sufficiency Outcomes Matrix (TSSOM)—to demonstrate what details can be uncovered when using a multidimensional measure of food insecurity and how it can connect to policy conversations in Nebraska. This chapter begins by providing an overview of the TSSOM tool, which is followed by the methodology to conduct the research for this chapter. We conclude with a set of research findings and how they connect to current policy conversations in Nebraska.

THE TOGETHER SELF-SUFFICIENCY OUTCOMES MATRIX

The TSSOM is a multidimensional tool aiming to provide clearer definitions and new, more flexible standards of measurement in order to capture the complexity of social issues surrounding food insecurity. The TSSOM was developed in 2018 by the authors in response to the rise in food insecurity and related issues in Omaha, Nebraska. Design of the TSSOM was also informed by the Arizona Self-Sufficiency Matrix, the LifeWorks Self-Sufficiency Matrix, Project Everlast Survey for transitioning foster youth, the USDA Community Food Security Module, and the U.S. Department of Housing and Urban Development assessment and measurement tool (2017), with modifications made to reflect the population served by Together, a nonprofit organization in Omaha, Nebraska.

The TSSOM measures levels of stability or vulnerability across ten key domains: education, housing stability, employment, income, access to health care, access to transportation, mental health status, support networks, community involvement, and food security. These domains were developed from best practices research, local and national standards, and tools used by other social services agencies, and contribute to our understanding of food insecurity in two unique ways (Rossi and Curtis 2013).

First, inflexible and narrow measurements provide limited effective and sustainable policy solutions addressing the root causes of food insecurity. For example, the Snohomish County Self-Sufficiency Taskforce found that while "self-sufficiency" came into vogue as a measurement standard in the mid-1980s, it lacked a concise definition (Snohomish County Self-Sufficiency Taskforce 2010). Self-sufficiency first focused on questions of income and calculated a household's self-sufficiency according to the basic expenses a working family must have in order to meet their basic needs without public assistance. In contrast, multidimensional measures provide a clearer picture of a person's needs than the Federal Poverty Level, and have spurred social service agencies to view self-sufficiency as more than a simple economic calculation. Expanding measurements of self-sufficiency allows us not only to understand the causes and consequences of an individual's food security but also helps to develop targeted interventions that reduce chronic reliance on emergency food services and the causes of food insecurity (Hart 2009). While public assistance programs are effective in reducing food insecurity, we must consider the informal support systems that impact the vulnerability of low-income households (Gunderson and Ziliak 2018). This research signals that social support and social cohesion reduce the risk of food insecurity, of remaining food insecure, and of becoming food insecure.

Second, the TSSOM is intended as a case management and a capacity-building tool for local nonprofit organizations. It can also inform policy. For example, the tool invites organizations to design comprehensive programs impacting more facets of a client's life, and helps define what poverty looks like for its clients. Further, the TSSOM allows organizations to use data to understand clients using both quantitative and qualitative data as a guide. This information helps organizations provide better services to clients and can educate the broader community and policymakers about the systemic issues and needs of the people served by nonprofits.

METHODOLOGY

Between 2019 and 2020, the research team conducted 200 semistructured interviews at a food pantry in Omaha, Nebraska using the TSSOM tool as a framework and guide. Operational definitions for each variable are based on established measures, such as USDA food insecurity standards and U.S. Department of Housing and Urban Development (HUD) guidelines relating to housing status. During these semistructured interviews, detailed notes were taken by the researchers. These interviews took place while study participants were visiting the food pantry, and each interview lasted between ten to forty-five minutes.

Participant responses were then coded using a Likert scale to represent the individual's level of vulnerability in each area of the SSOM. The numerically-coded responses informed descriptive statistics and patterns from the research, which was helpful in demonstrating trends of self-sufficiency along demographic lines such as age, gender, race and ethnicity, family size, and geographic location. Researchers were then able to determine whether or not there were any significant correlations between the reported levels of vulnerability across the different variables assessed by the SSOM. The useful-ness and efficacy of this approach were already evidenced by pilot interviews conducted for internal purposes. This study was approved by the Institutional Review Board of the University of Nebraska at Omaha/University of Nebraska Medical Center. Pseudonyms have been used throughout this chapter to pre-serve the privacy of TSSOM interview subjects.

FINDINGS

Of the 200 participants, 82.5 percent indicated that they were experiencing some degree of food insecurity, with 18.5 percent reporting severe to critical levels of hunger (see table 6.1). Across all participants, the mean food secu-rity score was 3.50 (+/− 1.12). Food security was found to be significantly positively correlated with a number of other variables, to include housing stability ($r = 0.388$, $p < 0.01$), employment ($r = 0.147$, $p < 0.05$), income ($r = 0.333$, $p < 0.01$), transportation ($r = 0.242$, $p < 0.01$), mental health status ($r = 0.255$, $p < 0.01$), support networks ($r = .284$, $p < 0.01$), and community involvement ($r = .232$, $p < 0.01$).

Hunger disparities varied among study participants (see figures 6.1 and 6.2 for mean food security scores by race/ethinicity and gender, as well as by age and gender). Individuals experiencing homelessness were significantly more likely to be food insecure than those who were housed ($r = −0.419$, $p < 0.01$). For perspective, homelessness was also significantly negatively correlated with potential protective factors against hunger, to include com-munity involvement ($r = −.330$, $p < 0.01$) and support networks ($r = −0.313$, $p < 0.01$). Although there were no statistically significant correlations found between race or ethnicity and hunger, food security levels did appear to vary slightly by gender among certain racial groups. Black/African American men reported higher food security than women, and the same was true for White men and women. Food security also seemed to increase with age ($r = 0.141$, $p < 0.01$), which is possibly a side effect of becoming more stable, form-ing families, developing a career, and the accumulation of resources (e.g., purchasing a home) over time. A degree of variability was also observed between men and women in certain age categories. Among younger people, primarily those who were between twenty-five to forty-four years old, women were more food secure than men on average. On the other hand, women aged

Table 6.1   **Distribution and Description of Food Security Scores among TSSOM Participants**

Score	Description	Participants
1	Critical Food Insecurity	14 (7.0 %)
	Participant has not eaten a full meal in 24 hours; frequently does not know where next meal is coming from; does not feel confident that they will be able to access food when needed.	
2	Very Low Food Security	23 (11.5 %)
	Often does not have enough to eat; often worried about whether food would run out before there was money to get more; often cannot afford to eat balanced meals; frequently cuts size of meals so others in the household can eat; has lost weight because of lack of food; a child has skipped meals because there wasn't enough money for food.	
3	Episodic Food Insecurity	47 (23.5 %)
	Concerns about food access occur relatively infrequently and are in response to changes in circumstances such as income, medical care, or behavioral/mental health issues.	
4	Low Food Security	81 (40.5 %)
	There is sometimes not enough to eat, and not enough of the kinds of food participant wants to eat; participant is sometimes worried that food would run out before there was money to buy more; sometimes could not afford to eat balanced meals; has not skipped a meal due to lack of food or resources in the last 6 months.	
5	High Food Security	35 (17.5 %)
	Participant feels comfortable accessing food when needed; has enough money (or is otherwise able) to feed themselves and their family; eats the kinds of food they want; feels they can provide balanced meals.	
Total		200

Source: Created by Authors

forty-five to fifty-four were approximately 17.8 percent less food secure than their male-identifying counterparts. One plausible explanation for this would be the significant positive relationship between the forty-five to fifty-four age grouping and households consisting of five to six people ($r = 0.144$, $p < 0.05$). At this stage of life, many participants described caring not only for themselves, their partners, and their own children, but also sometimes for grandchildren or aging parents. As family sizes grow, this could put additional pressure on participants, particularly women, as they attempt to provide adequate nutrition for the entire household.

It is worth recognizing that TSSOM is largely a self-report measure. Many participants who might seem food insecure to an outside observer expressed

Mean Food Security Scores by Race/Ethnicity and Gender

Together Self-Sufficiency Outcomes Matrix, 2019-2020

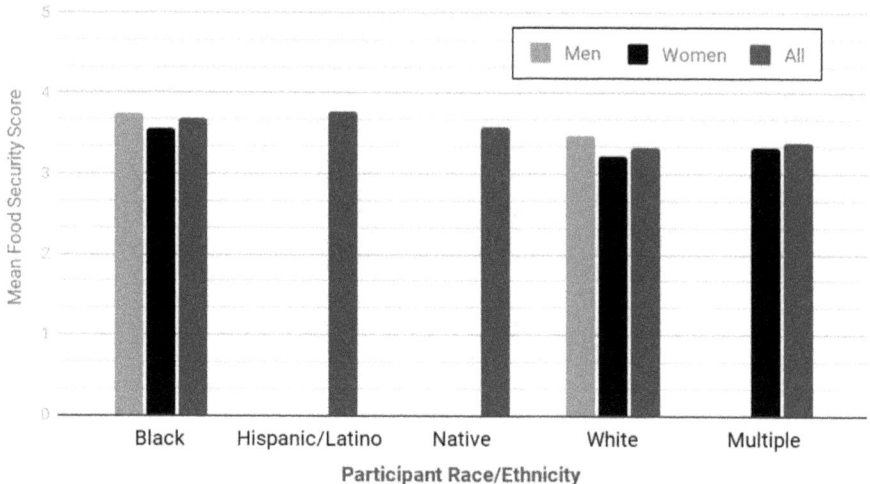

Figure 6.1   **Mean Food Security Scores by Race/Ethnicity and Gender.** *Source*: Authors

Mean Food Security Scores by Age and Gender

Together Self-Sufficiency Outcomes Matrix, 2019-2020

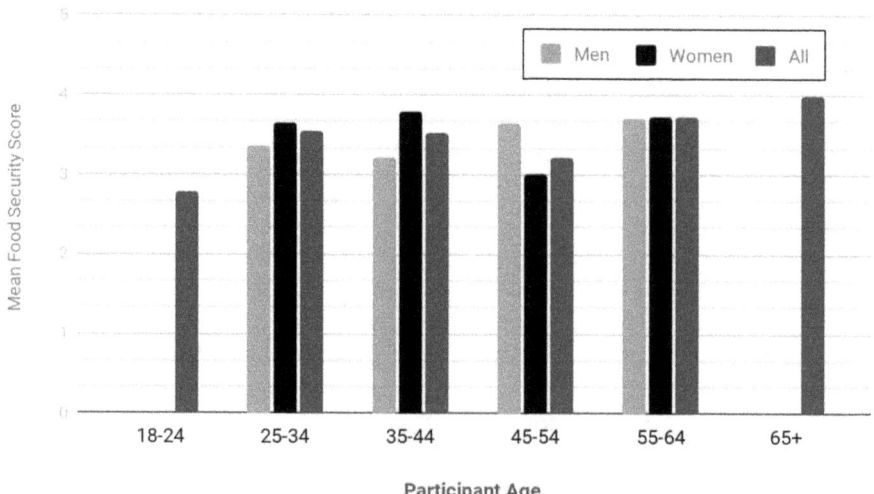

Figure 6.2   **Mean Food Security Scores by Age and Gender.** *Source*: Authors

they still felt able to feed their families. Although these respondents may not have had enough money to buy groceries at the supermarket, their confidence in pantries, family members, or other supports had lent them an increased degree of food security.

The Successes and Shortcomings of SNAP

Over half of TSSOM participants ($n = 110$, or 55%) received some amount of Supplemental Nutrition Assistance Program (SNAP) benefits. While there was no significant correlation identified between SNAP and food security among TSSOM participants, many respondents still felt that SNAP increased their food security. "I'd be starving to death without it," said one man. "[SNAP] helps balance the scales," another participant affirmed. SNAP was also the only form of income received by some participants; this was especially common among people experiencing homelessness. For one such respondent, SNAP was helpful for more than just buying food. "It helps me get into a warm place," he explained. In the middle of winter, having the ability to enter a store for a "legitimate" purpose was an added benefit.

However, the perceived utility of SNAP was far from unanimous for a number of reasons. Among those TSSOM respondents who received SNAP, household allotments averaged $45.76 per person per month, or $2.19 per person per day. Many participants expressed frustration with receiving stagnant, or even decreasing, benefits in the face of rising costs of living. Respondents told of sudden SNAP reductions or being cut off from the program entirely due to marginal increases in their income. Many older participants, for instance, saw their SNAP cut to amounts as low as fifteen dollars per month when their Social Security benefits kicked in at age sixty-five. Other respondents detailed how they had lost access to SNAP after taking on more hours or some other change in their employment circumstances. This phenomenon is commonly known as the "cliff effect" (Polkey 2019). Whether due to accepting a promotion at work, taking on a second job, or the activation of other benefits, a significant number of people found themselves paradoxically more food insecure after making exactly the type of good-faith efforts toward self-sufficiency that policymakers assert they should.

While most respondents did receive SNAP, many others were not able to access these funds. Some families found themselves just slightly above income limits, despite their struggling to make ends meet. As one woman put it, "[my husband] is a garbage man and he makes 'too much money . . . ' figure that one out." A number of participants stated they had received SNAP in the past, but received such small amounts and had decided it was not worth the hassle of recertifying every few months. For others, the application process itself was a deterrent to requesting assistance. Perhaps it is for this reason that participants who received other benefits, such as Section 8 housing vouchers or Social Security, were more likely to receive SNAP; having already determined the correct answers to questions from interviewers and figured out how to navigate government websites could make applying for SNAP seem less intimidating. Other commonly-cited barriers to seeking SNAP included the extensive work requirements or the possibility of a background check.

As of 2019, Nebraska was one of twenty-one states with a modified ban on providing SNAP benefits to individuals with certain drug felony convictions (Polkey 2019). In practice, this policy has resulted in stories such as that of John, a fifty-five-year-old diabetic who relies on food pantries to get by. Despite fifteen years of sobriety, he was not able to access SNAP benefits. Dante, a fifty-year-old landlord who was now sober, explained that he would have to complete a state-certified rehabilitation program in order to apply for SNAP. This was also the case for Amaya, a forty-four-year-old mother who had recently taken a ten-week substance abuse class. When she went to apply for SNAP for her family, she was informed by the Department of Health and Human Services that the course did not qualify because it was a "seminar."

Informal Supports

For many TSSOM participants, better food security was a matter of who they knew. It became apparent that networks of friends, family, and neighbors sharing food or other resources play a major role in mitigating hunger in Omaha. Quantitatively, this is most apparent through the positive correlation between support networks and food security ($r = 0.284$, $p < 0.01$). Although some respondents felt they had people they could turn to for emotional support, relatively few knew of someone they could reach out to for financial assistance in a time of need. As one participant put it, "everybody's kinda hurtin'." Nonetheless, it became clear that many people still found ways to feed each other (see table 6.2). Qualitatively, a number of themes arose, including sharing food purchased with SNAP benefits, providing transportation to pantries, educating peers on topics such as cooking and storing food, helping peers to find or navigate resources, and delivering groceries to those who are homebound, among others.

Guadalupe lost her job of nearly twenty years and her house as a result. "It was rock bottom," she said in her interview. She began working at a fast-food restaurant and found her SNAP benefits reduced because of the new income. Her sister or uncle would help make up the difference. Chantal, a woman in her thirties who struggled with mental health issues, also turned to relatives in times of need. After her Social Security benefits were cut, she was finally able to access SNAP. It helped, she explained, but it was not enough to feed her growing sons. "I don't like nobody to know I'm suffering," she said quietly.

Table 6.2   Instances of Formal and Informal Support Themes among TSSOM Participants

Type of Informal Support	Number of Instances
Skipping meals so that others can eat	20
Supporting the food security of others	13
Giving food, teaching cooking/budgeting skills, peer resource referrals, providing rides to pantries, among others.	
Relying on family members for food/resources	8
Receiving food, sharing SNAP, among others.	
Relying on friends or neighbors for food/resources	5
Receiving food, rides to pantries, among others.	
Total Instances	46
Type of Formal Support	Number of Instances
Increased food security through the use of pantries	71
Increased food security through the use of other agencies	8
Churches, homeless services providers, community meal sites, among others.	
Total Instances	79
Total Instances—*All support themes*	125

Source: Created by Authors

Despite this, she had called her nephew the day before to ask for help. "My refrigerator's empty," she lamented.

Families were not solely responsible for helping their food insecure members. Bill, who lived in permanent supportive housing, said he was grateful for his friends in the recovery community. Aisha had moved to Omaha from California and described how her neighbors used to pool their resources to help feed her before she found a job. Even with the help of her new friends, Aisha still found herself skipping meals frequently.

Some participants explained how other people relied on them for their food security. Lonnie, for example, described herself as a "volunteer social worker," providing meals and free rides to appointments and pantries to people experiencing homelessness. The sixty-five-year-old sometimes found it difficult to afford food, but as she put it, "there's agencies around." Lester, a sixty-eight-year-old veteran with heart disease and cancer, often found himself giving away the red meat and processed items that he received at food pantries. Due to his illnesses, he relied on staples such as fish, fresh produce, and almond milk, which were much harder to find at pantries. Another man, Chris, lived with his partner, who was disabled. His partner paid the bills using her Social Security and purchased food with SNAP benefits. In return, Chris took care of her, doing the cooking, running errands, and connecting her to community resources. "I got the frigerator [*sic*] full," he proclaimed. Chris also shared groceries with his neighbors, several of whom were also disabled and could not always access food when they needed it. "I run it," Chris said, referring to his neighborhood. "They come and knock on my door like it's the pantry." Mary spent her free time mentoring young mothers and teaching them skills such as cooking, storing food, and maximizing their grocery budgets. "If you know what you're doing, you can stretch it," she declared. Mary also helped her son with his catering business and prepared meals for neighbors. When she had leftovers, she brought them to the homeless. Regarding her own food security, Mary often depended on local agencies. "I thank God for the pantries."

Formal Supports

A significant number of TSSOM respondents relied on formal supports, such as food pantries, churches, or other social service agencies. The positive correlation ($r = 0.232$, $p < 0.01$) between community involvement and food security suggests that participating in local groups, organizations, or community activities is a helpful factor in being able to feed one's family. Respondents who were more involved in and aware of their neighborhood were often more aware of the resources that were available in the area. The habitual proximity to, or participation in, these community assets may lend a sense of familiarity that lowers barriers to entry. For example, those who were active in faith-based organizations felt more comfortable turning to their "church family" for help during months when money ran out. In addition, participants made use of formal support resources in a number of creative ways, such as using food pantries and community gardens to supplement what they could buy with SNAP or to stretch their grocery budget. A number of individuals also explained that they were using these resources in order to help increase their self-sufficiency. By sourcing food at pantries, money was freed up that could be used to pay down debts or even to help build up savings. Furthermore, some participants visited social service agencies in order to access programs such as SNAP, WIC (Special Supplemental Nutrition Program for Women, Infants, and Children), or Social Security, which can be hard to apply for without a phone or computer (see table 6.2 in previous section).

Terrell, a forty-eight-year-old who lived in a nearby public housing tower, told of using pantries to get through the month. "It's kinda scary," Terrell stated. "Thank God for y'all pantry . . . I eat like a bird to budget it out." Patty, a fifty-year-old artist with a heart-related disability, also relied on community agencies. "The food stamps you receive just are not enough," she remarked. "It's always a little tight at the end of the month." Even when SNAP ran out, she felt that she was able to get food when she needed it by visiting several local pantries. For Jeanetta, who had custody of six of her twenty-one grand-children, her church was a huge support. In addition to helping with food, Jeanetta's church had also helped with the rent in the past. To give back, Jeanetta volunteered when her church organized lunches for the homeless. Natisha, who had recently moved to Omaha and was staying with family, said that her daughter was struggling to adjust to their economic situation. When Natisha would come home from the pantry, she would tell her daughter that she had been to the grocery store. "[Together] is a better way for me to get my nutritions [*sic*] in," she stated. Rita, a sixty-two-year-old part-time school bus driver, said that she visited food pantries when she was unable to afford groceries. "You ain't hungry in Omaha!" she laughed. "You just have to ask." Rita voiced a common sentiment among participants: food security, at least in this city, was a matter of being willing and able to look for help. "You starve in Omaha, you're not trying," said one man. "If you go hungry in Omaha, Nebraska, you're just lazy," opined another. "You don't starve in Nebraska," yet another participant observed. Despite this sentiment, he later confessed, "I'm only eating now just enough to stay alive."

Another theme centered around the ability to access resources. Rebecca, a fifty-four-year-old mother of four, expressed concerns about drugs and criminal activity in her neighborhood. She desperately wanted to move out of Omaha, but she was worried that she would not be able to find food pantries in her new city. "Living [in poverty], I have to think about everything more," Rebecca explained. "There's a lot of hoops to jump through." For thirty-nine-year-old Timothy, who was staying at a local shelter, the centralization of food pantries, churches, and homeless services providers in Omaha was essential to his ability to feed himself and to make it to his appointments without reliable transportation. Timothy had discovered Together by chance several years earlier. After stealing Timothy's vehicle, the thief eventually ditched the car in the pantry parking lot.

Making the Choice: Who Benefits?

For many low-income families, dinnertime brings about more than just the decision of what to eat: it may also be a matter of who gets to eat. Throughout the TSSOM, stories arose of people acting against their own self-interests for the preservation of others. There were many instances identified of parents skipping meals so that their children would have enough food. "My daughter eats, but I don't eat," said Morgan, a single mother who received fifteen dollars in SNAP each month. James, a young father, explained that SNAP helped to feed his baby, but it wasn't enough to put food on the table for himself or his girlfriend. There was also Luisa, a thirty-year-old mother who called herself "the garbage disposal for scraps the kids don't eat." Similarly, a number of participants expressed that they would not eat until their aging parents had been fed. Bethany worked to support a family of seven and found it difficult to feed both her mother and her children. "I have to sneak mashed potatoes into my infant's milk," she stated. Sometimes, she would go until dinner without eating. There were even a few stories of people skipping meals in order to provide for beloved pets or service animals. Naomi, who was living with depression and a physical disability, relied on her dogs for emotional support. In return, she had gone without food in the past to feed them.

It is also important to note that those who give help to others and those who receive it are not mutually exclusive. Many participants described simultaneously providing aid and needing help within the same month. Others found themselves asking family members for food one week and sharing extra produce with neighbors the next. The permeability of the "helpers" and the "helped" speaks as much to the resilience and resourcefulness of the community as it does to the failings of current food policy. When families can fluctuate so quickly between having food to spare and scarcity, it is clear that whatever resources or supports they are using may not be adequately meeting their needs. This also indicates that the current policies in place may not actually be promoting the goal of long-term self-sufficiency.

POLICY IMPLICATIONS AND CONCLUSION

The stories collected from the TSSOM have the potential to contribute to the broader question of: Whose job is it to feed those in need? Policymakers may tend to overestimate the responsibility and capacity of people living in poverty to feed themselves and each other, assuming that nonprofits or well-resourced individuals will step in to bridge the gap between food insecurity and food security. In this way, an overreliance on informal networks could be framed as having the potential to perpetuate hunger because it abdicates responsibility for policy interventions.

Specifically, the TSSOM tool reveals several important policy implications for reducing food insecurity. First, food insecurity is more pervasive than the numbers show, as each pantry visitor could in turn be supporting several others. Second, effectively addressing system-wide, compounding deficiencies in other life domains can positively impact food security so that expanding access to childcare subsidies reduces the burden of affording food, or increasing the number of jobs that pay a livable wage will also increase food security. Third, SNAP alone is not as effective a tool to increase food security because of too-strict eligibility requirements and the cliff effect. Finally, reducing unnecessary barriers to accessing programs like SNAP will increase the long-term self-sufficiency of people experiencing food insecurity.

In 2019, Legislative Bill (LB) 255 introduced in Nebraska was the latest attempt to expand income eligibility for SNAP, this time from 130 percent to 140 percent of the Federal Poverty Level, and two other bills sought to change the lifetime ban on SNAP for certain drug felony convictions. The hearing in front of the Legislature's Health and Human Services Committee amounted to a long line of advocates and community organizations on the one side, and the Nebraska Department of Health and Human Services (DHHS) as the lone opponent on the other. Representatives from DHHS stated in Nebraska LB255 that SNAP and other economic assistance programs are meant to increase self-sufficiency and end reliance on government assistance but did not acknowledge that DHHS policies such as limiting eligibility undermine long-term solutions for self-sufficiency as voiced by TSSOM participants (LB255a 2019).

If policymakers seek to reduce reliance on government assistance that assistance must be expansive enough to give people the stability they need to build a foundation for self-sufficiency. Instead, government assistance is made as limited as possible because of the perception that a lack of assistance will somehow encourage the recipient to "lift themselves up by their boot-straps." Opponents of expanded SNAP eligibility remain resistant to reform because they say it would cost too much. This can be perceived as a short-sighted argument that negates the long-term savings of increasing stability across the economic spectrum, not to mention ignoring the dignity of each person. As TSSOM respondents demonstrated and the data affirmed, increas-ing the ability of people to afford food translates positively to self-sufficiency in other life domains.

Expanding gross income eligibility for SNAP would allow a person to increase their earnings to a sustainable level without losing the assistance they rely on to feed their families, low-income senior citizens to receive both Social Security and adequate SNAP benefits, and households with school-age children to make it through the summer when their children are not receiving meals at school (LB225b 2019; LB225c 2019; LB225d 2019). Repealing the lifetime ban on SNAP, as Nebraska attempted with Nebraska Legislative Bill 402 would both reduce recidivism and increase food security because economic assistance reduces vulnerability for that person and their family, and not to mention is the rational and compassionate response to a person who has served their sentence (LB402a 2019). If policymakers want to reduce reliance on the government for assistance, they must build on and leverage existing community supports rather than relying exclusively on those supports to make up the difference (LB 402b 2019). Practitioners who work on food insecurity know that food pantries are a short-term, immediate fix to the issue of hunger, and does not solve the why of the problem, which can only be solved through smart, effective, and compassionate policies that get at the root cause of food insecurity.

Means-tested policies addressing food insecurity, in both design and implementation, also come with administrative burdens, such as eligibility and accessibility (Herd and Moynihan 2018). As demonstrated through this research, these burdens have significant distributive effects on the compounding and cumulative challenges facing food insecure individuals and communities. Future research and policy work must continue to use multidimensional approaches like the TSSOM not only to inform policy work that creates more food-secure communities but also for reducing disparities that are often rooted in other overlapping social and economic disadvantages.

REFERENCES

Coleman-Jensen, Alisha, Matthew P. Rabbitt, Christian A. Gregory, Anita Singh. 2019. "Household Food Security in the United States in 2018." *U.S. Department of Agriculture Economic Research Service.* https://www.ers.usda.gov/webdocs/pu blications/94849/err-270.pdf.

FAO, IFAD, UNICEF, WFP and WHO. 2020. *In Brief to The State of Food Security and Nutrition in the World 2020. Transforming Food Systems for Affordable Healthy Diets.* Rome, FAO. https://doi.org/10.4060/ca9699en.

Gundersen, Craig, and James P. Ziliak. 2018. "Food Insecurity Research in the United States: Where We Have Been and Where We Need to Go." *Applied Economic Perspectives and Policy* 40, no. 1 (2018): 119–35. https://doi.org/10.1093/aepp/ppx058.

Hart, TG B. 2009. "Exploring Definitions of Food Insecurity and Vulnerability: Time to Refocus Assessments." *Agrekon* 48, no. 4: 362–383.

Herd, Pamela, and Donald P. Moynihan. 2018. *Administrative Burden: Policymaking by Other Means.* New York: The Russell Sage Foundation.

LB255a: Change Provisions Relating to the Supplemental Nutrition Assistance Program: Hearing before the Health and Human Services Committee, 106th Nebraska Legislature (2019) (statement of Matt Wallen, Director of Children and Family Services, Nebraska Department of Health and Human Services).

LB255b: Change Provisions Relating to the Supplemental Nutrition Assistance Program: Hearing before the Health and Human Services Committee, 106th Nebraska Legislature (2019) (statement of Kathy Siefken, Nebraska Grocery Industry Association).

LB255c: Change Provisions Relating to the Supplemental Nutrition Assistance Program: Hearing before the Health and Human Services Committee, 106th Nebraska Legislature (2019) (statement of David Holmquist, AARP).

LB255d: Change Provisions Relating to the Supplemental Nutrition Assistance Program: Hearing before the Health and Human Services Committee, 106th Nebraska Legislature (2019) (statement of Steve Sheridan, Center for People in Need).

LB402a Eliminate an Eligibility Provision Relating to Nutrition Assistance Benefits as Prescribed: Hearing before the Health and Human Services Committee, 106th Nebraska Legislature (2019) (statement of Senator Robert Hilkemann).

LB402b Eliminate an Eligibility Provision Relating to Nutrition Assistance Benefits as Prescribed: Hearing before the Health and Human Services Committee, 106th Nebraska Legislature (2019) (statement of Shelley Mann, Assistant Director of SNAP, Food Bank for the Heartland).

Polkey, Chesterfield. 2019. "Most States Have Ended SNAP Ban for Convicted Drug Felons." *National Conference of State Legislatures.* https://www.ncsl.org/blog /2019/07/30/most-states-have-ended-snap-ban-for-convicted-drug-felons.aspx.

Roncarolo, Federico, Caroline Adam, Sherri Bisset, Louise Potvin. "Traditional and Alternative Community Food Security Interventions in Montreal, Quebec: Different Practices, Different People." *Journal of Community Health* 40, no. 2 (2015): 199–207; Healthy People 2020. "Social Determinants of Health." https://www.healthyp eople.gov/2020/topics-objectives/topic/social-determinants-of-health.

Rossi, Michelle M., and Karen A. Curtis. 2013. "Aiming at Half of the Target: An Argument to Replace Poverty Thresholds with Self-sufficiency, or 'Living Wage Standards.'" *Journal of Poverty* 17, no. 1 (2013): 110–130.

Snohomish County Self-Sufficiency Taskforce. 2010. "Self-Sufficiency Matrix: An Assessment and Measurement Tool Created Through a Collaborative Partnership of the Human Services Community in Snohomish County." http://www.selfsuffi ciencystandard.org/sites/default/files/selfsuff/docs/SelfSufficiencyMatrix2010.pdf.

U.S. Department of Agriculture. "Definitions of Food Security." Last modified September 4, 2019. https://www.ers.usda.gov/topics/food-nutrition-assistance/fo od-security-in-the-us/definitions-of-food-security.aspx.

Chapter 7

Growing a Greener Lens

Connecting Concepts of Public Affairs and Sustainability from a Food Systems' Frame

Rachel Emas

INTRODUCTION

Counter to traditional economic development which fails to incorporate environmental and equity concerns, sustainable development (SD) presents a new paradigm of decision-making in which current societal needs are met without compromising the ability of future generations to meet their own needs (Brundtland Commission 1987). This intergenerational SD paradigm presents unique governance challenges. First, sustainable development issues are systemic and cross geopolitical borders, but policy mechanisms are often national or subnational. SD issues also evolve over various timelines, but rarely within a politically convenient timeframe, and require intergenerational decision-making. SD is also comprehensive, complex, interdisciplinary, and requires integration across governments, objectives, policy areas, and sectors. From these complexities, an SD paradigm requires a participative process of feedback, adaptation, and revision of policies led by an engaged society and a collaborative government (Dovers 1996).

As an academic field, Public Administration (PA, or Public Affairs) is the study of decisions, people, and institutions involved public service delivery, and their intersections and overlap (UNCEPA 2006). Given these definitions of sustainable development and public affairs, we can see why PA scholars increasingly acknowledge SD as central to governance. This chapter connects sustainability and public affairs by analyzing the Sustainable Development Goals (SDGs) of the United Nations (UN) using the Grand Challenges of the National Academy of Public Administration (NAPA). The chapter then connects three NAPA challenges with the SDGs framework from a food system perspective.

The UN's SDGs and NAPA's Grand Challenges are influential sets of broad objectives for the future of sustainability and public service, respectively. And, in seeking to achieve these goals, we must understand how the practice of public affairs is comprehensively connected to the future of sustainability. Just as with the Grand Challenges, the systemic issues of sustainability cross traditional policy and geographical boundaries and reflect the development of communities, nations, and societies. As such, PA research should expand its insight into the practical linkages between sustainability and public administration. To appreciate the interdependencies between public administration and sustainability, PA scholars should look to the interdisciplinary field of food policy.

Given the universal importance and impact of food in people's lives, we can deepen our understanding of the relationship between PA and sustainability by studying food issues. Food, just like sustainability and public administration, operates across traditional policy and political borders and requires the collaboration of stakeholders from all sectors. Food issues also reflect the delicate balance between environmental protection, economic development, and social equity—the heart of sustainability and three core responsibilities of public administrators. Thus, understanding the connections between public affairs, sustainability, and food can help confront challenges across government silos for a sustainable food system. The next section explores the relevant concepts from these fields. Following that, I explain the method of inquiry. The chapter then presents connections between SD and PA and extends the framework from a food systems' frame. In its analysis, this chapter helps to identify connections, create shared language, and grow the groundwork for future research of food systems and sustainable development in public administration.

BACKGROUND AND TERMS

This section offers an overview of public administration, SD and sustainability, and food systems as a foundation for the inquiry into the connections between these fields.

Public Administration

While public policies are passed by elected officials, they are implemented by public administrators; in day-to-day implementation, these administrators interpret and influence these policies to provide public goods and services (UNCEPA 2006). As an academic field, public administration (PA) is defined as the study of the decisions, people, organizations, and institutions involved public service delivery and policy implementation, and their intersections and overlaps (UNCEPA 2006). The organizations, actions, and decisions of administrators have enormous policy impacts.

Governments are traditionally organized into sectoral departments, and this works reasonably well until the system encounters a multifaceted and complex challenge, like sustainable development. Just as administrators confront sectoral silos, academics do as well. In Fiorino's 2010 plea for PA to better acknowledge sustainability, he draws on a 1963 article by Caldwell which called for a focus on environment because these issues cut across policy concerns. This shift would require PA research to "overcome 'segmental' thinking and decision making" to a more integrated understanding of policy issues (Fiorino 2010, S85). Integrating the environment, equity, and economy guides sustainable development and, as government is generally responsible for dealing with issues of environment and development, this focus on SD has increased demands on government (Dovers 1996).

Sustainable Development to Sustainability

The first UN Conference on the Human Environment was held in 1972 and, fifteen years later, the Brundtland Report (1987), *Our Common Future*, offered the widely used definition of sustainable development as development which meets the current generation's needs without compromising the capacity of future generations to meet their needs. Given the constraints of governance, how could society shift to a sustainable development paradigm that works to balance the environment, economy, and equity over multiple generations? The 178 governments at the 1992 UN Earth Summit ratified Agenda 21 and the Rio Declaration, which offered local- and national-level SD policy models for the integration of three pillars: environment, economy, and equity. This three-pillar model underlies our current understanding of the concept of sustainable development (Dovers 1996).

A related term, sustainability is used in myriad fields, including ecology, engineering, economics, planning, among others, as well as many interdisciplinary and specialty areas. As with the linked concept of sustainable development, this chapter understands sustainability as a paradigm of decision-making and not as a discrete, achievable objective. While SD refers specifically to developmental decision-making, sustainability is understood as a broader paradigm of all public decision-making; still, these terms are often used interchangeably (Salas-Zapata and Ortiz-Munoz 2018).

Sustainability requires the integration of intergenerational societal needs of environmental protection, economic stability, and social equity using participative processes in the creation and implementation of public decisions (Emas 2015). This integration of objectives is an inherent challenge of sustainability in traditionally siloed governance systems (Dovers 1996). Given that it requires overcoming isolated decision-making and cutting across policy areas and government levels, sustainability offers a paradigm for PA (Leuenberger 2006) and scholars have increasingly recognized this notion.

Sustainability in Public Administration

Sustainability is a complex and continuous challenge regarding governance and administration of public policies, goods, and services in a manner that balances the environment, economy, and equity (Bartle and Leuenberger 2006). From this understanding, scholars have argued for incorporating sustainability throughout public administration research based on PA's focus on managing resources (Bartle and Leuenberger 2006; Dovers 1996), managing risks (Leuenberger 2006), balancing between public values (Bartle and Leuenberger 2006; Fiorino 2010), and engaging the public in governance and policy (Hawkins and Wang 2012; Leuenberger and Wakin 2007; Portney 2005).

There is significant scholarship on sustainability in U.S. local government broadly (Hawkins and Wang 2012; Krause, Feiock, and Hawkins 2016; Leuenberger 2012; Wang, Van Wart, and Lebredo 2014; Zeemering 2018) and in urban settings specifically (Portney 2005; Swann and Deslatte 2019). Some PA scholars have linked sustainability to specific administrative subtopics, such as government purchasing and public procurement (Smith et al. 2016; Trammell and Dimand 2019) or budgeting (Oh, Jeong, and Shin 2019; Tommasetti et al. 2020). PA research has also applied sustainability to specific policy areas such as infrastructure (Grant, Beed and Manuel 2018), transit and transportation (Leuenberger, Bartle, and Chen 2014), water (Garcia et al. 2019) and waste management (Entwistle 1999; Pollans 2017), and land use and zoning (Leuenberger 2006). There has also been some work on the administration of sustainable food systems (Candel and Pereira 2017; Ingram and Zurek 2018).

Food Systems

A food system describes the stakeholders involved and processes by which food gets from the ground to the table and back; these stages are generally identified as production, processing, distribution, retail and consumption, and waste management (Ingram and Zurek 2018). Food policy was traditionally viewed as an agricultural and rural issue; however, modern crises, such as safety failures, price volatility, and food apartheids and insecurity, have revealed the complexities and interdependencies of food system issues. Traditional government efforts to influence these complex relationships often "get stranded in 'siloed' administrative systems" (Candel and Pereira 2017,

89). With this evolved understanding of the system's complexities, food policy is the range of policy efforts impacting food system outcomes, including the "integrative strategies that align these policy efforts into a concerted whole" (Candel and Pereira 2017, 89).

It is now understood that food policy cuts across other policy areas such as land use and zoning; water, waste, and recycling management; economic development; transit, transportation, and infrastructure; and health and food safety (Candel and Pereira 2017; Ingram and Zurek 2018). An effective food system approach recognizes the objectives, activities, resources, and relationships of "different food system actors and the range of policy, market, social, technological, and biophysical environments, or drivers, that influence" them (Ingram and Zurek 2018, 551). A food system approach should also acknowledge the nested natures of systems, such as other policy systems, local/regional food systems exist within national systems, which are situated within the global food system. The food system approach aligns with PA's focus on governance and sustainability's call for integration of economic, environmental, and equity concerns. Building on this background, this chapter connects PA and sustainability and then offers linkages from a food system frame. The next section explains the analysis methods used.

METHOD OF INQUIRY

This chapter links sustainability, public affairs, and food systems by aligning the Grand Challenges of the National Academy of Public Administration (NAPA) with the UN Sustainable Development Goals (SDGs, or Global Goals) and relevant SDG targets and indicators. The chapter then goes on to link PA, sustainability, and food systems using food-specific SDG indicators and selected NAPA Challenges. This section identifies the data sources and then outlines analysis processes.

Data Sources

In 2015, the UN General Assembly adopted the 2030 Agenda for SD, which laid out a fifteen-year plan to achieve the following seventeen SDGs:

(1) No poverty; (2) Zero hunger; (3) Good health and well-being; (4) Quality education; (5) Gender equality; (6) Clean water and sanitation; (7) Affordable and clean energy; (8) Decent work and economic growth; (9) Industry, innovation and infrastructure; (10) Reduced inequalities; (11) Sustainable cities and communities; (12) Responsible consumption and production; (13) Climate

action; (14) Life below water; (15) Life on land; (16) Peace, justice and strong
institutions; and (17) Partnerships for the goals. (DSDG 2020)

In July 2017, the UN General Assembly adopted the SDGs' framework
which incorporates 174 targets and 231 unique indicators; there are 247 indicators, but 12 indicators repeat under two or three different targets (DSDG
2020). This framework was accessed from the UN Division for SDG website
and downloaded to Excel. The processes by which this research analyzes the
SDGs framework is described in the next subsection.

Chartered by Congress in 1984, the National Academy of Public
Administration (NAPA) is a nonpartisan and nonprofit organization that
supports government leaders with guidance to develop more efficient,
accountable, and effective public organizations (NAPA 2019). In late 2018,
NAPA launched "the Grand Challenges in Public Administration campaign to identify the biggest challenges that government will face during
the 2020s" (NAPA 2019, 1). These selected challenges must work toward
an ambitious and valuable goal, be large in scope, require "significant
innovation and long-term commitment," entail a paradigm shift, and have
"significant individual, governmental, and societal impacts" (NAPA 2019,
1). A year of public and expert dialogues was facilitated by a fourteen-
member Steering Committee and NAPA entities to identify the twelve
Grand Challenges:

(1) Ensure electoral integrity and enhance voter participation; (2) Modernize
and reinvigorate the public service; (3) Develop new approaches to public
governance and engagement; and (4) Advance national interests in a changing
global context; (5) Foster social equity; (6) Connect individuals to meaningful
work; (7) Build resilient communities; and (8) Advance the nation's long-term
fiscal health; (9) Steward natural resources and address climate change and (10)
Create modern water systems for safe and sustainable use; (11) Ensure data
security and individual privacy and (12) Make government AI ready. (NAPA
2019, 2)

The 2019 NAPA Report also acknowledges that ensuring "environmentally
sustainable operations" is a foundational issue which cuts "across the Grand
Challenges in Public Administration as a whole and must be addressed within
each of them" (NAPA 2019, 2). Both the NAPA Challenges and the SDGs
lay out overarching governance challenges to be addressed by 2030. The
SDGs framework offers information which is used to link these two sets of
broad goals.

Data Analysis

Initially, the SDGs were assessed, and those relevant were preliminarily linked to each Challenge. To make modifications to the initial selections, the SDGs, targets, and indicators were then searched for keywords. The 2019 NAPA Report was used to identify appropriate terms for each of the Challenges. For instance, in analyzing data for Challenge 1, to ensure electoral integrity and enhance voter participation, keywords included elect, vote, and participate, and their grammatical variations (i.e., election, voter, participation, etc.). This process was followed for each Challenge and their relevant terms, and these results helped to modify the initial connections.

The third stage assessed which target within each relevant SDG best fit the associated Challenge. For instance, SDG 11, Sustainable Cities and Communities, is linked to several NAPA Challenges, but the Goal has ten targets, some of which may be more appropriate for one Challenge than another. This step was repeated to identify the best indicator of the selected target. Finally, these connections were critically reviewed to ensure clear connections between each Challenge and SDGs, and that each indicator was used only once. Though some indicators are expressed at the global level, the concepts presented can be understood as critical at all governance levels.

To deepen the discussion on sustainability in PA from a food system frame, the analysis process followed the same steps described above. But given the large number of linkages between PA and sustainability identified, only three Grand Challenges are assessed with a focus on food systems: (5) Foster Social Equity; (7) Build Resilient Communities; and (9) Steward Natural Resources and Address Climate Change. After initial identification of the relevant SDGs, the targets and indicators were searched for keywords such as agriculture, nutrition, food, farming, and hunger, and grammatical variations of these terms relevant to each specific Challenge. Based on the search and a more detailed assessment, the specific SDG was confirmed, and data was reviewed to identify which target of each selected SDG best connects to each Challenge. The previous step was repeated to select the indicator within the selected target. Finally, these connections were critically assessed to verify connections between each Challenge and the selected SDG, target, and indicator focused on food systems. For each relevant SDG, this analysis selects only one indicator to illustrate the connections between PA and sustainability and repeats this process from a food system perspective.

Finally, because SDG 16 and 17 are so closely connected to public administration (Bouckaert et al. 2016; UNCEPA 2006; UNDESA 2016) and underlie all twelve NAPA Challenges, they are excluded from the results. Future research should assess connections between SDGs 16 and 17 and the NAPA Challenges. While the analyses here included the selection of relevant SDGs,

targets, and indicators for each Challenge, the analyses in the following section do not present the selected targets; indicators are determined by their
target and the indicators are displayed. The following section presents the
results of the analyses.

CONNECTING PUBLIC ADMINISTRATION, SUSTAINABILITY, AND FOOD SYSTEMS

This section identifies linkages between sustainability and public affairs by
aligning the NAPA Grand Challenges with the SDGs framework. Then, the
chapter presents the links between three NAPA Challenges and food-relevant
indicators of selected SDGs.

Links between Public Administration and Sustainability

To illustrate the linkages between PA and sustainability, this analysis presents the
SDGs and indicators closely aligned with each NAPA Challenge. Besides Goals
16 and 17, the SDGs make only one reference to elections and voting issues, the
first NAPA Challenge. Indicator 10.6.1 evaluates voting rights of nations but
could be interpreted as the need for expanded and more equitable voting rights
within nations, an ongoing problem in the United States (NAPA 2019). SDG 16
and 17 speak directly to participatory decision-making and future research should
evaluate the links between these Goals and the NAPA Challenges.

Challenge 2, modernizing the public workforce, is closely aligned with
SDGs 16 and 17, which were excluded from analysis. However, Challenge 2
is also linked to SDG 12's focus on government's consumption via sustainable procurement policies (indicator 12.7.1). As mentioned, sustainable public procurement has become a growing area in PA research (Trammell and
Dimand 2019) and has links to sustainable food systems (Smith et al. 2015).

Developing new approaches to public governance and engagement,
Challenge three, is linked to Goal 6's focus on the establishment and operation of local policies for "community participation in water and sanitation
management" (indicator 6.b.1) (DSDG 2020). Reflecting the public engagement of Challenge 3, indicator 11.3.2 assesses local governments with "direct
participation structure of civil society in urban planning and management that
operate regularly and democratically" (DSDG 2020). Participatory water and
sanitation management, already a focus in urban planning, is also increasingly
recognized in PA scholarship (Entwistle 1999; Garcia et al. 2019; Pollans
2017). Both indicators look at local-level public participation and engagement.

Advancing national interests in a changing global context, Challenge 4,
includes increased innovation, technological capacity, and scientific research.

This is connected to indicator 9.5.1, which measures proportion of GDP spent on research and development. While several SDG 9 indicators fit the Challenge, other SDGs have no connected indicators. It is important to note that, in describing Challenge 4, NAPA states that it will work with stakeholders to "make progress on the UN SDGs," and this is the only reference to the SDGs in the report (NAPA 2019). While Challenge area 1 presents limited SD linkages, area 2 offers broader connections. The next four Grand Challenges work toward strengthening social and economic development.

Fostering social equity, Challenge 5, aligns with SDGs 1, 2, 4, 5, and 10 and selected indicators address disparity, inequity, or access issues. For instance, indicator 1.4.1 gauges the population with access to basic services and 2.1.2 assesses the pervasiveness of a population's food insecurity. Indicator 4.5.1 measures disparities in education and 5.5.1 evaluates inequity in governmental representation. Finally, indicator 10.4.1 measures impacts of social protection policies. A great deal of PA research looks at equity and access, but few from a sustainability perspective (see Leuenberger and Wakin 2007; Nijaki 2015).

Challenge 6, to connect individuals to meaningful work, is linked to the SDGs' focus on participation in education and training (indicator 4.3.1), average earnings of employees (8.5.1), and strength of the manufacturing sector (9.2.2). Challenge 6 is connected to much of SDG 4, on education, and SDG 8, on work and economic growth, but only one indicator was selected for each. While the SDGs refer to employment and work, there are no mentions of meaningfulness or intrinsic value to the work. The indicators selected are linked to the Challenge's notions of lifelong learning, education and training, and industry workforce (NAPA 2019).

Challenge 7, building resilient communities, connects to multiple SDGs. Resilience includes the capacity to adapt to and overcome disasters and shocks to society (NAPA 2019). While many of these resiliency concepts are identified in the SDGs, this analysis narrowly links NAPA Challenges with specific SDG indicators and used each indicator only once. Indicator 4.a.1 evaluates resiliency features of school structures, 6.1.1 measures provision of safely managed drinking water, and 11.7.1 assesses urban areas set aside as open space for public use. Most directly linked is indicator 13.1.3, which looks at "local governments that adopt and implement disaster risk reduction plan" (DSDG 2020) to assess municipal resiliency planning.

Challenge 8, to advance the nation's long-term fiscal health, is connected to indicator 1.2.2 regarding poverty in the population and 10.5.1 which measures a nation's financial soundness. Very little in the SDGs mentions government's debts and fiscal sustainability, considered national concerns. Instead, the SDGs speak to foreign investment, technology transfers, and international issues (DSDG 2020). The next two NAPA Challenges regard environmental sustainability.

Several NAPA Challenges have more connections to the SDGs than others. Challenge 9, to steward natural resources and address climate change, is clearly and closely connected to multiple SDGs. Linked to Challenge 9's stewardship of natural resources for intergenerational use, indicator 2.5.1 measures food resources secured in "medium- and long-term conservation facilities" and 7.1.2 addresses reliance on "clean fuel and technology" (DSDG 2020). Challenge 9 also discusses waste and overconsumption, associated with adequate waste discharge in cities (indicator 11.6.1), and material consumption (12.2.2). In its focus on sustainable natural resource management, Challenge 9 relates to indicators 14.2.1 and 15.2.1 which address sustainable management of marine areas and forests, respectively. One could argue that all SDGs have indicators linked to Challenge 9, and future research can address this notion.

Challenge 10 is to create modern water systems for safe and sustainable use, and this is closely linked to all elements of SDG 6, but also an indicator of Goal 3 regarding health. Indicator 3.9.2 evaluates deaths "attributed to unsafe water, unsafe sanitation and lack of hygiene" (DSDG 2020). While Challenge 10 and SDG 6 have many linkages, only one was selected for presentation: shifts in water-use efficiency over time (indicator 6.4.1). Efficiency is considered a central value of PA (Leuenberger 2006), and this indicator helps illustrate the connections between PA and sustainability. The final two challenges focus on technology.

Challenge 11, to ensure data security and individual privacy, is aligned with indicator 9.c.1 which gauges the population covered by different mobile network technologies. While the challenge more closely addresses issues of data privacy and security, these topics are not mentioned in the SDGs. The goals discuss supporting technology for equity, in education and training, throughout energy, water, and sanitation administration, and for more sustainable development, but no mention of privacy or security. Challenge 12 is to make government AI ready and, as with the previous challenge, the SDGs do not mention AI, big data, robotics, among others. However, Challenge 12 can be connected to a population's ICT skills (indicator 4.4.1) and the value added by the tech industry (9.b.1). The next global SD agenda should address these growing concerns over AI and data security. The following section presents the connections between PA and sustainability from a food system perspective.

Links between Public Administration, Sustainability, and Food Systems

Given the number of connections between PA and SD identified, only three NAPA Challenges are used to assess the SDGs from a food system perspective. Several indicators of SDG 2, No Hunger, are associated with food, but this work illustrates the interdependencies of food and PA with multiple SDGs. For instance, fostering social equity, Challenge 5, is related to food in the SDGs by looking at stable financial access to food (indicator 2.c.1) and gender equity in agricultural land ownership (5.a.1); these link to food distribution and production, respectively. Equitable access to and distribution of food is a major challenge of governance, especially in a sustainability paradigm.

Challenge 7 regards resiliency, which is the ability to withstand, adapt, and recover from adverse shocks and the "potential and actual stresses facing communities" (NAPA 2019, 22). A community's capacity to overcome disasters, specifically threats to food production or distribution, is central to resiliency. Indicators 2.4.1 and 6.5.1 address sustainable and integrated management of agriculture and water resources, respectively, both of which are necessary for a resilient community.

Challenge 9, to steward natural resources and address climate change, is linked to several food system elements. Related to the sustainability of food production resources is the "change in water-related ecosystems over time" (6.6.1) and the shift to clean energy "in a manner that does not threaten food production" (13.2.1) (DSDG 2020). There are also connections to unsustainable consumption and waste regarding local breeds at risk of extinction (indicator 2.5.2), food loss and waste (12.3.1), protection of marine areas (14.5.1), and reducing land degradation (15.3.1). As with sustainability, stewardship speaks to intergenerational equity of resources and these indicators look at shifting patterns and ensuring the long-term use of resources.

RECOMMENDATIONS

Though we recognize the centrality of PA to the SDGs, implementation of the 2030 Sustainable Development Agenda "also requires significant departures from the usual way of administering public affairs. It calls for radical shifts in understanding administration," developing a flexible, capable, and innovative public workforce, and it "requires moving towards a 'whole of government' or 'whole of society' approach" (HLPF 2018, 17). To achieve these shifts toward sustainability, governments should integrate the SDGs in policies and institutional frameworks, support inclusive partnerships, mobilize financial support toward sustainability, and establish effective participative policy and budget processes (HLPF 2018). Research on these topics should continue to build on these connections between PA and sustainability.

There have been criticisms of the Global Goals for their minimal focus on food interdependencies, and lack of acknowledgement of food as a human right, as water, education, and health are declared to be. The next global SD agenda should better integrate and address food issues instead of assuming that global markets will correct the problems (Vivero Pol and Schuftan 2016). Government agencies at all levels have a role to play in balancing food system issues, but the Global Goals reflect the reliance on the free market in solving food problems, despite decades of evidence to the contrary.

Public affairs addresses managing resources and risks, social equity, and public engagement, and these topics are all deeply connected to sustainability and food systems. And, as administrators at all levels face increasingly complex challenges in meeting their constituents' needs, public administration research can provide a theoretical lens and a common language that speaks to the interdisciplinary areas of sustainability and food systems. The SDGs' lack of attention to food issues and interdependencies reflects the need for more research connecting public administration, food systems, and sustainability.

While this chapter presents the connections between sustainability and PA from a food system frame, the SDGs framework, and public administration more broadly, does not adequately reflect the intricacies and interdependencies of food system issues. PA scholarship should pay greater attention to the complexities of the food system, especially issues of food sovereignty, sustainability, and security and food system governance and interdependencies. In doing do, public administration will be better prepared to face the governance challenges of the twenty-first century.

CONCLUSION

Government and public policy are central to ensuring environmental protection, strengthening social equity, and encouraging economic development. As these are the three tenets of sustainability, it is critical to recognize the links between public administration and sustainability. Sustainability is a complex public service challenge, and PA scholarship must increase its focus on this critical topic. Sustainability's call to incorporate economic, environmental, and social objectives across sectors, territories, and generations via participative policymaking is well-illustrated by a food systems frame.

Food issues deeply impact the economy, environment, and equity of a society; and food policy decisions involve multiple spheres of government, levels of decision-making, and sectoral stakeholders. If communities and nations want to successfully meet the major governance challenges of the twenty-first century, public administration should emphasize issues of sustainability and food systems. While the UN SDGs must improve to adequately address the complexities of food challenges, this chapter draws out some of the connections between PA, sustainability, and food systems. By linking the SDGs and the NAPA Grand Challenges, this chapter illustrates the critical and complex connections between PA, sustainability, and food systems.

Given that public administration, policy, and governance are integrally linked to equity, the environment, and economy, it follows that PA would feature prominently in the SDGs. As scholars have stated, "public administration is everywhere in the SDGs" and this chapter's assessment illustrates this point (Bouckaert et al. 2016, 8). While this analysis selects only one SDG target and indicator to highlight the connections between PA and sustainability, future research can build on this initial framework linking the NAPA Challenges and SDGs. It is also important to again note the significance of PA in SDG 16 and 17, and UN bodies also have acknowledged that these two goals are foundational for progress toward the other fifteen SDGs (HLPF 2018).

PA is inherently multi- and interdisciplinary, as are sustainability and food issues, which can create challenges for both researchers and practitioners. Understanding the ties between public affairs, sustainability, and food may help confront challenges across governmental and scholarship silos to address twenty-first century challenges. This chapter connects public administration and sustainability by aligning the UN SDGs and indicators with Grand Challenges of the National Academy of Public Administration. The chapter then draws out these connections from a food systems' frame for three NAPA Challenges. In its assessment, this work identifies practical linkages between public affairs, sustainability, and food systems, develops a common language, and helps strengthen the foundation of research on food systems and sustainability in public affairs.

REFERENCES

Bartle, John, and Deniz Leuenberger. 2006. "The Idea of Sustainable Development in Public Administration." *Public Works Management and Policy* 191–194.

Bouckaert, Geert, Rolet Loretan, and Steve Troupin. 2016. "Public Administration and the Sustainable Development Goals." Written Statement by the International Institute of Administrative Sciences Submitted to the 15th session of the UN Committee of Experts in Public Administration.

Brundtland Commission. 1987. *Presentation of the Report of the World Commission on Environment and Development to the Commission of the European Communities, the EC and EFTA Countries.* Brussels: World Commission on Environment and Development.

Candel, Jeroen, and Laura Pereira. 2017. "Towards Integrated Food Policy: Main Challenges and Steps Ahead." *Environmental Science & Policy* 89–92.

Division for Sustainable Development Goals (DSDG). 2020. The 17 Goals. UN Department of Economic and Social Affairs. https://sdgs.un.org/goals.

Dovers, Stephen. 1996. "Sustainability: Demands on Policy." *Journal of Public Policy* 303–318.

Emas, Rachel. 2015. "The Concept of Sustainable Development: Definition and Defining Principles." *United Nations Global Sustainable Development Review.* United Nations.

Entwistle, Tom. 1999. "Towards Sustainable Waste Management: Central Steering, Local Enabling or Autopoiesis?" *Policy and Politics* 375–388.

Fiorino, Daniel. 2010. "Sustainability as a Conceptual Focus for Public Administration." *Public Administration Review* S78–S88.

Garcia, Margaret, Elizabeth Koebele, Aaron Deslatte, Kathleen Ernst, Kimberly Manago, and Galen Treuer. 2019. "Towards Urban Water Sustainability: Analyzing Management Transitions in Miami, Las Vegas, and Los Angeles." *Global Environmental Change* 101967.

Grant, Jill, Timothy Beed, and Patricia Manuel. 2018. "Integrated Community Sustainability Planning in Atlantic Canada: Green-Washing an Infrastructure Agenda." *Journal of Planning Education and Research* 54–66.

Hawkins, Christopher, and XiaoHu Wang. 2012. "Sustainable Development Governance: Citizen Participation and Support Networks in Local Sustainability Initiatives." *Public Works Management and Policy* 7–29.

High-level Political Forum on Sustainable Development (HLPF). 2018. "Report of the Secretary-General on Synthesis of Voluntary Submissions by Functional Commissions of the Economic and Social Council and Other Intergovernmental Bodies." Note by the Secretariat, UN Economic and Social Council.

Ingram, John and Monika Zurek. 2018. "Food Systems Approaches for the Future." In *Agriculture and Food Systems to 2050*, by Rachid Serraj and Prabhu Pingali, 547–567. World Scientific.

Krause, Rachel, Richard Feiock, and Christopher Hawkins. 2016. "The Administrative Organization of Sustainability Within Local Government." *Journal of Public Administration Research and Theory* 113–127.

Leuenberger, Deniz. 2006. "Sustainable Development in Public Administration: A Match with Practice?" *Public Works Management and Policy* 195–201.

Leuenberger, Deniz. 2012. "Sustainability in Action: Local Applications for Public Administration." *Public Works Management and Policy* 4–6.

Leuenberger, Deniz Zeynep, John Bartle, and Can Chen. 2014. "Sustainability and Transportation." *Public Works Management and Policy* 316–321.

Leuenberger, Deniz Zeynep, and Michele Wakin. 2007. "Sustainable Development in Public Administration Planning: An Exploration of Social Justice, Equity, and Citizen Inclusion." *Administrative Theory & Praxis*, 394–411.

National Academy of Public Administration (NAPA). 2019. "Grand Challenges in Public Administration." NAPA.

Nijaki, Laurie Kaye. 2015. "Justifying and Juxtaposing Environmental Justice and Sustainability: Towards an Inter-Generational and Intra-Generational Analysis of Environmental Equity in Public Administration." *Public Administration Quarterly* 85–116.

Oh, Youngmin, Seong-ho Jeong, and Heontae Shin. 2019. "A Strategy for a Sustainable Local Government: Are Participatory Governments More Efficient, Effective, and Equitable in the Budget Process?" *Sustainability* 5312–5328.

Pollans, Lily. 2017. "Trapped in Trash: 'Modes of Governing' and Barriers to Transitioning to Sustainable Waste Management." *Environment and Planning A: Economy and Space* 2300–2323.

Portney, Kent. 2005. "Civic Engagement and Sustainable Cities in the United States." *Public Administration Review* 579–591.

Salas-Zapata, Walter Alfredo, and Sara Milena Ortiz-Munoz. 2018. "Analysis of Meanings of the Concept of Sustainability." *Sustainable Development* 1–9.

Smith, Julie, Gunilla Andersson, Gunilla Gourlay, Sandra Karner, Bent Mikkelsen, Roberta Sonnino, and David Barling. 2015. "Balancing Competing Policy Demands: The Case of Sustainable Public Sector Food Procurement." *Journal of Cleaner Production* 249–256.

Swann, William, and Aaron Deslatte. 2019. "What Do We Know about Urban Sustainability? A Research Synthesis and Nonparametric Assessment." *Urban Studies* 1729–1747.

Tommasetti, Aurelio, Riccardo Mussari, Gennaro Maione, and Daniela Sorrentino. 2020. "Sustainability Accounting and Reporting in the Public Sector: Towards Public Value Co-Creation?" *Sustainability* 1909–1928.

Trammell, Evelyn, and Ana-Maria Dimand. 2019. *2019 Local Government Entity Sustainable Procurement Study*. The Institute for Public Procurement.

United Nations Committee of Experts on Public Administration (UNCEPA). 2006. *Definition of Basic Concepts and Terminologies in Governance and Public Administration*. United Nations.

United Nations Department of Economic and Social Affairs (UNDESA). 2016. *Compendium of Innovative Practices in Public Governance and Administration for Sustainable Development*. NY: United Nations.

Vivero Pol, Jose Luis, and Claudio Schuftan. 2016. "No Right to Food and Nutrition in the SDGs: Mistake or Success?" *BMJ Global Health* 1–5.

Wang, Xiaohu, Montgomery Van Wart, and Nick Lebredo. 2014. "Sustainability Leadership in Local Government: The Administrator's Role in the Process." *Public Performance and Management Review* 339–364.

Zeemering, Eric. 2018. "Sustainability Management, Strategy and Reform in Local Government." *Public Management Review* 136–153.

Section III

REGULATION

Chapter 8

Informationism in Food Politics

How the U.S. Food and Drug Administration Came to Regulate Food Through Informative Labels

Xaq Frohlich

It is a commonplace complaint today in food policy circles to lament the lack of information available to consumers to make informed decisions. Food politics is often framed in terms of "read the label" or "better labels" campaigns. As more cooking is done away from the home, with consumers buying more prepreared packaged foods, social concerns about nutrition and health or food waste are converted into policy discussions about the "choice architecture" of labels such as the Nutrition Facts panels (Frohlich 2010) and "best by" date labels (Milne 2013). Such policies are lauded for enabling the "active consumer" (Trentmann 2006) without infringing on her freedom to make choices at the supermarket. When informative labels do exist and social problems persist, the failure is often seen to be one of consumer comprehension and the need for consumer education or calls for better labels.

This chapter examines the emergence of this tendency to focus on labels in food politics, characterizing it as "informationism," by which I mean both information reductionism and what has been described as the "conduit metaphor" of information, that "information is supposed to be objective and existing independently of human agents" (Tsoukas 1997, 831). Informative labels are regularly treated as self-evident, eliding the translation work and framing that experts had to invest in selecting and condensing information onto food packages. When put forward as a solution to social problems, part of the political "sell" of labels is that they are a self-contained tool. Information is presented as descriptive or declarative, rather than relational and situational.

One of the most widely criticized examples in food studies is "nutritionism," the marketing and reformulating of the foods we eat based on the nutrition information. It can have profound effects on where value resides in food chains, such that an omega-3 fatty acids food fad can lead to the design of new genetically modified "SDA soybeans" to express a higher percentage of omega-3 fatty acids in soy products. In other words, with the substantial vertical integration in farm-to-fork food systems, small changes in information markets can ripple back through the food chain creating substantial material shifts in food production. Gyorgy Scrinis and others have amply documented how marketers distort health claims to reduce food to not only its nutritional value, but also sometimes to just single nutrients or nutritional properties (Scrinis 2015). Scrinis attributes nutritionism to the broad popularity of scientism and to deliberate and deceitful marketing by food manufacturers to construe processed foods as normal and healthy. I will argue that much of the critique of nutritionism is not specific to nutrition, but instead reflects changes in information-mediated interactions due to changes in food systems.

A key theoretical framework here is that informationism is not simply an ideology or discourse, but something that emerges out of a new arrangement in "food infrastructures" (Frohlich et al. 2014). I use the example of the history of U.S. Food and Drug Administration's (FDA) regulation of food labels in the second half of the twentieth century, and what elsewhere I call an "informational turn" (Frohlich 2017), to illustrate how and why food politics get reframed as a problem of good or bad labeling. First, I will describe how the focus on labeling emerged out of the post-World War II restructuring of food retailing in America. Next, I describe two stages in the informational turn in food politics: the development of food "standards of identity" in the 1950s and 1960s, using the metaphor of the recipe, and then informative labeling from the 1970s to present, where food is represented as interchangeable ingredients and health properties. Last, before concluding, this chapter lists some of the transformations that come with focusing policy on labels, what I describe as the "logics of labeling."

ENABLING A NEW FORM OF CONSUMERISM: NEW LEGAL, MARKET, AND PRODUCTIVE INFRASTRUCTURES FOR CHOICE AT THE SUPERMARKET

The interest in informative labeling in food markets emerged in a broader context of industrialization, and in particular the increased marketing of consumer packaged goods and processed foods whose quality, having placed a barrier between consumer and food, was harder for end consumers to assess unaided. The challenges posed by industrial manufacturing were technological, how to ensure quality control on mass-produced goods, but they were also legal and entrepreneurial. Branded manufacturers looked to design in package labeling and marketing as a means to build trust in the quality and loyalty to their brand, and to distinguish their products in retailing environments where such "credence goods" might otherwise look very little different from competitors (Strasser 1989).

In the first half of the twentieth century, food safety officials, backed by courts, began to overturn the earlier legal philosophy of caveat emptor, or buyer beware. They saw the policing of labels and marketing claims as a fix to the imbalance in market information between buyer and seller, what economists call "information asymmetry," which results in adverse product selection and market fraud. A wide variety of food policy interest groups in government, industry, and consumer advocacy began to view food fraud as partly a problem of uninformed consumers. They attributed its rise to two trends: first, the way in which industrial foods were too complicated for the ordinary consumer to make sense of without help, and second, the urbanization of consumption. Urban housewives were less familiar with where food came from and by extension how to assess food, and less women were cooking and thus knew less about food preparation. Home economics was a field born out of the concern with addressing this consumer knowledge gap (Goldstein 2012).

Food technologists were redesigning food and food packaging in ways that both accommodated the changes in home cooking caused by refrigeration and more women entering the workforce. This meant that much of cooking was shifting increasingly away from the home upstream into food-processing factories. New food processing technologies such as flash freezing "fish sticks" were reconstructing the notion of convenience and what was "food" (Josephson 2008). Automating the disassembly of standardized chickens in meat-packing plants meant chicken growers could now sell family friendly packages of pieces of chicken for daily consumption instead of the whole chickens sold more infrequently for the Sunday roast or special occasions (Horowitz 2004). New packaging materials such as cellophane made it possible to wrap perishable foods like meat in a transparent skin, so that customers could still see the food they buy, but they also fueled the market for color dyes and related techniques for ensuring standard and familiar colors for foods (Hisano 2019). Fabricating foods that met the chief food concerns of postwar suburban middle-class housewives, convenience, and nutritiousness, not only led to a transformation in what was food but also transformed the kinds of choices consumers could make about food at the supermarket. Consumers buying packaged goods delegated the direct, physical tasting, instead testing products based on their labeled attributes. Insofar as food technologists were creating new packaged food opportunities, they were also contributing to this shift from consumers tasting to testing foods.

A second important professional group reconfiguring the postwar food market was retailing and manufacturing food businesses, who were using new marketing techniques and changes in retailing spaces to change the way consumers got their food. While histories of consumption often focus on consumer movements to articulate changing tastes, scholars have recently argued such consumer choice is in fact highly orchestrated and structured through the design of spaces of consumption, in particular supermarkets. Tracey Deutsch describes how grocery chains deliberately reconfigured the organization of stores, building modern supermarkets—"large, centrally managed stores that limited personal attention"—that emphasized the virtues of "convenience" and the "refinement of clean, well-lit, and orderly" spaces. They molded these new spaces of consumptions around "a conservative, middle-class model of femininity" so as to transform the housewife's role from an actively engaged, locally knowledgeable customer to a passive (or pacified), literate consumer (Deutsch 2010). In this way, the rise of the supermarket was an extension of postwar interest in forming a suburban America. One head of a chain of supermarket stores in the 1960s linked the chain's successful turn to a new self-service model to "the increasing importance of the written word amongst an educated population." Information labels catered to this educated consumer, who is interested in "[l]ess talk, more print; [. . .] who, instead of engaging in conversation with store assistants or her peers, becomes a solitary, silent reader of innumerable printed text on packages offered for her perusal" (Bowlby 2002, 194). Such changes required new tools to aid the consumer with this new paradigm of self-service (Cochoy 2015). Hand in hand with the rise of self-service supermarkets was the growth in market research and consumer studies seeking to unpack the hidden rational and irrational motivations for housewives selecting certain foods over others off the grocery shelf. Marketers were moving away from the focus on mass-markets of the first half of the twentieth century, developing increasingly fine taxonomies of consumers to aide in niche marketing.

The result was that food was increasingly less something an ordinary person could assess with the unaided eye, and increasingly more an industrial "credence good," the assessment of its value requiring some kind of expert opinion or information aid. Given this new food economy, regulators, in the case here, the U.S. FDA, sought to position themselves as an activist state that would protect consumers by standardizing common food product and thereby rationalize the marketplace. Throughout the 1940s and 1950s, the FDA actively defended its authority, often through litigation, to remove products from the marketplace that it believed to be "misbranded," products that were either directly or implicitly not what they "purported to be" or did not conform to the FDA's system of product classification. Courts supported the FDA's position that any and all marketing materials, including industry pamphlets and grocery shelf labels or flyers, which shaped the consumer's understanding of the package label, would be considered "labeling" and therefore under the purvey of the FDA's regulations. The result was a system where standards on food labeling and product classification were used to structure food markets and the kinds of foods that could be produced.

In a process that I have elsewhere described as "imagining consumers" (Frohlich 2011), experts at the FDA, in consultation with industry and consumer advocates, drew upon different models of the consumer and legal standards of what was a "reasonable expectation" to justify its food label policies. Through these labeling rules, the agency thereby sought to enable certain kinds of consumers. Initially, the focus in postwar America was on protecting the "ordinary consumer," who was seen to be a housewife buying familiar foods and following time-honored traditions and recipes. But increasingly the FDA, under pressure from industry and consumers especially in the 1960s, came to see its role as aiding the "informed consumer," an active and literate consumer who might have a variety of lifestyle concerns to balance and was therefore not interested in the FDA making choices for her.

THE INFORMATIONAL TURN IN FOOD POLITICS, PART 1: FOOD AS RECIPE

The 1938 Federal Food, Drug, and Cosmetic Act (FDCA) directed the FDA to develop "standards of identity" for all mass-produced foods, which would state a fixed identity or common name, such as "peanut butter" or "tomato soup," and then provide a description listing preapproved ingredients and acceptable ranges. Lawrence Busch notes that "standards always incorporate a metaphor or simile, either implicitly or explicitly" (Busch 2011), and in this case, the FDA standards were explicitly modeled on a generic recipe out of which companies could create their unique branded variations. The FDA sought to use the recipe format to prevent any changes to basic food formulas which might cause consumer deception and to restrain the increasing use of chemical additives, which regulators saw as untested with unknown health risks (Merrill 1974). Standard foods would *not* carry informative labels, such as ingredient lists, because the goal was that an ordinary food labeled with a common name would be recognized for what it was by a consumer. Information beyond the name wasn't necessary.

Through the 1950s and 1960s, the FDA held numerous food standards hearings where companies and anyone interested could offer comments and evidence for what they believed to be the consumer's expectation of a "customary recipe" for the food in question. Nonstandard foods were treated like substandard foods and labelled "imitation," in order to deter cheap imitations from crowding out quality goods. A notorious example was imitation milk or "filled milk" that had substituted nondairy fat. An important dimension of this regulatory system was the food-drug line. The FDA also drew a clear distinction between standard food products and products intended for medical use, which were either classified as "drugs," requiring substantial premarket testing and approval, or "special dietary foods," which were intended for use by patients under the recommendation of their physician. The agency was, at least early in this period, very aggressive in policing food products that it saw as "misbranded" when they made health claims. The overriding presumption was that one could draw a line between ordinary, healthy consumers, who should be protected from sensational health marketing, and special-needs consumers, that is, patients, who should be directed to expert market "gatekeepers" that could help them manage the "calculus of risk" between treatment and illness (Frohlich 2021).

The problem the FDA ran into with this system was how to ensure the proper channeling of "special dietary foods" to special-needs patients and ordinary foods to mass markets. A variety of new diet foods appeared in the 1950s and 1960s that helped to undermine confidence in the food standards system and generate interest in informative labeling, especially nutrition labels. Three areas of the emerging diet food market were especially problematic: (1) vitamin supplements and vitamin-enriched foods, (2) low-calorie products made with new artificial sweeteners, and (3) low-saturated fat foods and fatty acids labeling. Each of these products raised different concerns for regulators. The first were health tonics, raising the perennial concern with "nutrition quackery," the selling of ordinary products as if they had magical properties. The second group, artificially sweetened foods, were embroiled in debates in this period about risk-taking and new food additives. FDA regulators approved cyclamate- and saccharine-sweetened foods for use by diabetics, whose immediate health needs justified the unknown risks of these new additives. However, they did not want companies to market such foods to otherwise healthy consumers who might be buying them for mere vanity-dieting. The third group of low-fat foods posed a new medical question, hotly debated in the 1960s among medical professionals: was preventive care just for the sick or for everyone? America had undergone a "nutrition transition," which brought with it higher standards for well-being and also an increase in "diseases of the affluent," chronic degenerative diseases associated with overeating. The idea that diet was linked to future risk for heart disease, for example, expanded the notion of "at risk" to healthy people. Many medical experts were advocating that even ordinary consumers explore nonstandard and special dietary health foods as part of a healthy lifestyle. Under the FDA's standards of identity system, these popular new foods would be labeled imitation or declared misbranded and removed from the market.

By the end of the 1960s, a wide variety of interest groups saw the standards system as a straightjacket on innovation. The American Medical Association felt that it was slow to adapt to the emerging health paradigms of preventive medicine and risk factors. Food technologists noted with irony the day was coming when certain novel foods might have to be marketed as "*superior imitation*," as these foods would have value-added features not yet adopted in official standards. Consumer advocate Michael Jacobson complained that the current system resulted in the existence of "silent labels" for "foods whose labels list none or only a few of the ingredients and additives that the food contains" (Jacobson 1972). Progressive grocery chains, such as Giant Food in the Washington DC area, began to experiment with private informative labels to cater to its customers' interest in "right to know" campaigns in favor of more detailed food labels.

THE INFORMATIONAL TURN IN FOOD POLITICS, PART 2: FOOD AS INTERCHANGEABLE PARTS

These disagreements between FDA officials, industry lawyers, medical professionals, and eventually consumer advocates about what were standard foods and nonstandard consumers resonated with a core political question of the 1970s: What should the relationship between the state and individuals be on matters of personal lifestyle? The broader cultural dimensions of this question cannot be overstated. Civil rights movements and consumer advocacy groups were challenging many social conventions, health orthodoxies, and the value of social conformity itself, casting doubt on the belief that the government had their alternative interests at heart. The power to prescribe the birth control pill, for example, to women who now demanded control over their bodies pitted the women's rights movement against both conservative physicians, who dithered about sexual risk-taking, and a cautious FDA that hesitated on the need for such risky lifestyle drugs (Watkins 1998). The industrialization of the food supply and the entrance of women into the workforce had also changed the value of home cooking. Convenience foods and instant meals were potentially domestic work liberators, yet they inverted basic norms about what was food and who was responsible for making it nutritious. The FDA's rigid food standards system became embroiled in these broader consumer politics. By the early 1970s, there was widespread disenfranchisement in government, on the Left and the Right, and growing enthusiasm for private solutions to what had before been considered public problems (Tuck 2008). The interest in informative labeling and access to nutrition information reflected a broader transition from a "domestic politics" of the first half of the twentieth century (Twarog 2017) to a consumer lifestyles politics and "drugs for life" model of health in the in the second half (Dumit 2012).

On January 19, 1973, the FDA published its final rules on food labeling in the *Federal Register*. The substantive changes in the FDA's food labeling rules were wide-ranging and significant. The proposals listed twelve separate, but interrelated policy changes.[1] Three specific areas of reform stood out for how they marked a significant turn away from the FDA's earlier food standards system: the introduction of a "voluntary" Nutrition Information panel, a universal Ingredient label requirement, and the shift away from the punitive imitation label.

The principal change was the FDA's new embrace of nutrition labeling and nutrient disclosures. Before informational panels were seen to be only needed for special dietary foods used under special care. Now the agency was expanding information disclosures to cover all foods that made "voluntary" health claims. As FDA Chief Counsel Peter Hutt reasoned at a 1973 background conference for the new label:

> As we started to put together the idea of nutrition labeling, it became clear that what was once "special" is now "ordinary." The idea of nutrient fortification is commonplace; it's almost beginning to be the rule rather than the exception, and therefore these are no longer special dietary foods, they are conventional foods. They are intended for use by the entire population, not by small groups of people.[2]

The idea was to reframe labeling around the recognition that certain nutritional properties and health-promoting tools do not have to be limited to special groups. Hutt and his colleagues reasoned that, while some nutrients were of special interest to particular patient populations, other ingredients had popular appeal. The challenge was to design labeling policies in a way that didn't confuse or interfere with these different uses of the nutrition label.

While the FDA claimed its new labeling policies were impartial, not designed to promote one food over another, in practice they accelerated the trend toward tinkering with foods to make them diet-friendly. The FDA would now only impose the imitation label on substitute foods deemed to be "nutritionally inferior to the food for which it is a substitute." This change effectively freed up industry to introduce a whole host of new diet recipes without first seeking FDA approval. To underscore this change, the FDA included a new food standard for mellorine, an ice cream substitute using vegetable oil, which since 1955 had been labeled imitation ice cream. Mellorine now had to be fortified with protein and vitamins to be "nutritionally equivalent" to ice cream, but could be marketed as its own independent kind of food, not unlike margarine for butter, without facing legal challenges from ice cream producers. Mellorine was a model for creating novel industrial foods with health-promoting properties. It was also a model for thinking of food as something engineered from different ingredients rather than made whole through traditional agrarian production.

LOGICS OF LABELING

The FDA was able introduce such sweeping reform in the 1970s because it presented informative labeling as politically neutral and catering to Americans' demand for new consumer lifestyles. "Informational regulation," regulating markets through information disclosure, would become an increasingly popular style of governance since then because of its cross-partisan appeal (Sunstein 1998). It was neither a simple dismantling of the state, the deregulation feared by the Left, nor the bureaucratic ramping up of direct state controls, which might result in onerous procedures feared by the Right. A risk studies scholar in the 1980s summed up this view of regulating through information as noninterfering: "Information provision is an indirect means of regulation, since it assumes that individuals will use what they know to make choices best suited to their own preferences" (Hadden 1986, 34).

The turn to information labeling, however, did reframe debates about how to regulate food markets. By the 1990s, there was a widespread reflection on the ways that the "Information Age" would require changes in the economy, including food and health. When announcing an initiative to rework the FDA nutrition information panel in 1989, Secretary of Health and Human Services Dr. Louis W. Sullivan criticized the proliferation of dubious health claims on food, stating, "The grocery store has become the tower of Babel, and consumers need to be linguists, scientists, and mind readers to understand many of the labels they see" (Lyons and Rumore 1993, 249). Public debates centered less on banning questionable ingredients or enforcing standards of quality. Instead, they focused on the problem of "information overload" created by an abundance of choice at the supermarket. The FDA's new rules in 1993 creating the Nutrition Facts label, the label one sees on foods today, embodied this new paradigm of indirect information management replacing direct market management of standards used before. On the one hand, it was an expansion of the FDA's oversight of food labeling and marketing, since the Nutrition Facts label was now required on all food products, had a standard design, and all health information about food had to link back to it. It helped to position the FDA as a primary information broker for food and nutrition. On the other hand, the Nutrition Facts label reflected something akin to a path dependency for the idea of information labels in food policy, without re-examining many of the contested assumptions about whether it works.

What are those assumptions? Informational regulation has been popular across political parties because of its purported neutrality and fairness, and that notion of fairness was predicated on two assumptions. The first is the belief that markets are an equitable and legitimate terrain in which to enact public initiatives. The turn to information labeling reflects a governance choice to translate questions of public health and the management of citizens' health into questions of markets and the management of consumers. The FDA's history of policing health claims on foods, and especially its "nutrition education" turn in the 1970s, fits within a broader history of the state's role in cultivating the "consumer-citizen" (Spring 2003) and a recent turn to "lifestyle politics" (Giddens 1991). The FDA's long struggle to demarcate the line between educating, informing, advertising, and deceiving can be seen in this light as an effort to negotiate the extent to which citizens' health ought to be a consumable good distributed through markets. The marketization of diet and nutrition information since the 1970s should be situated in a larger cultural shift toward market-embedded ethics and health libertarianism, what sociologist Ronen Shamir argues is the neoliberal state's "responsibilization" of the individual as a tactic to diminish the state's activist role and streamline state resources. Using the food label as a public health tool presumes that all consumers will have equal access to the labeled information and equal competence to weigh its value and that differences in lifestyles should subsequently determine how the label is used.

Second, the idea that nutrition labeling was fair is predicated on the notion that there exists objective information about food in the marketplace. The myth of nutritionism is that nutrition science merely represents food, that it does not intervene in our relationship to food by reducing food to health. The FDA's dramatic changes to food labeling in the 1970s needed an external system of evaluating food that was sufficiently general, capable of being applied to the wide variety of foods found in the American market, and objectively measurable such to be characterized as a factual information disclosure rather than discretionary advice. The construction of nutrition labels as mere information disclosures was a necessary fiction for the label's legal viability—such information could be required under the FDA's authority to mandate product disclosures—and for its politically viability, as nutrition numbers could be characterized as value-neutral facts.

This is the institutionalized fiction Scrinis critiques as nutritionism. Nutrition was seen to be objective because it didn't target a specific food industry. There is no saturated fats industry as there is a meat industry. Nutrition also provided a global language for food, one that disguises the translation work needed to make comparisons across vastly different categories of food and food groups. The FDA's adoption of nutrition information labeling entailed a kind of "double boundary work" of validating certain forms of expert knowledge and legal practice (Jasanoff 1990), favoring a specific kind of quantifiable objectivity and trust in numbers over other forms of objectivity such as "truth-to-nature" (Daston and Galison 2007). The FDA took great pains to present the label within this scientific frame of food objectivity and neutrality, even while medical specialists continued to dispute alternative ways to institutionalize healthy eating. The practical effect was to shift attention from foods as whole foods to foods as combinations of interchangeable ingredient and nutrient parts.

The idea of nutrition as an objective, politically neutral criteria is just a part of a larger logic of labeling that the new FDA rules institutionalized. Packaging and informative labeling created a mediating platform that transformed production and consumption, and in Marshall McLuhan's famous words, "the medium is the message." Science studies scholars have shown how the design of technical interfaces, such as personal computers or ICT networks, can "configure the user experience" and thereby shape user agency without predetermining it (Oudshoorn et al. 2004; cf. Miller and Rose 1997). The same can be said for how package and label design configures consumers. Enacting social agendas, such as healthier eating, through better labeling results in certain inescapable tensions and policy traps:

1) *The transformation of public policy into market mechanisms.* Labels work through their ability to change food purchases, yet not every citizen has the same purchase power nor liberty to prioritize health over price and convenience. What's more, differences in access to healthy foods, an issue "food desert" research has drawn attention to, foregrounds the limited impact labels will have if there are not real choices available to all consumers.

2) *The nichification of policy.* Since informative labels work through market mechanisms, labels contribute to the increasing importance of product differentiation and market segmentation or consumer niches. If producers reformulate foods to create a nutrition profile that attracts the 10 percent of consumers who are reading the Nutrition Facts panel, they have changed the food for the other 90 percent whose interests may have not been addressed. Active readers' concerns are driving market policy. For any label-centered initiative, the question becomes, who is the target audience? The nutrition label favors the ideal of a literate, health-conscious consumer.

3) *The false promise of information as a rational tool.* Informative labeling is touted as form of rational governance because of the assumption

that rational information will be used rationally. The fact that consumers often react to information through forms of what behavioral economists call "rational irrationality" really just proves that labels are always about trust in those who provide the information and institutions that certify that it is what it promises to be.

4) *The performativity of labels.* Most critics of different labeling systems tend to focus on the gap: the gap between what is labeled and the reality of what is in the package, or the gap between consumer expectation and comprehension of what they are reading and what they are getting. This kind of critique ignores how labels are not simply a reduction or misrepresentation of the food, but are instead performative: the label is both not only the expression of the ideal of what is being described, but also a target that producers use to change what is in the package to make it conform more closely to the label. Historically, when food labels are changed, foods changed.[3] This reveals certain ironies about how "healthy" is a moving target.

In these ways, the reliance on labeling transforms political debates about food quality and safety and redirects discussion away from whose interests are being protected and toward discussions about how to shape the flows of information through markets and "choice architectures" for consumers at the supermarket.

CONCLUSION: BEWARE INFORMATIONISM AS A POLITICAL OPT OUT FROM RESPONSIBLE GOVERNANCE

The introduction of nutrition labeling in the 1970s, and I would argue other food labeling campaigns in decades since, should be understood as a political compromise, or even at times a political opt out, introduced when citizens are advocating some sort of institutional change but are disenchanted with politics and suspicious of heavy-handed public governance. Policies built on informationism ignore the important role that market intermediary "gatekeepers" and interpersonal relationships play in driving what we eat. Label campaigns transform difficult questions about what citizens think food should be and who they should trust to remediate risk in the marketplace into choices at the supermarket that consumers can make for themselves. The FDA's switch from food standards to labeling nutrition and ingredients not only dramatically reconfigured the way food was represented in the marketplace, flattening the distinction between traditional whole foods and nonstandard processed foods, but it also transformed the state's relationship to citizens-as-consumers on questions of diet, risk, and health.

This chapter seeks to resituate political critiques of the marketization of food information, such as "nutritionism" (Scrinis 2015) or "healthism" (Crawford 2006), in a broader context: the disintermediation of markets brought about by changes in twentieth-century information environments (John 2000).[4] In the case of food, this transformation was due to the rise of packaged foods and with it new forms of representing food through a variety of media no longer directly controlled by traditional social, medical, and regulatory institutions. A fuller examination of nutritionism, informationism, and food consumerism more generally should address not only the message but also the medium of information used as a solution to food-related social problems. The recent popularity of "nudgeology" among policymakers, "nudging" people toward specific social agendas by designing "information architecture" (Thaler and Sunstein 2008), continues this longer history of technocratic control through information infrastructure.

As this chapter has shown, the use of information fixes such as product labels by public administration, in the name of empowering consumers, is at best problematic and at worst a means of offloading the responsibility of the government to safeguard food and consumers. The implications for policy today are twofold. First, food reform campaigns must confront the reality that reform cannot end with new label regulation. Instead, to be effective, new labels must be accompanied by a substantial investment in sustained education campaigns to equip consumers with the knowledge needed to use labels well. This did not happen with the 1990s Nutrition Facts panel. As the FDA's resources and attention turned away from promoting the label and nutrition education, a knowledge void was filled by private commercial campaigns, including food industry and retailing front-package and shelf labels designed to coopt the public health message to sell more products (Taylor and Wilkening 2008a, 2008b). Second, contrary to many "right to know" consumer campaigns, more information doesn't necessarily mean more satisfied consumers. Consumers in the 1950s had less information available to them on the labels of standard foods, but they could reasonably expect the FDA to police those standards and ensure foods would approximate consumers' expectations of what that food should be. Nowadays, consumers are expected to be self-taught nutritionists yet confront an explosion of choice at the supermarket designed to exploit an overburdened and attention-weary public. Confronted with more and more labels, consumers perceive a greater moralization of their food choices without a comparable empowerment to shape those choices. The result is a restless consumption (Lezuan and Schneider 2012), a continued search to satisfy unmet needs.

NOTES

1. These were (1) the "information panel" concept, (2) the "nutrition information" disclosure concept, (3) "setting a standard of identity for vitamin-mineral supplements," (4) a "label declaration of ingredients in standardized foods" (i.e., universal ingredients labeling), (5) "food flavor labeling," (6) designated difference between natural and artificial flavoring, (7) a policy change on fortified foods, (8) "special dietary food regulations," (9) "Incidental Food Additives" (exemptions for disclosing trace elements), (10) "Imitation Food Labeling," (11) a "Standard of Identity for Mellorine and Parevine," and (12) a uniform effective date for the labeling changes.

2. "Background Conference: Nutrition Labeling," FDA (February 1973), p. 23, as found in the binder "FoodNutritionLabeling1_1970–1983" in the personal archives of Hutt, Peter Barton. Private library of Covington & Burling Law Firm, Washington, D.C.

3. A clear example of this can be seen in David Schleifer's study of trans fats. He shows a shift in campaigns that demonized saturated fat and elevated trans fats as a healthy substitute, to campaigns that demonized trans fats, leading to the introduction of trans fats labeling in the early 2000s and the near disappearance of the ingredient in most American foods (Schleifer 2012).

4. This disembedding feature of food labeling can also be seen in other areas of food. Efforts to regulate food's "purity" (Singerman 2015; Berenstein 2016; Veit 20019), "freshness" (Freidberg 2004), and "organic" naturalness (Guthman 2004) through labels led to similar transformations of those ideals with consequences for the foodways they represented.

REFERENCES

Berenstein, Nadia. 2016. "Making a Global Sensation: Vanilla Flavor, Synthetic Chemistry, and the Meanings of Purity." *History of Science* 54, no. 4: 399–424.
Bowlby, Rachel. 2002. *Carried Away: The Invention of Modern Shopping.* New York: Columbia University Press.
Busch, Lawrence. 2011. *Standards: Recipes for Reality.* Cambridge, MA: MIT Press.
Cochoy, Franck. 2015. *On the Origins of Self-Service.* London: Routledge.
Crawford, Robert. 2006 "Health as a Meaningful Social Practice." *Health* 10, no. 4: 401–420.
Daston, Lorraine, and Peter Galison. 2007. *Objectivity.* Princeton, NJ: Zone Books.
Deutsch, Tracey. 2010. *Building a Housewife's Paradise: Gender, Politics, and American Grocery Stores in the Twentieth Century.* Chapel Hill, NC: University of North Carolina Press.
Dumit, Joseph. 2012. *Drugs for Life: How Pharmaceutical Companies Define Our Health.* Durham, NC: Duke University Press.
Freidberg, Susanne. 2004. *French Beans and Food Scares: Culture and Commerce in an Anxious Age.* Oxford: Oxford University Press.

Frohlich, Xaq. 2010. "Buyer Be-Aware: The Ethics of Food Labelling Reform and 'Mobilising the Consumer.'" In *Global food security: ethical and legal challenges*, edited by Carlos M. Romeo Casabona, Leire Escajedo San Epifanio and Aitziber Emaldi Cirión, 221–227. Wageningen, Netherlands: Wageningen Academic Publishers.

Frohlich, Xaq. 2017. "The Informational Turn in Food Politics: The US FDA's Nutrition Label as Information Infrastructure." *Social Studies of Science* 47, no. 2: 145–171.

Frohlich, Xaq. 2021. "The Rise (and Fall) of the Food-Drug Line: Classification, Gatekeepers, and Spatial Mediation in Regulating U.S. Food and Health Markets." In *Risk on the Table: Food Production, Health, and the Environment*, edited by Angela N. H. Creager and Jean-Paul Gaudillière, ##–##. New York: Berghahn Books.

Frohlich, Xaq, Mikko Jauho, Bart Penders, and David Schleifer. 2014. "Preface: Food Infrastructures." *Limn Magazine* no. 4 (Spring): 2–3.

Giddens, Anthony. 1991. *Modernity and Self-identity: Self and Society in the Late Modern Age*. Redwood City, CA: Stanford University Press.

Goldstein, Carolyn M. 2012. *Creating Consumers: Home Economists in Twentieth-Century America*. Chapel Hill, NC: University of North Carolina Press.

Guthman, Julie. 2004. *Agrarian Dreams: The Paradox of Organic Farming in California*. Berkeley, CA: University of California Press.

Hadden, Susan. 1986. *Read the Label: Reducing Risk by Providing Information*. Boulder, CO: Westview Press.

Hisano, Ai. 2019. *Visualizing Taste: How Business Changed the Look of What You Eat*. Cambridge, MA: Harvard University Press.

Horowitz, Roger. 2004. Making the Chicken of Tomorrow: Reworking Poultry as Commodities and as Creatures." In *Industrializing Organisms: Introducing Evolutionary History*, edited by Susan Schrepfer and Philip Scranton, 215–235. New York: Routledge.

Jasanoff, Sheila. 1990. *The fifth branch: Science advisers as policymakers*. Cambridge, MA: Harvard University Press.

Jacobson, Michael F. 1972. *Eater's Digest: The Consumer's Fact-Book of Food Additives*. New York: Doubleday.

John, Richard R. 2000. "Recasting the Information Infrastructure fo the Industrial Age." In *A Nation Transformed by Information: How Information Has Shaped the United States from Colonial Times to the Present*, edited by Alfred D. Chandler and James Cortada, 55–105. Oxford: Oxford University Press.

Josephson, Paul R. 2008. "The Ocean's Hot Dog: The Development of the Fish Stick." *Technology and Culture* 49, no. 1: 41–61.

Lezuan, Javier and Schneider, Tanja. 2012. "Endless Qualifications, Restless Consumption: The Governance of Novel Foods in Europe." *Science as Culture* 21, no. 3: 265–391.

Lyons, Jean and Martha Rumore. 1993. "Food Labeling—Then and Now." *Journal of Pharmacy & Law* 171, no. 2: 249.

Merrill, Richard A., and Earl M. Collier. 1974. "'Like Mother Used to Make': An Analysis of FDA Food Standards of Identity." *Columbia Law Review* 74, no. 4: 561–621.

Miller, Peter and Nikolas Rose. 1997. "Mobilizing the Consumer: Assembling the Subject of Consumption." *Theory, Culture & Society* 14, no. 1: 1–36.

Milne, Richard. 2012. "Arbiters of Waste: Date Labels, the Consumer and Knowing Good, Safe Food." *The Sociological Review* 60, no. 2 (December): 84–101.

Oudshoorn, Nelly, Els Rommes, and Marcelle Stienstra. 2004. "Configuring the User as Everybody: Gender and Design Cultures in Information and Communication Technologies." *Science, Technology, & Human Values* 29, no. 1: 30–63.

Scrinis, Gyorgy. 2015. *Nutritionism: The Science and Politics of Dietary Advice.* New York: Columbia University Press.

Schleifer, David. 2012. "The Perfect Solution: How Trans Fats Became the Healthy Replacement for Saturated Fats." *Technology and Culture* 53, no. 1: 94–119.

Singerman, David Roth. 2015. "Inventing Purity in the Atlantic Sugar World, 1860–1930." *Enterprise & Society* 16, no. 4: 780–791.

Spring, Joel H. 2003. *Educating the Consumer-Citizen: A History of the Marriage of Schools, Advertising, and Media.* Mahwah, NJ: Lawrence Erlbaum Associates.

Strasser, Susan. *Satisfaction Guaranteed: The Making of the American Mass Market.* New York: Pantheon Books, 1989.

Sunstein, Cass R. 1998. "Informational Regulation and Informational Standing: Akins and Beyond." *University of Pennsylvania Law Review* 147: 613–675.

Taylor, Christine Lewis, and Virginia L. Wilkening. 2008a. "How the Nutrition Food Label Was Developed, Part 1: The Nutrition Facts Panel." *Journal of the American Dietetic Association* 108, no. 3: 437–442.

Taylor, Christine Leiws, and Virginia L. Wilkening. 2008b. "How the Nutrition Food Label Was Developed, Part 2: The Purpose and Promise of Nutrition Claims." *Journal of the American Dietetic Association* 108, no. 4: 618–623.

Thaler, Richard H., and Cass R. Sunstein. 2008. *Nudge: Improving Decisions About Health, Wealth, and Happiness.* New Haven, CT: Yale University Press.

Trentmann, Frank. 2006. *The Making of the Consumer: Knowledge, Power and Identity in the Modern World.* Oxford: Berg Publishers.

Twarog, Emily E. 2017. *Politics of the Pantry: Housewives, Food, and Consumer Protest in Twentieth-Century America.* Oxford: Oxford University Press.

Tuck, Stephen. 2008. "Introduction: Reconsidering the 1970s—The 1960s to a Disco Beat?" *Journal of Contemporary History* 43, no. 4: 617–620.

Veit, Helen Zoe. 20019. "Eating Cotton: Cottonseed, Crisco, and Consumer Ignorance." *The Journal of the Gilded Age and Progressive Era* 18: 397–421.

Watkins Elizabeth Siegel. 1998. *On the Pill: A Social History of Contraceptives, 1950–1970.* Baltimore, MD: Johns Hopkins University Press.

Chapter 9

Contested Regulations in the Organic Foods Sector

Public Administration's Challenging Encounter with Alternative Food Activism

Michael Haedicke

The National Organic Program, housed within the Agricultural Marketing Service of the U.S. Department of Agriculture, is the public authority that regulates the production and trade of organic foods in the United States. Since its implementation in 2002, the National Organic Program (hereafter NOP) has been charged with maintaining the integrity of organic agriculture as a distinctive system of food production and with ensuring that products sold as organic in the United States meet this system's standards. NOP's overall purpose is to support the organic foods market by enhancing public trust in organic products, and in this, it has been successful. The trade in organic products in the United States totaled over $55 billion in 2019, as compared to only $8.6 billion during the year of NOP's implementation (Organic Trade Association 2020).

Despite this market growth, NOP is a controversial program within the organic sector. Regulatory proposals have fed into debates about the program's legitimacy, and on occasion, these debates have sparked wider "episodes of contention" in which critics have mobilized consumers and used the legal system to pressure regulators in innovative ways (McAdam, Tarrow, and Tilly 2001, 6). This chapter examines four such debates, including the response to the initial draft of the regulations, a lawsuit disputing rules related to processed organic products, debates about the validity of hydroponic growing techniques in organic farming, and struggles about animal welfare requirements in the program. I focus on these four debates because they represent some of the most important disagreements that have emerged around the organic regulations, and also because they illustrate the recurring nature of contention in the sector and the range of issues it encompasses. Using a sociological lens, I trace how these debates were shaped by (1) organizational and cultural divisions in the organic sector and (2) the institutional context of the regulatory program. I argue that these underlying factors have played into each episode and largely account for why disparate technical issues in organic agriculture have become emotion-laden conflicts that are difficult to resolve.

I sketch out my sociological framework in the next section of this chapter, and then turn to a historical examination of the regulatory program itself. I describe NOP's design and provide an overview of the content of the organic regulations. Then, I explore each of the four contentious episodes in turn, discussing the immediate stakes in each dispute and making connections to deeper factors at play. In the chapter's conclusion, I consider the insights that this analysis of NOP might offer into other forms of food policy that bring together state regulators and civil society advocates for food system reform. This is an important question, since recent decades have witnessed both an expansion of social activism that focuses on environmental, cultural, and social dimensions of food systems and a greater willingness of regulators and policymakers to engage constituencies beyond the agricultural interests that have traditionally guided food policy (Lang, Barling, and Caraher 2009). NOP's struggles reveal complexities involved in these shifts and illuminate governance challenges associated with this emerging food policy landscape.

CONCEPTUAL FRAMING: THE ORGANIC FIELD AND THE NOP'S INSTITUTIONAL CONTEXT

A Divided Field

Two related perspectives from organizational sociology guide this chapter's analysis. First, I approach the organic foods sector using Neil Fligstein and Doug McAdam's concept of "strategic action fields" (Fligstein and McAdam 2012). Thinking of the organic foods sector as a strategic action field means paying attention to differences in how members of the sector interpret and engage in the business of producing organic foods. The concept highlights a long-standing tension within the sector between *commercial orientations*, which emphasize increasing the scale of organic production and consumption, and *movement orientations*, which emphasize the creation of an alternative food system based in small-scale production and face-to-face relationships. Some observers (e.g., Jaffee and Howard 2010; Vos 2000) have suggested that this division reflects the cooptation of the countercultural organic foods movement by mainstream food businesses, but the reality is more complex. Historically, organic farming has been linked to various movements for food system (and broader social) change, including the New Left of the 1960s, environmentalism, and natural foods campaigns (Guthman 2004). However, some of these early participants were also quite enthusiastic about the idea of shifting as much of American agriculture as possible to the organic model. Advocacy for commercial growth thus preceded the entry of mainstream food businesses into the organic sector in the late 1990s (Haedicke 2016). Even today, some of the staunchest proponents of the commercial orientation have deep personal roots in the organic sector (Obach 2015).

Despite their long coexistence, these two orientations have also generated tension within the sector. In particular, they shaped debates about federal organic regulations. These debates began even before NOP came into existence as a regulatory program by informing different evaluations of the Organic Foods Production Act (hereafter, OFPA), the law that authorized NOP's creation. To offer one illustration, Senator Patrick Leahy, a longtime supporter of organic farming and one of OFPA's Congressional sponsors, justified the law in *commercial* terms, noting that "this bill sets one tough national standard . . . Supermarkets, able to trust the organically produced label, will be more willing to carry organic food, generating increased consumer demand, thus contributing to more profitable farming." In contrast, the organic farming advocate Elizabeth Henderson, who operated a small farm in rural Massachusetts, criticized the law from a *movement* perspective, explaining that "the impulse for the [program] came from people who wanted to 'help' organic farming become real agri-business. That is a very different conception of our mission than that held by most of the people who are farming . . . We have to stay in business to survive, but we would prefer our businesses to be ethical and personal rather than competitive and aggressively expanding" (Haedicke 2016, 73). These two examples illustrate this important cultural division within the organic foods sector, showing how commercial and movement orientations can lead to very different evaluations of the same policy.

The strategic action field concept also highlights the work of advocacy groups and organizations that have formed to assert these different orientations in discussions about organic farming policy and regulations. As Fligstein and McAdam (2012) point out, a field that is divided culturally is not necessarily one that will be characterized by ongoing controversy and contention. If people are disorganized and isolated, they may experience individual dissatisfaction but lack the ability to mount a sustained challenge. Advocacy groups and organizations help to coordinate people, craft political strategies, and collect the resources that are needed to support sustained challenges. In the organic sector, advocacy groups have played a leading role in the repeating rounds of debate and contention that characterize NOP's history. In some of these episodes, groups that embrace commercial orientations have found themselves at odds with groups that claim a movement affiliation.

In other cases, groups that represent both orientations have formed common cause against federal regulators who work for NOP.

NOP's Institutional Context

The strategic action field perspective, which illuminates cultural and organizational divisions within the organic sector, is essential for understanding why controversies related to federal organic regulations have been so persistent. However, this perspective leaves ambiguous the factors that shape the behavior of the Department of Agriculture (hereafter USDA) staff members who run NOP. These regulators do not simply respond to the (often contradictory and changing) demands of organic sector members, but possess a degree of autonomy and independence (Skocpol 1985). For insight in this area, I turn to institutionalist approaches to policy analysis. Institutional theory focuses on the context of regulators' decision-making and action (Perrow 1986). It seeks to identify "higher-order factors"—that is, ones that operate beyond the level of individuals—which shape the ways that regulators understand policy problems and go about solving them (Schneiberg and Clemens 2006, 195). Among other things, these factors can include legal frameworks within which policymakers act, bureaucratic routines that guide policy formation and implementation, and shared norms and values within policy communities. These contextual elements create "structural biases" that result in consistent policy patterns over time, often to the frustration of activists and other constituencies that seek to create change (Lang, Barling, and Caraher 2009).

This means that career regulators, including those who run NOP, are attuned both to public demands and expectations and to the restrictions and pressures placed upon them by the institutional environment in which they operate. In NOP's history, two institutional factors have emerged as particularly important. First, the program's staff members face ongoing pressure to ensure that NOP's rules do not go beyond the authority assigned to the program by the Organic Foods Production Act. In some cases, this has led regulators to act in ways that frustrate significant portions of the organic sector. In other situations, ambiguities in the law have created opportunities for advocacy organizations to try to influence regulatory decision-making, often using contentious strategies. Second, because NOP is a relatively small program within the Department of Agriculture, staff members have been sensitive to the agendas of the agency's leadership as well as to pressures from other agencies in the federal bureaucracy. On several occasions, this has caused the program to make abrupt policy changes that have sparked outcry from the organic sector.

In sum, understanding the controversies that surround NOP requires attending to the actions of three parties—advocates for commercial

expansion, advocates for systemic transformation, and regulators themselves—as well as to the cultural orientations and institutional factors
that guide these actions. I apply this framework to analyze each of the
four contentious episodes that I examine in this chapter. Before engaging
in this analysis, I provide a brief introduction to the main features of the
organic regulatory program.

NOP'S DESIGN AND THE CONTENT OF
FEDERAL ORGANIC REGULATIONS

When it was signed into law in 1990, OFPA created an outline for the National
Organic Program. First, the law directed the Department of Agriculture to
develop a set of regulatory standards for the production and handling of
organic foods. Only foods produced and handled in accordance with these
standards would be allowed to be sold as "organic." Second, OFPA instructed
USDA to create a program to certify producers that complied with these standards. Rather than inspecting producers directly, the agency was to delegate
this work to private and public organic certifiers that had developed during
the 1970s and 1980s. This meant that USDA's actual charge was to define
procedures for reviewing and accrediting these certifiers. Implementing the
law involved elaborating these two components, which continue to be at the
core of NOP's activities (Figure 9.1).

This chapter will focus mainly on NOP's production and handling standards, since questions related to these standards have catalyzed the most vig-
orous episodes of contention in the program's history. While OFPA did not
spell out the content of these standards (this job was left to USDA staff during
the implementation process), it did identify two foundations upon which the
standards were to be built. This reflected an effort by the law's architects to
find a compromise between commercial and movement orientations in the

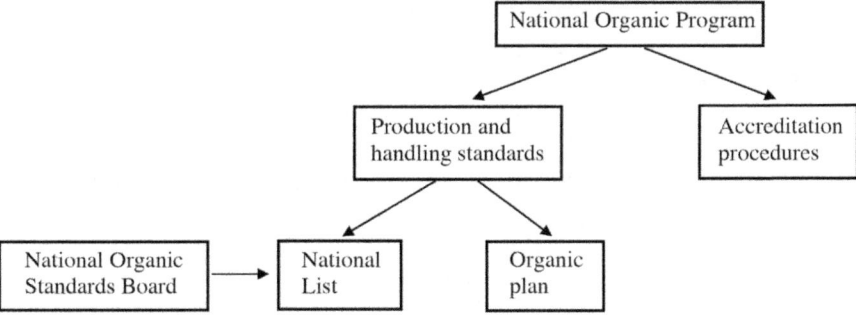

Figure 9.1   OFPA's Regulatory Framework. *Source*: Constructed by author.

organic sector (Haedicke 2016). On the commercial side, the law-directed USDA to create a registry of materials that would be permitted and prohibited in organic production and handling. Known as the National List, the registry would be based on a principle known as "origin of materials" (Meyer 1990). Simply put, inputs that originated in nature would generally be permitted in organic farming, while those that were synthetically produced would generally be prohibited. This requirement was seen as necessary to meet consumers' expectations that organic products would remain free from synthetic pesticides, fertilizers, and additives—an essential condition for increasing consumer demand for these products. On the movement side, the law also indicated that certification would involve review of an "organic plan" created by each farm or business seeking certification. This plan would discuss the operation's impact on various indicators of ecological health, such as soil fertility. The "organic plan" requirement was an effort to codify a principle known as "agronomic responsibility," which emphasized that organic agriculture should be guided by the effort to farm in ways that avoided negative effects on "soil life, water and environmental quality, non-renewable resource use, livestock health, and nutritional value and safety of the foods produced" (Meyer 1990, 20).

While OFPA gave equal weight to the National List and the organic plan, the former has emerged as a more prominent feature of NOP. There are a variety of reasons for this, including the fact that OFPA explicitly gave USDA the task of creating the National List and spelled out relatively precise criteria for the review of materials. Probably the most important factor in the prominence of the National List, though, is that OFPA formalized a process by which organic sector members could influence (and in some readings of the law, control) how materials were placed on the list. This mechanism was the National Organic Standards Board (NOSB), an advisory committee comprised of fifteen representatives from the organic sector. The law indicated that, in addition to providing general advice and representing public interest, the NOSB had the specific responsibility of conducting the initial review of materials for the National List and of proposing exceptions for natural materials that should be *prohibited* and synthetic materials that should be *permitted* in organic farming. Since the law elsewhere indicated that USDA could not create exceptions for materials that had not been proposed by the NOSB, many members of the organic sector assumed that this committee had ultimate authority over the National List. As we will see, uncertainty about the legality of this provision contributed to at least one episode of contention related to NOP—but at least in the program's early years, the NOSB's statutory prerogative focused a great deal of attention on the National List.

FOUR EPISODES OF CONTENTION

With this thumbnail sketch of NOP in mind, I will now turn to an examination of the four episodes of contention identified at the beginning of this chapter. I will consider each episode separately, beginning with a brief summary of major events and then employing the analytic framework described above to identify and draw out underlying catalysts of conflict.

Episode #1: The First Proposed Rule, 1997–1998

Summary

The process of developing organic regulations stalled for several years after OFPA's passage because of resistance within USDA and the failure of Congress to appropriate funds for the new program. NOP did not have a professional staff to begin the process of writing regulations until 1994, although the NOSB had begun meeting two years earlier to draft the National List. A period of intense work during the subsequent three years culminated with the release of a provisional version of the organic regulations in December 1997. According to federal law, the members of the public had sixty days to provide comments on the draft, although this period was doubled as a result of the volume of responses that the USDA received. More than 275,000 comments arrived, setting a record in the history of USDA rulemaking. Most of these comments followed the spirit of leaders in the organic sector, who labeled the proposed rule "deplorable" and "a boon for the conventional food system" (Haedicke 2016, 75). In the face of such widespread opposition, NOP scrapped much of the proposed rule and returned to work, issuing a second, and more widely accepted, version of the organic regulations in 2000.

Analysis

Many participants in the organic sector interpreted the First Proposed Rule as an intentional effort by staff at NOP to undermine organic agriculture at behest of large farmers and mainstream food companies, pointing in particular to sections of the rule that suggested that genetic engineering and food irradiation might be allowed in the production of organic foods. However, there is little evidence to support this position. In fact, most of the NOP staff members were sympathetic toward the organic sector, and some had personal experience with organic farming. A closer look suggests that NOP staff encountered institutional pressures that, combined with broad skepticism toward government regulation in the organic sector, precipitated this episode of contention. One source of institutional pressure had to do with NOP's relationships with other offices in the USDA and other agencies in the federal government. Grace Gershuny, a respected organic advocate who worked for NOP during this period, has described an ongoing need to "convince the hierarchy that we did not pose a threat to business as usual" (Gershuny 2016, 149). While Gershuny and others at NOP worked to include language that explicitly prohibited genetic engineering in the organic regulations, these sections ran counter to the agendas of other offices and were removed by the Office of Management and Budget during the interagency review process that preceded the release of the proposed rules to the public. In response, NOP staff "settled on a desperate 'Hail Mary' tactic of using the [proposed rule] to ask for public comment about [genetic engineering] . . . once we had the resounding public comment we knew would come, we could then safely put those prohibitions back into the Final Rule" (Gershuny 2016, 153).

Institutional pressures also contributed to tensions that emerged between NOP staff and the NOSB. Recall that, according to OFPA, only the NOSB could propose exceptions for materials on the National List. This provision was interpreted as granting the NOSB final authority over the content of the list. However, this portion of the law contradicts a separate statute, the Federal Advisory Committee Act of 1972, which governs the operation of stakeholder committees like the NOSB and which explicitly prohibits those committees from setting policy and engaging directly in rulemaking. From the perspective of NOP staff, allowing the NOSB to have authority over the National List was illegal and risked invalidating the regulations as a whole if the rulemaking process was found to be out of compliance with the law. These fine points were not widely understood within the organic sector, though. Rather, perceptions of the USDA as an agency that existed to support the interests of conventional farmers and food conglomerates led to a perception that staff were trying to force the NOSB into a "subservient" position and usurp control of the rulemaking process from the organic sector's representatives (Haedicke 2016, 74). This fear about the cooptation of organic regulations added greatly to the fervor of protest that met the release of the first proposed rule.

Episode #2: The Harvey Lawsuit, 2002–2005

Summary

The revised organic regulations went into force in the fall of 2002 but were challenged in federal court only a few days later by a Maine organic farmer named Arthur Harvey. Harvey's lawsuit took several years to make its way through the initial decision and appeal, and during this time, it gained support from a number of organizations that affiliated with the movement orientation to organic agriculture, including organizations formed to help coordinate the campaign against the First Proposed Rule. In January 2005, an appellate court in Boston ruled in Harvey's favor on several counts, including that NOP's decision to allow the use of synthetic ingredients in organically labeled processed food products violated the Organic Foods Production Act. The commercially oriented Organic Trade Association responded to the ruling by sponsoring an effort to amend OFPA, much to the consternation of the groups that supported the lawsuit. When the amendment was signed into law later in the year, it eliminated the grounds for Harvey's lawsuit and ended this challenge to NOP. However, it contributed to an enduring rift between groups that only a few years earlier had joined together in protesting the First Proposed Rule.

Analysis

Understanding how this episode of contention developed requires attention both to NOP's institutional context and to cultural divisions within the organic sector. In the first place, considering the institutional context clarifies why NOP developed regulations that were vulnerable to legal challenge, despite regulators' constant effort to ensure that that their rulemaking followed the framework established by the law. In the case of processed products, defined in the law as those subjected to "cooking, baking . . . preserving, dehydrating, freezing, or otherwise manufacturing" prior to sale, OFPA contradicted itself. At one point, OFPA indicated that processed products that contained synthetic ingredients could not be sold as "organic" (although they could advertise that they contained organic ingredients), while at another point, it seemed to permit exceptions to this rule for essential ingredients that had no natural substitutes. On the basis of the latter provision and following the guidance of the NOSB, NOP staff included a limited list of common synthetic ingredients that had no natural alternatives, such as ferrous sulfate (for iron enrichment) and ascorbic acid (vitamin C), in the regulations. It was this list that the lawsuit targeted.

OFPA's ambiguity prepared the ground for Harvey's legal challenge, but does not explain why the lawsuit garnered so much attention or proved to be so polarizing within the organic sector. After all, innocuous ingredients like vitamin C do not normally generate the sort of passion that characterized arguments during this period. To answer this question, it is necessary to consider cultural divisions in the organic field. While the lawsuit focused on the legality of the list of permitted synthetic ingredients, the larger debate went far beyond this point by considering how processed organic foods would affect the sector as a whole. Groups affiliated with the movement perspective argued that the regulations would encourage mainstream food companies to develop organic versions of conventional food products, undermining the

organic sector's ability to cultivate a food system anchored in regional networks and relationships. The nutritionist Joan Gussow expressed this concern
in a widely read article titled "Can an Organic Twinkie Be Certified?" Noting
the important role that processed products like Twinkies played in creating
a "global industrialized food system [that] has flourished on the destruction
of human community," Gussow argued that organic foods, when minimally
processed, connected consumers with "a particular place, a particular time of
year . . . and to a set of values that care for nature implies" (Gussow 1997,
150). In contrast, groups that affiliated with the commercial orientation, such
as the Organic Trade Association, emphasized the possible effects of the
court's ruling on the trade in organic products. If manufacturing companies,
whether large conglomerates or small independents, could not label products that used *mostly* organic ingredients as organic, they might stop buying
organic ingredients altogether. The collapse in demand would affect farmers
who grew wheat organically for flour and who raised chickens organically for
eggs, causing bankruptcies and farm closures. As the association's executive
director Kathleen Merrigan put it, "if this goes through, in the worst case
scenario, it could devastate the industry" (Fromartz 2006, xii). Despite their
opposing positions in this debate, movement-affiliated and commercially
affiliated groups agreed that allowing synthetic ingredients in organic products would support the sector's growth, and restricting synthetics would limit
it. They simply disagreed about which outcome was more in keeping with the
spirit of organic agriculture.

Episode #3: Hydroponic Production, 2010–2017

Summary

Along with food processing, a second regulatory issue to highlight differences between commercial and movement orientations in the organic sector
concerned the status of growing systems that avoid open-air planting in soil.
Chief among these was hydroponic production, which involves cultivating
plants in containers that bathe roots in a nutrient-rich solution. In 2010, the
NOSB recommended against allowing hydroponic operations to be certified,
although it also indicated that container-based operations that raise plants
in soil should be eligible for organic certification. NOP, noting a growing
number of applications from operations that were neither clearly hydroponic
nor clearly soil-based (e.g., operations that raised plants in containers filled
with compost and provided nutrients through a recirculating water system),
requested further clarification. The NOSB revisited the issue in 2017, by
which point several dozen partially or completely hydroponic operations had
become certified. This 2017 meeting was divisive, with anti-hydroponics
demonstrators rallying outside the NOSB's meeting room, and the board's

narrow decision not to recommend a more expansive definition of hydroponic production that would have rendered ineligible many of the certified operations was met with dismay by some and relief by others.

Analysis

As was the case in the food processing debate, disagreements related to hydroponic certification were driven as much by cultural divisions within the organic sector as by technical features of hydroponic systems. For movement-affiliated supporters of the more expansive definition, the concept of "soil" had enormous symbolic resonance. As the hydroponics critic Eliot Coleman explained, it was organic farmers' intimate knowledge of and nurturing relationship with soil that enabled organic farming to become "an elegant dance, a partnership between the farmer and the living systems of the earth." In contrast, he noted, "hydroponics exists in the technosphere along with the chemists" (Coleman 2017). Advocate and scientist Linley Dixon similarly argued that "the most important, and challenging, aspect of organic farming is ensuring that organic matter and fertility in the soil is maintained or increased . . . [so] the controversy over whether or not hydroponics could be considered for USDA organic certification gets at the very heart of the definition of organic agriculture" (Dixon 2017). Commercially affiliated groups, including the Organic Trade Association, offered a different set of reasons for opposing the new definition. They emphasized the importance of diversity and innovation within the organic sector provided that all approaches to organic farming avoided prohibited inputs and worked to minimize negative environmental impacts. As one business leader put it, "I believe they made the right decision not to prohibit these out-of-soil production methods. It would have put hundreds of growers out of business, taken valuable supply away from organic consumers, and squelched innovation in our movement" ("U.S.: NOSB Votes Not To Ban Hydroponics From Organic Certification" 2017).

The NOSB's decision not to adopt a more expansive version of hydroponic production meant that the status quo did not change. NOP has continued to allow crops grown in complete and partial hydroponic systems to be certified as organic. This outcome is not surprising, since it would have been difficult for NOP to impose new regulations on hydroponic production without clear support from the NOSB. However, NOP's earlier disregard of the NOSB's 2010 recommendation to exclude hydroponic crops from organic certification needs explanation. Given that this recommendation received near-unanimous support from the NOSB, why did NOP fail to act? An institutionalist perspective highlights two factors that likely made a difference. First, as noted above, there were ambiguities in the NOSB's recommendation, which defined hydroponic systems as those which raised plants in "an inert, solid, porous matrix bathed in nutrient-rich solutions" but made an exception for container-grown crops rooted in "organic matter capable of supporting the plant root system and a natural and diverse soil ecology" (National Organic Standards Board 2010). The recommendation did not specify how "a natural and diverse soil ecology" would be measured, nor explain how regulators should distinguish between "inert" and "organic" container filling. This ambiguity posed practical difficulties when NOP considered actual growing practices, which included, for example, raising plants in containers partially filled with shredded coconut husks, a material that is "organic" but that generally cannot support "a natural and diverse soil ecology." Second, OFPA did not provide NOP with a clear mandate to exclude hydroponic systems from organic certification. The term "hydroponic" did not appear in the law, and while it indicated that maintaining soil fertility should be an important part of an operation's organic plan, it did not specifically indicate that soil-free growing systems were not eligible for organic certification (Morath 2018). Combined, these factors help contextualize NOP's inaction on the hydroponics issue.

Episode #4: The Organic Livestock and Poultry Practices Rule, 2016–2018

Summary

Finally, issues related to animal confinement have drawn concern from many members of the organic sector. When they were implemented in 2002, the organic regulations included a limited number of requirements that dealt the treatment of animals on organic farms. For instance, organic farmers had to provide dairy cows with "access to pasture" and laying hens with "access to exercise areas, fresh air, and direct sunlight." In practice, these rules were interpreted broadly. Some dairy farms allowed cows to graze for only a few months at a time, while keeping them in confined feedlots for the remainder of the year, and some egg producers added only small, concrete "porches" to the large barns in which they raised their flocks. Others provided constant access to pasture for cows and allowed hens to forage outdoors. In 2016, NOP released a draft Organic Livestock and Poultry Practices (OLPP) rule that tightened requirements for outdoor access and also prohibited some practices, such as the amputation of pigs' tails and chickens' beaks, that enabled animals to be raised in close quarters without harming one another. OLPP was supported by most groups in the organic sector, although it was criticized by groups that represent conventional farming interests, such as the American Farm Bureau Federation. To the surprise of organic sector supporters, the USDA abruptly withdrew the rule in the spring of 2018, prompting a round of intense criticism and a lawsuit from the Organic Trade Association that, as of this writing, continues to progress through the courts.

Analysis

While food processing and hydroponics questions exacerbated cultural divisions in the organic sector, animal welfare concerns united sector members. For groups that affiliated with the movement orientation to organic agriculture, the logic of this position is not difficult to understand. Raising livestock in confinement is a core practice in conventional agriculture. For critics, this practice is not only inhumane and exploitative but also contributes to the disappearance of small-scale farms and imposes heavy burdens on the environment and on nearby communities. Indeed, the handful of movement-affiliated groups that withheld support for OLPP did so only on the grounds that it did not go far enough in ensuring that these practices would be excluded from organic agriculture. Groups that affiliated with the commercial orientation not only agreed with many of these ethical concerns but also highlighted the potential for vague rules and disparate practices to erode consumer demand for organic foods. For instance, Organic Trade Association noted in its comments on the draft rule that consumers' "concerns about the living conditions and health care practices for livestock have the potential to impact the industry in widespread and significant ways" and that "loss of confidence in the manner in which organic livestock and poultry are raised will jeopardize the continued success of organic in the marketplace" (Lewis 2016).

The withdrawal of OLPP was thus not a response to a lack of support from within the organic sector. Instead, two institutional factors affected NOP's decision to withdraw this rule. The first was the fact that, as was the case with hydroponics, OFPA did not explicitly authorize NOP to include animal welfare considerations in the national organic standards. Additionally, the "origin of materials" framework that OFPA established to guide the standards did not justify incorporating such considerations, since they were unrelated to the materials used in organic livestock production. The lack of explicit authorization placed OLPP on shaky ground, making it especially vulnerable to the second institutional factor: the priorities of the USDA's leadership. While NOP staff are career civil servants and not political appointees, the Secretary of Agriculture, who has ultimate authority over NOP, is appointed by the president. The draft version of OLPP was released under Secretary Tom Vilsack, an Obama appointee who was relatively receptive to the concerns of sector members. By the time, the USDA withdrew the rule, the leadership of both the USDA and the Executive Branch had changed. Soon after the 2016 election, the Trump Administration announced a requirement that federal agencies eliminate two regulations for each new regulation drafted or implemented. In this context, the new Agriculture Secretary, Sonny Perdue, who had little personal connection to the organic sector, had a clear incentive to direct NOP to withdraw OLPP in order to focus on areas of higher regulatory priority.

CONCLUSION

Many observers have noted that NOP has been the target of recurring debates, but the tendency has been to explain these episodes mainly as flare-ups of grassroots resistance to the co-optation of federal organic regulations by the mainstream food industry. While corporate participation in organics is certainly a point of tension, this chapter's examination of the First Proposed Rule, the Harvey lawsuit, hydroponics, and the Organic Livestock and Poultry Practices Rule suggests that the underlying drivers of debate are more complex. Some of these episodes pitted commercially oriented and movement-oriented wings of the organic sector against one another, while in other episodes, advocates from across the sector joined forces to challenge regulatory staff at NOP. Nor did these regulators simply enact agribusiness interests. They faced a variety of institutional pressures that shaped their actions, which sometimes led them to diverge from organic advocates to whom they felt personal sympathies.

NOP is somewhat unique among USDA regulatory programs in that it sets production standards for an entire category of products on the basis of cultural principles developed by a community of alternative agriculture practitioners (Gershuny 2016). Nevertheless, it reflects broad trends that are shaping contemporary food policy. One of these trends involves a gradual move away from a production-focused orientation, which aims mainly to encourage the use of practices and technologies designed to maximize yields of a limited set of agricultural commodities. A second has to do with the diversification of voices in the policymaking and implementation processes, which are increasingly likely to include environmental and social advocates as well as traditional farming and food industry interests. In this context, food governance involves "an interactive process of state and public laws and policy with private interests and actors . . . [who] may be corporate led or originate from civil society" (Lang, Barling, and Caraher 2009, 81).

We can thus ask what NOP's history has to teach us about the implications of these shifts, as well as what practical lessons it holds for policymakers and regulatory professionals. Two insights stand out. First, the program's history suggests that including new voices in policymaking and implementation multiplies opportunities for disagreement and debate, as new participants bring historically excluded cultural frameworks to bear on policy issues. These debates can enliven the rather staid world of food policy, but in a practical sense, it is important for policymakers and professionals to be aware of the potential for seemingly obscure technical questions to become flash points of controversy. Second, the experiences of NOP reveal how the legacies of earlier policy approaches, which appear in the form of institutionalized rules and procedures, can produce unexpected roadblocks as policy takes a new turn. One example of this is how the role of the NOSB was thrown into question by a contradiction between the Federal Advisory Committee Act, which was intended to limit the influence of powerful industries on regulators charged with overseeing them, and the Organic Foods Production Act, which sought to assure representatives from the organic sector that they would have input into rules developed by a federal agency that many viewed with suspicion. Awareness of the institutional context may allow for policies to be designed in ways that avoid such roadblocks, or failing this, enable policymakers and regulators to foster transparent conversations about the structures that slow the pace of change.

REFERENCES

Coleman, Eliot. 2017. "The Adventure of Organic Farming." Accessed July 14, 2020. https://www.keepthesoilinorganic.org/letter-from-eliot-coleman.

Dixon, Linley. 2017. "Why Hydroponics Is Not Organic." Accessed July 14, 2020. http://www.cornucopia.org/2017/10/the-significance-of-soil/.

Fligstein, Neil, and Doug McAdam. 2012. *A Theory of Fields*. New York: Oxford University Press.

Fromartz, Samuel. 2006. *Organic, Inc.: Natural Foods and How They Grew*. Orlando: Harcourt, Inc.

Gershuny, Grace. 2016. *Organic Revolutionary: A Memoir of the Movement for Real Food, Planetary Healing, and Human Liberation*. Lexington, KY: Joe's Brook Press.

Gussow, Joan Dye. 1997. "Can An Organic Twinkie Be Certified?" In *For All Generations: Making World Agriculture More Sustainable*, edited by J. Patrick Madden and Scott G. Chaplowe, 143–153. Glendale, CA: WSAA Publications.

Guthman, Julie. 2004. *Agrarian Dreams: The Paradox of Organic Farming in California*. Berkeley: University of California Press.

Haedicke, Michael A. 2016. *Organizing Organic: Conflict and Compromise in an Emerging Market*. Stanford: Stanford University Press.

Jaffee, Daniel, and Philip Howard. 2010. "Corporate Cooptation of Organic and Fair Trade Standards." *Agriculture and Human Values* 27 (4): 387–399.

Lang, Tim, David Barling, and Martin Caraher. 2009. *Food Policy: Integrating Health, Environment, and Society*. Oxford: Oxford University Press.

Lewis, Nathaniel. 2016. "OTA Comments on the Proposed Organic Livestock and Poultry Practices Rule." Accessed July 14, 2020. https://ota.com/sites/default/files/indexed_files/OTA_OLPP_AMS-NOP-17–0031.pdf.

McAdam, Doug, Sidney G. Tarrow, and Charles Tilly. 2001. *Dynamics of Contention*. New York: Cambridge University Press.

Meyer, Harlyn. 1990. "Position Papers." *Organic Farmer: The Digest of Sustainable Agriculture*, Winter, 18–20.

Morath, Sarah J. 2018. "Hydroponics: The End of Organic." *Natural Resources and Environment* 33 (1): 36–39.

Obach, Brian K. 2015. *Organic Struggle: The Movement for Sustainable Agriculture in the United States*. Cambridge, MA: MIT Press.

Organic Trade Association. 2020. "U.S. Organic Industry Survey 2020." Accessed September 24, 2020. https://ota.com/organic-market-overview/organic-industry -survey.

Perrow, Charles. 1986. *Complex Organizations: A Critical Essay*. New York: Random House.

Schneiberg, Marc, and Elizabeth S. Clemens. 2006. "The Typical Tools for the Job: Research Strategies in Institutional Analysis." *Sociological Theory* 24 (3): 195–227.

Skocpol, Theda. 1985. "Bringing the State Back In: Strategies of Analysis in Current Research." In *Bringing the State Back In*, edited by Peter B. Evans, Dietrich Rueschemeyer and Theda Skocpol, 3–37. Cambridge, UK: Cambridge University Press.

"U.S.: NOSB Votes Not To Ban Hydroponics From Organic Certification." 2017. FreshFruitPortal.com. Accessed July 14, 2020. https://www.freshfruitportal.com/ news/2017/11/08/u-s-nosb-votes-not-prohibit-hydroponics-organic-certification/.

Vos, Timothy. 2000. "Visions of the Middle Landscape: Organic Farming and the Politics of Nature." *Agriculture and Human Values* 17 (3): 245–256.

Chapter 10

Seed Libraries in the United States

Regulations, Seed Saving, Seed Sharing, and Seed Sovereignty

Nurcan Atalan-Helicke, Andrew
J. Schneller, Clarivel Gonzalez,
Carolyn Lois, and Helen Mebrate

INTRODUCTION

Seeds are the carriers of genetic diversity and express agro-ecological traits that vary over time and space, as the product of evolution or human manipulation (Conner 2015, 17–18). Historically, seed saving and sharing have contributed to the domestication of agriculture, advancing food security, human culture, local food economies, and biodiversity (Musser 2014, 14). Moreover, seed propagation and breeding in the hands of farmers (and gardeners) have helped agro-ecological adaptations and built resilience within agri-food systems (Nabhan 2013, 174–175). Unfortunately, globally, 75 percent of edible plant varieties have been lost in the last century, paralleling the industrial, green, and biotech revolutions (Seed Savers Exchange 2020). The loss of adaptable seed varieties and agricultural biodiversity poses a threat to human welfare. Moreover, crop uniformity, due to the consolidation[1] of seed markets and genetic homogenization[2] (Soleri 2018, 332), exacerbates risks from pests, disease, and climate change (Atalan-Helicke 2015, 641).

There are several factors that contribute to agricultural biodiversity loss, including the industrialization of agriculture, aging of farmers, reduction of farming population, cash crop cultivation, globalization of agribusiness, homogenization of global diets, and competition from hybrid and genetically engineered seeds (Atalan-Helicke 2015, 637) Technological advances and legislative factors that promote commercialization and privatization of seeds favor the interests of big business and disincentivize farmers' participation in plant breeding (Atalan-Helicke and Mansfield 2012, 136–138; Kloppenburg 2010, 368). The regulatory environment may also restrict the rights of farmers to grow, save, and exchange open-pollinated seeds[3] (Dove 2016, 24).

In response to these problems, a movement of community seed projects has developed globally. Community seed projects have existed in the United States since the 1970s as a reaction to the passage of the Plant Variety Protection (PVP) Act of 1970, giving plant breeders exclusive control over new, distinct, uniform, and stable sexually reproduced plant varieties (Ramsey 2018, 201) In the United States, there has been a notable surge in this movement since the 2000s that incorporates initiatives to maintain and improve open-pollinated varieties (Atalan-Helicke 2015, 637). Developed amid concerns about food security and farmers' rights, these initiatives connect to the alternative food movement (AFM) in terms of resisting and challenging corporate control and consolidation by localization (Soleri 2018, 332). Additionally, they aim to address long-term and more recent policy and fiscal trends related to scientific plant breeding. The purpose of this chapter is to examine the work of seed libraries in the United States and the extent to which they contribute to building sustainable food systems.

As of June 2020, there are about 1,400 self-identified seed libraries in the United States (Seed Libraries 2020). Seed libraries facilitate democratic and semiformal seed collection and distribution systems. They have grown significantly in number since the opening of the first seed library at California in 2000.[4] While the work of seed libraries represents a renewed interest in community seed stewardship, increased local food access, and resiliency (Musser 2014, 15), it has also revealed tensions surrounding regulations and policies on seeds. An incident in 2014, when a Pennsylvania seed library was closed by the state's Department of Agriculture (DOA) for violating the state's seed law, has raised questions about the "legal grey area" in which seed libraries operate (Ramsey 2018, 201). This incident sparked a conversation about existing federal and state legislation on commercial seeds. It also led seed library activists to craft new laws to protect noncommercial seed exchanges from burdensome policy requirements (Soleri 2018, 332).

Seed libraries (and the movement) are an understudied phenomenon in the American food system. While there is growing attention to the seed libraries in public media (Wang 2010; Shea 2014; Sproul 2017), there is a gap in the literature regarding the policy framework in the United States, and how that intersects with the work of seed libraries. Librarians embrace seed libraries as "an innovative mechanism" to serve the community challenges around food, poverty, health, and sustainability (Peekhaus 2018, 273). Others argue that seed libraries hold the promise of restoring seed sovereignty and provide broader access to regionally adaptable seeds for building resilience (Dove 2016, 46; Soleri 2018, 332). Seed libraries also work to protect local knowledge and the rare and heirloom seeds[5] that may not be maintained or distributed commercially (Musser 2014, 15).

Our research examined the priorities and concerns of seed libraries in the United States, tensions related to access to seeds, and the policy frameworks that at times challenge the work of seed libraries. This qualitative research employed online surveys and semistructured interviews to better understand: (1) The major concerns of farmers, activists, and seed savers within the seed library movement in the United States; (2) The goals of seed libraries and through what means they are accomplished; and (3) The extent to which seed library effectiveness can be explained. Through archival analysis, we additionally documented the legal and policy framework of six U.S. states (California, Colorado, Massachusetts, New York, Virginia, and Wisconsin), and argue that while the uncertain and challenging legal environment renders seed libraries an underused component in the AFM (Ramsey 2018, 217), seed library expansion nationwide, and their attempts at institutionalization and networking, have increased their significance for access to seeds and resilience of the American agri-food systems. The changes in state policies also raise interesting questions about policy diffusion, and the potential role of state legislatures in shaping and managing relations and transactions related to seeds across the United States.

LITERATURE REVIEW

Governance of Seeds and U.S. Legal Landscape

While the Patent Office Division of Agriculture existed in the United States since the 1850s, broader application of patents expanded in the twentieth century with the development of more sophisticated and scientific techniques in plant breeding. By the 1900s, seed saving, exchange, and cultivation practices of farmers started to change with the establishment of seed certification programs in the United States. These focused on improving seed quality and yields, particularly, through the development of hybrid seeds and publicly funded seed breeding programs. In the United States (during the late 1920s and early 1930s), this led to greater private sector interest in seed breeding (Kloppenburg 2005, 12). The use of hybrid seeds and modern cultivars expanded rapidly after the 1940s, during the green revolution, a technological and agricultural paradigm shift that coupled modern cultivars, often hybrid seeds, with agricultural chemicals, expanded irrigation models, and modern machinery (Kloppenburg 2005, 6).

There are different mechanisms at the global scale that regulate the use of commercial seed varieties for breeding. One of them is the PVP that provides breeders exclusive rights to propagate and sell the protected variety and derivatives. PVP was established in the 1961 International Convention for the Protection of New Varieties of Plants (the Convention), and it became effective in the United States in 1970 with the PVP Act. For a variety to be protected, eligibility criteria include distinctness, uniformity, stability, and novelty, a set of criteria that generally excluded traditional, farmer-saved seeds (Atalan-Helicke and Mansfield 2012, 134). With the PVP Act, the federal government set the broad parameters, and provided plant breeders control over new varieties for twenty years, and tree/vine varieties for twenty-five years (U.S. Department of Agriculture 2013).

In the United States, despite some exemptions, the 1970 PVP Act imposed limitations on farmers' rights to save and exchange seed, while seed industry's consolidation spawned seed sovereignty advocacy across different states: Civil society initiatives in the United States such as Seed Savers Exchange and Native Seeds/SEARCH emerged in mid-1970s and early 1980s, reflecting the concerns of gardeners, communities, food activists, and scientists about disappearing diversity and seeds, as well as access to seeds (Atalan-Helicke 2015, 644). Because the PVP Act provided exemptions that were not fully attractive to plant breeders, another regulation, a utility patent that involves the U.S. Patent and Trademark Office came into effect. A utility patent protects specific attributes of individual varieties, applicable to sexually reproducing and GE (genetically engineered) plants (Ramsey 2018, 202–203). A plant variety with a utility patent can only be used for crop production and can't be used for seed saving, resale, given away, or replanted (Johnny's Seeds 2017).

In the United States, there are also other rules at the federal- and state-level regarding the sale, labeling, breeding, testing of seeds, and their movement across state borders. These seed laws aim to protect the farmers and individuals from purchasing poor quality or mislabeled seed. (U.S. Department of Agriculture 1988). They also aim to protect patents and intellectual property rights for plant breeders and reward their innovation associated with modern cultivars (Atalan-Helicke and Mansfield 2012, 134).

The Federal Seed Act (FSA) of 1939 (amended in 1988) aims to regulate interstate and foreign commerce in seeds by requiring labeling with the goal of preventing misrepresentation in interstate commerce and setting standards for imported seeds. The FSA[6] requires that seed labeling information and advertisements pertaining to the seed must be truthful, further working to protect farmers from receiving wrong (or defective) seeds, thus losing expenses of seed and crops (Ramsey 2018, 202). Moreover, the FSA ensures that seeds planted by farmers are not contaminated with undesirable "weed seeds." Seeds must be certified by a seed certifying agency showing compliance with rules, regulations, and standards of its class (U.S. Department of Agriculture 1988).

FSA works to promote uniform state laws and since the 1940s, intersects with the work of the Association of American Seed Control Officials
(AASCO), representing the seed regulatory officials of the United States and
Canada. AASCO meets annually and updates its *Recommended Uniform
State Seed Law* (Association of American Seed Control Officials 2017),
which provides a model state seed law. This Uniform Law includes an
exemption on noncommercial seed sharing, which is critical, as the wording
of a state seed law distinguishes between commercial and noncommercial
seed distribution, and dictates whether a seed library can operate legally in a
given state (Ramsey 2018, 204).

Regulation of Noncommercial Seeds

The Uniform Law defines noncommercial seed sharing as the distribution and
exchange of seeds without monetary compensation. While it also clarifies rules
regarding the labeling and educational requirements of noncommercial seed
sharing, AASCO's model law is important for the functioning of seed libraries:
By definition, anyone distributing seeds under seed sharing "may not expect,
or create the expectation, that seeds must be returned in exchange for receiving
seeds" (Association of American Seed Control Officials 2017). The law also
defines the limit on the amount of seeds to be exchanged (Ramsey 2018, 204).

The nuances in state laws affect the legality of seed libraries, as they may
be held to the same labeling and testing requirements of commercial seed
companies. In 2014, the incident involving Cumberland County Library
System (CCLS) and DOA in Pennsylvania was related to violation of state
laws on the sale, distribution, and labeling of commercial seeds. The CCLS
seed library officials were informed that their seed library was a seed distribu-
tor, and should be licensed annually (for $25), follow labeling requirements,
and conduct purity and germination analyses (Carolan 2018, 88). Because
the state seed laws work to protect commercial seed quality, the DOA cited
violations of labeling requirements as a potential danger to the agricultural
system (SELC 2014). However, demanding that seed libraries comply with
testing and labeling regulations designed for commercial seed companies
places "an undue burden on the resources of nonprofit seed libraries and make
it impossible for them to operate as community-based, often volunteer-run,
organizations" (SELC 2017, 4). Such interventions facilitated seed activists
and the Sustainable Economies Law Center (SELC) to ensure the legality of
seed libraries, to clarify the ambiguity in the language of state laws about the
"sale" of seed, and to exempt seed that is not sold or offered for sale from
state laws (Musser 2014, 15).

The Pennsylvania DOA intervention led to a compromise for some seed
libraries, as they decided not to accept returns of seeds from home-grown

plants (Carolan 2018, 91). In other instances, some seed libraries, such as in Pennsylvania and California, decided to close (Soleri 2018, 332). A seed library administrator[7] interviewed for this research interpreted the incident:

> I think the concern in Pennsylvania was if you come to our seed library and I give you seeds that say Sunsweet watermelon, and it's not, I'm participating in some sort of business fraud . . . And my response to that is, we're giving it away. We're telling you it's a local donation. So . . . let the buyer beware. We're not selling you something that's causing you to lose money if it's not pure. We're giving seed away in earnest hope that it is pure and to serve a greater purpose. (Personal Communication 2016)

Following 2014's incident, SELC immediately launched the Save Seed Sharing Campaign to spread awareness and build support for legal protections for seed libraries and other community-based seed sharing initiatives (SELC 2020). In 2015, SELC helped coordinate the first International Seed Library Forum in Arizona, and worked to pass state laws to exempt noncommercial seed sharing from burdensome requirements[8] (SELC 2020). These new laws set a precedent to provide new guidance and to promote seed sharing among different stakeholders (Dove 2016, 24–25). Broadly, states interact with one another in the environmental policy arena, while interaction also occurs between states and the federal government. In our current interconnected world, understanding policy diffusion aids in the understanding of policy advocacy and change more broadly (Shipan and Volden 2012, 788). Studies demonstrate that strategic interactions in environmental policy are particularly prominent in the Northeast and Western United States (Billard et al. 2020, 15; Rabe 2008, 106). A close examination of select state policies can help us to better understand the broad array of interpretations that states have adopted, especially when confronted with the 2014 incident, and parameters set by the federal government. However, it is not a guarantee that these amendments or new interpretations will result in other states and policymakers following suit as there are several factors to consider, including intergovernmental networks, and time between federal and substate policy adoption (Beland et al. 2018, 535).

Select State Laws

We focus on policy in six states: New York, Massachusetts, Colorado, California, Virginia, and Wisconsin, as the representatives from their seed libraries completed both our survey and semistructured interviews. We focus on these six states to contrast the state-level approaches to seed libraries and provide a regional sampling across the United States. Moreover, some states have been examined in literature more than others (e.g., Pennsylvania,

California, Nebraska, Minnesota), and this research effort contrasts these highly examined states with other less-studied states. While all state laws address commercial seed sale and distribution, they differ in terms of how they address seed exchanges and seed libraries. While California's amendments specific to noncommercial seeds enabled room for seed libraries, several states (including Colorado) did not amend their laws because seed libraries did not work with patented seeds or engage with the "sale" of seeds.

California has long played a pioneering role in environmental protection and progressive policies. Indeed, the "California Effect" refers to the cross-state diffusion of its policies, pulling other states into its orbit when they adopt similar policies, as has been the case with climate change policy and efforts to reduce greenhouse gas emissions (Rabe 2008, 111). Because the first seed library was established there, and there is a well-established AFM,[9] California chose to amend its state law. Representing a "departure from California's previous stance on seed sharing" (Ramsey 2018, 207), California became one of the first states to amend its seed law for exclusions on noncommercial seed sharing. While emphasizing the seed industry's role and commitment "to improve the quality and variety of seed available to the consumer-buyer," the amendment clarified that noncommercial seed-sharing "activity does not include receiving, storing or distributing patented seed" and thus "does not violate the federal PVP Act" (California Seed Law 2016). Several seed libraries in California also make few requirements on seed borrowing to fulfill a seed distribution role[10] (Soleri 2018, 338).

The Colorado State Law regulates licensing, labelling, and sale of commercial seeds with specifications for germination and purity testing (Colorado Department of Agriculture 2020), emphasizing consumer and environmental protection. After the DOA's intervention in Pennsylvania, the Colorado DOA plant industry division released a statement clarifying seed sale and small-scale exchanges at seed libraries. The program manager Laura Pottorf stated: "The purpose of our seed law is to regulate business transaction with seed. At local seed libraries, no money is exchanging hands." These assurances gave a green light for seed libraries in Colorado to continue operations (Livick 2015).

Similar to Colorado's interpretation, seed libraries in Massachusetts also chose to emphasize the free nature of "borrowing" rare or heirloom seeds (Shea 2014). A similar emphasis also allowed the functioning of seed libraries in Wisconsin where policies exempt seed libraries from requirements of the state law provided there are no monetary or seed exchange requirements. The director of the Wisconsin Plant Industry Bureau, Brian Kuhn, emphasized that the state seed law's goal was "to create a system so that regulators know where all of the distribution points are," and thus, they asked seed libraries "to get a $25 license" (Shepel 2016). Whereas some seed libraries in Virginia adapted a Seed Protocol to ensure that "seed borrowers get accurately labeled seeds, and that participants share only healthy plants" (Lewis Ginter Botanical Garden 2020), others now emphasize a Borrow-Grow-Return policy with specific instructions on returning or donating seeds (Salem Public Library 2020).

Like California, New York had one of the first seed libraries established[11] in 2004, and as of March 2020, New York hosts more than twenty seed libraries (Beglinger 2020). While the state does not require licensing to sell or distribute seeds, its state law regulates the inspection and sales of seeds with a specific emphasis on "truth in labeling" (Westra 2016).

METHODS

Our qualitative case study research was conducted between January and April 2016 and triangulated both sources and methods (Creswell and Poh 2018, 53). We collected online (Qualtrics) and identical paper surveys from representatives at sixty-one U.S. seed libraries, and conducted ten semistructured interviews via phone and in-person with representatives from U.S. seed libraries (librarians or volunteer coordinators) and individuals involved in the organic agriculture movement in New York (e.g., garden manager, seed company representative).[12] Further, we conducted participant observation at two regional organic food conferences of the Northeast Sustainable Agriculture Working Group and the Northeast Organic Farming Association of New York. Respondents for semistructured interviews were selected among those who provided their contact information within our surveys, and agreed to follow-up with an in-depth interview. Semistructured interviews were conducted in English, recorded using digital voice recorders, transcribed, and coded. The participant observation during the conferences (where authors also *worked as volunteers*) provided a unique opportunity to document and collect data about seed-related conversations among stakeholders in the Northeastern United States, better understand emerging priorities and issues, assess concerns, and understand seed systems beyond what stakeholders say publicly (Creswell and Poh 2018, 18). Additionally, archival research was used to explore seed library websites, newsletters, and popular media articles.

FINDINGS

Functions and Priorities of Seed Libraries

As the literature suggests (Peekhaus 2018, 273; Soleri 2018, 332), a majority of seed library respondents were hosted in public libraries. Respondents described free membership and simple borrowing rules. The majority, 80 percent, of respondents described open access, while a mere 5 percent limited membership by geographic region. As many seed libraries aim to enhance access to seeds, they also described their role in distribution of organic, local, open-pollinated, and heirloom seeds, free to the public.

Seed library functional development was better understood after isolating emerging concerns and priorities from their mission statements. We categorized these priorities as (a) education of the public on topics related to gardening, seed saving, culture of sharing, and community building; (b) expansion of seed access; (c) access to locally sourced food for food security; (d) creating locally and/or regionally adapted seeds; (e) preserving biodiversity; (f) promoting health of local communities; (g) resistance to corporate control in the food system, and (h) empowering local communities (table 10.1). Surveys showed that "resisting the power of multinational seed corporations" was mentioned across mission statements, particularly due to the role of corporate dominance in the seed sector. In most cases, the lines between different priorities were blurred. For instance, one administrator stated that their mission is to provide alternatives to the genetically engineered seed and processed foods by promoting self-resilience and locally grown food. While most of them focused on bolstering access and availability of seeds to aid regional food system resilience, addressing global climate change was also repeatedly listed.

Several seed library mission statements emphasized their "free" services as they provide "a *free* source of locally adapted, open-pollinated seeds," "a *free* community service for home gardeners to exchange seeds," or "*free* information on seed saving and growing food." These statements highlight the sharing function that seed libraries emphasize to differentiate their role from commercial seed companies.

Effectiveness of Seed Libraries

We devised five measures to assess the relative resilience that seed libraries contributed to their regions: years active, partnerships, membership, funding, and volume of seed varieties (stored and exchanged) and categorized seed libraries regionally. We predicted that the most effective libraries would have been active the longest, established extensive partnerships, received external funding, maintained a large base of active members, and hosted a diverse seed collection.

External Partnership and Funding

In their rarity, heirloom seeds require expensive initial investments. The cost to build the original seed stock and replenish seed stocks require stable

Table 10.1 Seed Library Mission Statements Coded by Theme

Education	Seed Access	Local Food/Food Security	Regionally/Locally Adapted Seeds
"To create a culture of learning, sharing, and community through sustainable seed saving that reclaims seeds as a public resource." "To provide a free service committed to enriching our community by educating its members in the practice of gardening and seed saving . . ."	"To encourage seed saving in our local area and to make seeds available for low income and less experienced members of our community."	"To access locally grown food and to build authentic connections with neighbors to create a vibrant, thriving . . . community." "To crate sustainable local food sourcing as well as growing a healthier . . . community through feeding ourselves and learning together the skill and art of [seed] saving."	"To create a publicly accessible source of regionally adapted seeds that is maintained by our community of novice and experienced farmers and gardeners."

Preserving Biodiversity	Health	Food Sovereignty/Resistance to Corporate Control in Seed and Food System	Empower Local Communities/Gardeners
"To collect and share bio-diverse, locally adapted plant seeds, cultivated by and for area residents." "To increase biodiversity of locally adapted seeds . . . by providing open pollinated heirloom seeds, encouraging people to garden, and sharing the knowledge of seed saving."	"To provide our local populace with the seeds and the information to assist them in growing wholesome food for their families and communities."	"To educate patrons on the practice of saving seeds for self sustainability . . . provide information on [GE food] and organic alternatives to processed food, educate low income patrons on cost effective ways to grow their own food and replenish their own seed stock."	"To bring back seed-saving traditions of many ethnic groups; to empower individuals and communities to produce the foods and seeds that do best in their environment."

financial sources. "You can't run a seed program based only on donated seed," reads a survey response from one administrator who heads one of the most community supported seed libraries (over 1,000 active members). Although there is no clear trend that solidifies the relationship between community partnerships and financial assistance, 63 percent of libraries had at least one partner and received assistance in the form of seed and monetary donations. For the Northeast region, all seed libraries have at least one community partner and received financial assistance and seed donations.

Active Membership and Seed Varieties in Circulation

Our survey results found that 60 percent of seed libraries sampled were operating for only one to three years. The more years a seed library was active, the more connections they had to other seed libraries. Further, active membership was at the core of seed library functionality, with one respondent stating: "The folks who show up and make it run, [who] let their minds and hearts holds seeds" (survey respondent). To assess the true influence of membership, we looked at the relationship between the number of active members and the number of seeds in circulation (at each library) to determine a relative measure of resilience. The assumption was that seed libraries with most number of active members would also have the highest diversity of seeds in circulation. As a baseline assumption, we predicted that a robust base of twenty active members or more is likely to have more than 100 seed varieties in circulation. Nationwide, seed libraries boasting at least this level of active membership (twenty members) and seed circulation volume only comprised over a quarter of the total seed libraries that we sampled. Interestingly, we found that the limiting factor that yielded only a quarter of the seed libraries to qualify was not the number of members they had, but the number of seed varieties available for borrowing. Raising the stakes to fifty or more members but decreasing the benchmark of seed varieties from 100 to at least 50, we found that the same percentage of libraries qualified (about a quarter). At the extremes, active membership seemed to bear a positive correlation to the breadth of seed diversity. For example, the library with the topmost active membership circulated more than 1,000 seeds, while the least utilized library with no active members possessed only twenty-four varieties. This correlation was not an anomaly; seed libraries with the lowest active membership were often the same libraries that possessed the least diversity of seeds available. Meanwhile, the top five libraries with memberships exceeding 400 people had, on average, one hundred times more seed varieties in circulation (313 varieties) than the five seed libraries with the lowest membership (33 varieties). This trend was especially robust in the Northeast region, where we found that memberships of 100 or more also had over 100 seed varieties. This suggests that active community involvement in a given seed library increases seed diversity.

Years Active and Interconnectivity

Our research aimed to understand how years of being an active seed library influences the number of formal and informal connections to other libraries. Seed exchange between seed libraries magnifies the scope of opportunity for each heirloom variety to be saved, redistributed, and replanted. To assess the level of interconnectedness between seed libraries, we cross-tabulated the number of years each seed library had been active and the frequency of interlibrary seed exchanges (table 10.2). Out of 61 respondents, 77 percent of libraries do not exchange seeds with other libraries. For the remaining 33 percent that have swapped seeds with other libraries, we found the highest level of interconnectivity were among libraries that had been active for four to seven years. In this particular bracket, seed libraries were more than three times as likely to exchange with other seed libraries compared to younger libraries aged one to three years. In addition to the increased likelihood of exchange, libraries aged four to seven participated in double the frequency of those exchanges compared to the newcomers.

Since we found that interconnectedness tends to increase with number of years established, it is logical that only about a quarter of seed libraries have exchanged with other seed libraries before, since the majority were just getting established (figure 10.1). Contrary to our hypothesis that interconnectedness enhances with age, we found that only one out of the four oldest seed library respondents has ever exchanged seeds with another library. Overall, most seed library administrators described these exchanges as informal or need-based only. As one seed library representative attested, "we have done so, but only occasionally, and not in any highly organized manner." The hesitancy to exchange seed stocks with other seed libraries could also stem from limitations on interstate distribution of seeds specified in state laws, and a concern about limiting problems that could stem from purity to the specific local area in which the seed library functions.

Table 10.2   Inter Seed Library Loan in Relation to Years Active

Years Active	Do Not Interexchange	Percent Total (%)
1–3	5	87.5
4–7	8	55
8–11	1	0
12–15	1	66
All	46	75

		Do you exchange seeds with other seed libraries?	
		Yes (If yes, how often and with how many seed libraries?)	No
For how long has your seed library been active?	1-3 years	4	28
	4-7 years	9	11
	8-11 years	1	0
	12-15 years	1	2
	16-19 years	0	0
	20 or more years	0	0

Figure 10.1   Active Years of a Seed Library in Relation to Interlibrary Loan. *Source:* Authors

Limitations and Barriers for Effectiveness of Seed Libraries

We found that the majority of administrators facilitate seed exchange on a volunteer basis, many in the confines of local public libraries. Stemming from the volunteer basis of their jobs, interviewees explained: (i) gaps in financial and community support for their seed library, (ii) challenges and obstacles for implementation, and (iii) effective methods for long-term success. A volunteer seed library coordinator in Virginia expressed their concerns with entrusting the integrity and survival of heirloom seeds to inexperienced seed savers, but commended their operation for offering educational resources that address heirloom seed mismanagement: "[operating with volunteers], we're not going to be able to guarantee the biological efficacy of every seed. [Yet] I think we do pretty darn well because we educate people" (Personal communication 2016). The coordinator also noted "time constraints," and added the challenges due to "logistics of running a pretty functional program [without] having the connectedness that a full-time employee would have" (Personal communication 2016).

These findings confirm the literature that seed libraries require operating costs that mainly stem from purchasing seeds and paying for staff time. Peekhaus (2018) argued that the estimated operating costs of a seed library is $2,500 annually, and it tends to decrease as more patrons return seeds, or the library receives more seed donations (275). In general, a public library contributes to the seed library by providing staff time to facilitate seed library operation, although there is no specific line item for this budget. Because the labor requirements of a seed library tend to be seasonal, a public librarian can run seed library operations with volunteers (Peekhaus 2018, 276). Soleri's (2018, 332) findings also confirmed that public libraries are critical to the functioning of seed libraries, as they provide a physical space, access to library webspace, scheduling ease with complementary activities, and an opportunity to stay open for more hours.

Seed Return Policy

Seed libraries organize seed-saving workshops to teach about seed-saving skills, even though 50 percent of our respondents did not expect members to return seeds. While 15 percent encouraged returns on easy-save seeds, only 5 percent expected returns of borrowed seeds that exceeded double the amount borrowed. Similar to how seed libraries emphasize borrow and grow function, our respondents emphasized that "only those who attended educational workshops or are advanced gardeners" to return seeds, "take a class" before return, "return only the seeds that one is comfortable" with saving and identifying. Indeed, 30 percent of seed libraries had incorporated some criteria for returning seeds, including no hybrid or genetically engineered seeds accepted, only open-pollinated seeds accepted; only heirloom seeds accepted; donations from regional companies or regionally adapted seeds accepted. No seed library required lab germination tests upon return of the seeds to the library to ensure the quality and growth viability of the seeds being returned. While requiring germination tests would ensure heirloom purity, it could also pose a hurdle for members with a lack of time and/or funding.

DISCUSSION AND CONCLUSION

Seed libraries serve multiple functions in the American agri-food system to establish local food systems and build resilience. While concerns about agri-food system changes have facilitated the emergence and initial expansion of seed libraries, policy amendments and/or reinterpretations, particularly in the state seed laws, have facilitated their recent expansion. Policies that allow for noncommercial seed exchange and distribution are critical, as they allow public exchange of locally adaptable, open-pollinated seeds, and promote seed-saving knowledge in the hands of gardeners and local communities. Seed libraries have also bolstered broader conversations about seed sovereignty, as seed libraries emphasize the role of local farmers, gardeners, and the community, in conserving agricultural biodiversity (Atalan-Helicke 2015, 646). In the AFM, seed libraries, like farmers' markets and community gardens, also hold the promise of heightening equity, providing healthy food to low-income community members (Ramsey 2018, 216).

These case study findings suggest that (a) The more years a seed library is active, the more connected they are (formally/informally) to other seed libraries; (b) Active community involvement increases the manifold of seed diversity in exchange; and (c) Community partnerships, at least in the Northeast region of the United States, likely lead to financial assistance and a greater quantity of seed donations. Formal development of state and federal policies and the creation of supportive legal environments for seed libraries (to operate) is critical for providing broader access to locally adaptable seeds and preventing the loss of traditional seed saving knowledge and networks. While bolstering public education of gardeners, policymakers, and communities about the role of seeds in food systems, seed libraries also promote an interest in gardening among younger generations.

The quality of returned seed and the (sometimes) inadequately labelled seed packets are still a concern for seed libraries. With an emphasis on "free" services, seed libraries face challenges in terms of guaranteeing that patrons will return and exchange seeds. Because many seed libraries are understaffed, they may also have difficulty maintaining their return procedures, despite measures to maintain quality in their collection (Dove 2016, 44). Seed libraries are also cognizant of seed quality for agricultural purposes, and sometimes hesitant to accept donated seeds, or may limit donations to certain types of seeds. Further, seed libraries are not likely to exchange seed stocks with other seed libraries, due to concerns about purity and/or legal limitations on interstate distribution.

Our research found that policy decisions at the state level have at times addressed noncommercial seed exchange, with these interpretations serving as models for action in other states, which in turn could further protect seed libraries from uncertain legal environments. In the environmental policy arena, states interact with one another, as well as with the federal government. And while it is important to consider the role of federal legislation in shaping and managing intergovernmental relations, it is also important to consider the role of policy diffusion *across* states. State policy innovations may also trigger a national debate vis-à-vis seed systems instigating bottom-up policy changes. Yet, as the nuances in interpretations show, the outcomes of these debates vary by state. Enabling policies at the state level, coupled with supportive legal environments for seed libraries (to operate and expand), are critical for facilitating the suite of social and environmental benefits that we have documented above.

NOTES

1. The seed industry which was characterized by thousands of small, mostly family owned business before 1970s has now become dominated by just three agrochemical firms controlling more than half of the global proprietary seed market (Howard 2015, 2489).
2. Genetic diversity refers to the genetic variability among or within a sample of individuals of a variety, population, or species. "A broad genetic base is necessary to keep plant populations strong" (Conner 2015, 17). Unfortunately, the loss of seed varieties is connected to the loss of genetic diversity (Conner 2015, 19).

3. Open pollinated plants are those, if properly isolated from other varieties in the same plant species, will breed true. That is, the seed will produce a plant very similar to the parent (Conner 2015, 8).

4. The first seed library, Bay Area Seed Interchange Library (BASIL) was established at the Berkeley Ecology Center in CA by Sacha DuBrul and run by volunteers (Conner 2015, 13).

5. A seed can be rare for several reasons: A variety or strain that has been stewarded by a family or community for generations and not shared beyond or a family heirloom which has been passed down only through the hands of the same family would be rare. Some of these are also called heirloom varieties. An ex-commercial variety that has been dropped from seed catalogues or a new variety created by a producer would also be rare (Dove 2016, 25).

6. The FSA covers seed used in the agricultural production of food, feed, fiber, and turf, but does not regulate flower, tree, shrub, or seeds used primarily for revegetation purposes (United States Department of Agriculture 1988).

7. There are no interview subject names used in this chapter. Only pseudonyms were used during coding and analysis stage of the research.

8. The first state law for exemptions for noncommercial seed distribution passed in Minnesota. Nebraska followed suit (Ramsey 2018, 205–206).

9. Such initiatives emphasizing localization of food systems in California include "Good Food Purchasing Pledge" by school districts, "California Regional Seed System" chapter of Organic Seed Alliance's farmer-plant breeder collaboration to develop locally appropriate seed for organic production as well as passage of GE free agriculture measures in several countries in California (Soleri 2018, 333).

10. In a qualitative study with forty-five seed library managers in California, Soleri (2018, 336) found that annually 6,456 packets of seeds, mostly of commercial seeds from small seed companies, are distributed by seed libraries in California.

11. In 2004, Hudson Valley Seed Library was established by Ken Greene in Gardiner, NY. It went online in 2008, and in 2009, the Hudson Valley Seed company began. Since then, the company has propagated heirloom and open-pollinated vegetable and flower seeds for Northeast climate, and started collaborations across farmers and various stakeholders for seed sovereignty and sustainable and resilient food systems (Hudson Valley 2020).

12. We did not collect demographic data about the research subjects (gender, age).

REFERENCES

Association of American Seed Control Officials. 2017. "Recommended Uniform State Seed Law." Accessed August 1, 2020. http://www.seedcontrol.org/pdf/russ l_2017.pdf.

Atalan-Helicke, Nurcan, and Becky Mansfield. 2012. "Seed Governance at the Intersection of Multiple Global and Nation-State Priorities: Modernizing Seeds in Turkey." *Global Environmental Politics* 12, no. 4: 125–146.

Atalan-Helicke, Nurcan. 2015. "Seed Exchange Networks and Food System Resilience in the United States." *Journal of Environmental Studies and Sciences* 5, no. 4: 636–649.

Beglinger, Jan. 2020. "A Seed Library Sprouts in Batavia." *The Daily News Online*, March 9, 2020. https://www.thedailynewsonline.com/lifestyles/a-seed-library-spro uts-in-batavia/article_2696a394–9bf1–5ecc-bb21-acab8bb6a40e.html.

Beland, Daniel, Anahely Medrano, and Philip B. Rocco. 2018. "Federalism and the Politics of Bottom-Up Social Policy Diffusion in the United States, Mexico, and Canada" *Political Science Quarterly* 133, no. 3: 527–560.

Billard, Come, Anna Creti, Antoine Mandel. 2020. "How Environmental Policies Spread? A Network Approach to Diffusion in the U.S." *CEC Working Papers, 10.* Accessible at https://www.chaireeconomieduclimat.org/wp-content/uploads/2020 /11/WP-2020–10.pdf.

California Seed Law. 2016. "Assembly Bill-1810" https://leginfo.legislature.ca.gov/ faces/billTextClient.xhtml?bill_id=201520160AB1810.

Carolan, Michael. 2018. *The Food Sharing Revolution: How Start-ups, Pop-ups, and Co-ops are Changing the Way we Wat.* Washington, DC: Island Press.

Colorado Department of Agriculture. 2020. "Seed Law" https://www.colorado.gov/ pacific/agplants/seed.

Conner, Cindy. 2015. *Seed Libraries: And Other Means of Keeping Seeds in the Hands of the People.* B.C., Canada: New Society Publishers.

Creswell, John and Cheryl N. Poh. 2018. *Qualitative Inquiry and Research Design: Choosing Among Five Approaches.* 4th edition. Thousand Oaks: SAGE Publications.

Dove, Charlotte. 2016. *The Role of Community Seed Projects in Protecting Seed Diversity.* Winston Churchill Memorial Trust and The Frank Johnston Foundation report. Accesible at https://seeddiversity.wordpress.com/research-project/ .

Howard, Paul H. 2015. "Intellectual Property and Consolidation in the Seed Industry." *Crop Science* 55, no. 6: 2489–2495.

Hudson Valley. 2020. "Our history" Accessible at https://hudsonvalleyseed.com/p ages/history.

Johnny's Seeds. 2017. "Understanding Utility Patents and PVP." Accessed July 15, 2020. https://www.johnnyseeds.com/about-us/about-our-seed/understanding-util ity-patents-and-pvp.html.

Kloppenburg, Jack. 2005. *First the Seed: The Political Economy of Plant Biotechnology 1492–2000.* Madison: University of Wisconsin Press.

Kloppenburg, Jack. 2010. "Impeding Dispossession, Enabling Repossession: Biological Open Source and the Recovery of Seed Sovereignty." *Journal of Agrarian Change* 10, no. 3: 367–388.

Lewis Ginter Botanical Garden. 2020. "Seed Library." Accessed August 1, 2020. https://www.lewisginter.org/learn/library/seed-library/#:~:text=Is%20this%20seed %20library%20legal,obtained%20from%20the%20Seed%20Library.

Livick, Shannon. 2015. "Seeds of Discontent." *The Mancos Times*, February 11, 2015. https://the-journal.com/articles/23765.

Musser, Bill. 2014. "Seed Lending Libraries: Teaching Moments in Botany and Horticulture." *Council on Botanical and Horticultural Libraries Newsletter* 135: 14–15.

Nabhan, Gary. 2013. *Growing Food in a Hotter, Drier Land: Lessons from Desert Farmers on Adapting to Climate Uncertainty.* Hartford: Chelsea Green Publishing.

Peekhaus, Wilhelm. 2018. "Seed Libraries: Sowing the Seeds for Community and Public Library Resilience." *The Library Quarterly* 88, no. 3: 271–285.

Rabe, Barry G. 2008. "States on Steroids: The Intergovernmental Odyssey of American Climate Policy." *Review of Policy Research*, no. 2: 105–128.

Ramsey, Ursula. 2018. "Seed Libraries and Food Justice: Cultivating an Effective Legal and Policy Environment." *Georgetown Journal on Poverty Law & Policy* 25, no. 2: 194–220.

Salem Public Library. 2020. "Seed Library" Accessed August 1, 2020. https://salemva.gov/Departments/Salem-Public-Library/Seed-Library.

Seed Libraries. 2020. "Sister Libraries." Accessed July 15, 2020. http://seedlibraries.weebly.com/sister-libraries.html.

Seed Savers Exchange. 2020. "Our Story." Accessed August 15, 2020. https://www.seedsavers.org/story.

SELC. 2014. "Setting the record straight on the legality of seed libraries." Accessed August 1, 2020. https://www.shareable.net/setting-the-record-straight-on-the-legality-of-seed-libraries/.

SELC. 2017. "The Seed Democracy Advocacy Toolkit." Accessed August 1, 2020. https://d3n8a8pro7vhmx.cloudfront.net/theselc/pages/745/attachments/original/1483580476/2017.01.04_-_Seed_Democracy_Toolkit.pdf?1483580476.

SELC. 2020. "Save Seed Sharing." Accessed July 1, 2020. https://www.theselc.org/save_seed_sharing.

Shea, Andrea. 2014. "You Lend What? Seed Lending Libraries Crop Up Around Massachusetts." *WBUR News,* June 18, 2014. https://www.wbur.org/news/2014/06/18/concord-seed-lending-library-preserves-heirloom-seeds-and-their-stories.

Shepel, Jan. 2016. "Revised Rule Puts Seed Libraries Under State Regulation." *Wisconsin State Farmer*, December 5, 2016. https://www.wisfarmer.com/story/news/state/2016/12/05/revised-rule-puts-seed-libraries-under-state-regulation/95028316/.

Shipan, Charles R., and Craig, Volden. 2012. Policy Diffusion: Seven Lessons for Scholars and Practitioners. *Public Administration Review*, 72, no. 6: 788–796.

Soleri, Daniel. 2018. "Civic Seeds: New Institutions for Seed Systems and Communities—A 2016 Survey of California Seed Libraries." *Agriculture and Human Values* 35, no. 2: 331–347.

Sproul, Suzanne. 2017. "Local Seed Libraries Play Growing Role in Future of Crops." *The Orange County Register*, May 17, 2017. https://www.ocregister.com/2017/05/07/local-seed-libraries-play-growing-role-in-future-of-crops/.

United States Department of Agriculture. 1988. "Federal Seed Act." https://www.ams.usda.gov/sites/default/files/media/Federal%20Seed%20Act.pdf.

United States Department of Agriculture. 2013. "Plant Variety Protection Act." https ://www.ams.usda.gov/sites/default/files/media/Plant%20Variety%20Protection% 20Act.pdf.

Wang, Joy Y. 2010. "A Seed Library for Heirloom Plants Thrives in the Hudson Valley." *The New York Times,* October 6, 2020. https://www.nytimes.com/2010/1 0/07/garden/07seed.html.

Westra, Alan. 2016. "Selling Agricultural Seed in New York: The State Seed Law." Accessed August 1, 2020. https://cpb-us-e1.wpmucdn.com/blogs.cornell.edu/dist /e/1628/files/2016/02/Ag-Seed-Sales-177g9c9.pdf.

Section IV

BUDGET AND FINANCE

Chapter 11

Factors Affecting the Sustainability of Short-Term Collaborative Networks

A Case Study of Communities Putting Prevention to Work Nutrition Initiatives in Douglas County, Nebraska

Can Chen, A. Bryce Hoflund, and Carol Ebdon

INTRODUCTION

The United States is facing the harmful physical and social effects of chronic diseases such as diabetes, cancer, heart disease, and stroke. According to the U.S. Centers for Disease Control and Prevention (CDC), approximately 40 percent of adults are obese (Hales et al. 2020). High medical and productivity costs are associated with obesity. Finkelstein et al. (2009) estimated obesity-related medical care costs of $144 billion in 2008 dollars. Trodgon et al. (2008) estimate an economic impact of obesity-related absenteeism of $3.38 billion to $6.36 billion. In addition to adults, the CDC estimates that approximately 18.5 percent of children and adolescents aged two–nineteen-year-old are obese. Furthermore, Narayan et al. (2003) estimate that one-third of all children born since 2000 will suffer from diabetes, and many others will face chronic obesity-related problems such as heart disease, high blood pressure, cancer, and asthma.

Rising health care costs have made good health an issue of economics, as well as quality of life. Public health is related to community design, routine physical activity, and healthy eating. While we face challenges in creating environments that support healthy lifestyle choices, encouraging individuals and organizations to take responsibility for improving health may produce dramatic results. In 2010, the U.S. Department of Health and Human Services (DHHS) funded the Communities Putting Prevention to Work (CPPW) project through the CDC to support fifty communities working to reduce obesity and tobacco use.

Grants from one level of government to another have long been used as a tool of fiscal federalism. These grants serve a variety of purposes, including inducing lower-level governments to provide specific services, increasing equity, encouraging innovation, and offering flexibility to local officials who best understand community needs (Mikesell 2018). There is a substantial body of literature related to the "flypaper effect" concept that federal and state grants tend to increase local spending in the short-run (e.g., Bae and Feiock 2004; Deller and Maher 2005; Gamkhar and Shah 2007; Mehiriz and Marceau 2014). However, there is very little research related to the longer-term effects of grants. Douglas and Hartley (2011) is one of the very few studies to address these sustainability issues. They studied drug courts in four states and found that short-term seed grants led to uncertainty about continuation funding, which led to fragmentation in funding and increased the difficulty of sustainability. They concluded that "it is not rational for granting officials to promote their policies by offering seed grants unless there is a strong likelihood that these services can be sustained locally once the seed money is depleted. This holds true when offering grants to nonprofits organizations as well as lower-level governments. Simply providing money over the short-term and hoping programs will stick is unrealistic" (Douglas and Hartley 2011, 91). They term this the "fly ball" effect. Our study applies this theoretical framework, and network governance, to analyze the long-term sustainability of the CPPW grant activities in Douglas County, NE. We have three research questions:

- To what extent were program activities funded by the short-term federal grant sustained following the grant period?
- What factors affected the continuation of the program activities?
- What role did the grant and/or other incentives play in program sustainability?

Answering these questions helps us to better understand the benefits and challenges to sustaining long-term partnerships in a short-term collaborative network. This chapter makes several key theoretical and practical contributions. First, as noted above, there is a dearth of literature related to longer-term effects of short-term grant funding. Second, this research is valuable for theory-building for collaborative governance and fiscal federalism. Finally, our findings provide practical lessons for grant funders and program leaders in efforts to develop sustainable and collaborative activities to increase healthy eating habits.

The next section provides the research background of the Douglas County CPPW activities and a review of literature on CPPW activities, followed by an overview of the theoretical lenses. The third section describes the methodology, followed by the study results. The last section concludes with policy implications and a future research agenda.

RESEARCH BACKGROUND AND LITERATURE REVIEW

Communities Putting Prevention to Work Nutrition Initiatives in Douglas County, Nebraska

The Douglas County Health Department (DCHD), through the Live Well Omaha partnership, received a $5.5 million CPPW grant from the CDC for a two-year period from 2010 to 2012. The goals were to decrease overweight/obesity prevalence, increase physical activity levels, improve nutrition, decrease smoking prevalence, decrease teen smoking initiation, and decrease exposure to secondhand smoke. The CPPW grants were awarded to forty-four communities across the country.

The Douglas County grant partnership was comprised of approximately fifty non-profit, educational, and government organizations. The partners worked together to create a physical and cultural environment to support and sustain healthy, active lifestyles. Ten activities were funded by the grant: (1) Farm to School; (2) Share the Road Campaign; (3) Bike Share Program; (4) Transportation Master Plan Update; (5) Safe Routes to School; (6) Movin' After School; (7) School Gardens; (8) Healthy Neighborhood Stores; (9) Partners for a Healthy City; and (10) the City at Risk Marketing Campaign. Accomplishments over the two-year grant period included, for example,

- Initiating Farm-to-School programs in three school districts
- Building seven new school gardens in Omaha Public Schools
- Facilitating policy for healthy food options and increased daily physical activity in nearly 350 businesses, faith-based organizations, physicians' offices, and community organizations
- Partnering with eight neighborhood store owners to enhance their business models by carrying healthy options
- Creating Safe Routes to School to over thirty area schools
- Bringing Movin' After School programs to two thousand children in forty locations
- Collaborating on a pedestrian and bicycle-friendly community through infrastructure, safety, and sharing programs

Our study focuses on the CPPW activities that relate to nutrition: increasing healthy eating and decreasing use of foods with high calories and poor nutrition. This includes four activities: Movin' After School, Farm to School, School Gardens, and Healthy Neighborhood Stores.

Review of CPPW Literature

Bunnell et al. (2012) review the program progress during the first year of a two-year CPPW initiative. The authors contend that CPPW communities successfully adapted to their local circumstances and achieved at least one objective for a third of their planned strategies. They conclude that the CPPW program has the potential to reach over 55 million people within the funded jurisdiction and an estimated additional one hundred million people who could benefit from the CPPW community efforts.

Fagen et al. (2014) explore the major barriers and facilitators of policy, systems, and environmentally (PSE) oriented school-based obesity programs based on a case study of the CPPW program in Cook County, Illinois. The authors point out major barriers (lack of buy-in, funding limitations, legal roadblocks, and uncertain policy change) and facilitators (existing collaborations, effective communication, champions, and formal leadership) for school districts to implement PSE oriented obesity prevention initiatives.

Hoflund, Chen, and Ebdon (2014) explore issues of network governance and leadership in implementing the CPPW Farm to School program in Douglas County, Nebraska. Based on interviews, the authors identify four challenges: lack of coordination of activities, lack of information sharing among participants, difficulties with how to measure success, and sustainability. The authors conclude that successful Farm to School programs require an active champion, successful partnerships, and creative use of resources.

Cheadle et al. (2016) evaluate the policy, systems, environment, and infrastructure (PSEI) changes brought about by the CPPW initiative in King County, Washington, and identify the elements of the initiative that contributed most to the implementation of successful strategies. The two most important elements include a backbone organization to provide strong leadership and technical assistance in the form of outside consultants or content experts and working directly with champions implementing change in key sectors (Cheadle et al. 2016, 58).

Kane et al. (2017) analyze the organizational capacity for successful implementation of CPPW public health programs. Based on a qualitative analysis of twenty-two programs, they conclude that each awardee was unique and implemented different program structures. However, key elements in organizational capacity are essential for success: experience, history of collaboration, leadership support, and turnover.

Two studies estimate health impacts using the Prevention Impacts Simulation Model (PRISM). Kuo et al. (2016) assess the CPPW obesity prevention strategies in Los Angeles County, California. They predict that CPPW shows modest but promising results that will reduce obesity in youth by 29,870 and adults by 94,136 cases by 2040. Soler et al. (2016) forecast that sustained CPPW investment may avert 14,000 premature deaths, $2.4 billion (2010 dollars) in discounted direct medical costs, and $9.5 billion (2010 dollars) in discounted lifetime and annual productivity losses through 2020. In sum, although there is a growing number of studies on CPPW activities, no scholars have focused on the long-term sustainability of the CPPW grant. To fill this gap, this research aims at analyzing the degree to which CPPW grant-funded nutrition activities were sustained after the grant ends and the key factors that influenced the continuation of the CPPW activities in Douglas County, NE. The next section provides the theoretical lens to examine the long-term sustainability of a short-term grant-funded collaborative network.

THEORETICAL LENSES

This research applies the Douglas and Hartley (2011)'s "fly ball" theory and network governance theory to understand the factors of sustaining long-term partnerships in a short-term collaborative network.

Short-Term Grants and "Fly Ball" Theory

Short-term grants refer to grant-in-aid programs provided by upper levels of governments to lower levels of governments for a specified period of time (no more than three to five years) (U.S. GAO 1979). These grants are often used as seed money (start-up grants) to encourage grant recipients to take on particular activities deemed important by the grantor government (U.S. GAO 1979). Although there is substantial literature related to fiscal federalism, especially the "flypaper effect" concept that grants tend to increase local spending in the short-run (Hines and Thaler 1995), there is little research related to longer-term effects. In 1979, the U.S. General Accountability Office (GAO) found that federal seed money programs have limited success in generating self-sustaining projects which use significant amounts of non-federal funds. Meanwhile, many projects were reduced or discontinued when federal funds ended (U.S. GAO 1979).

Weiner et al. (1979) analyze the effect of terminating federal funds on the program continuation of community mental health centers. They confirm that these centers remained fiscally viable subsequent to termination of federal grants. This is because a variety of nonfederal revenue sources such as state and local government funding, third-party payors, and fee collections provided large amounts of financial assistance.

Douglas and Hartley (2011) propose the "fly ball effect" as a theoretical framework for understanding how seed money impacts program maintenance. Their theory suggests that long-run local preferences will not be strongly influenced by seed money and short-term seed grants by themselves lead to considerable funding uncertainty and program eliminations or stagnation once the initial grant money expires (Douglas and Hartley 2011). Based on a comparative case study of drug courts in four states, the authors find that using short-term grants to start-up drug courts resulted in a considerable amount of uncertainty concerning continuation funding and this uncertainty made program sustainability difficult (Douglas and Hartley 2011).

Sustainability of Collaborative Networks

In recent years, there has been a growing interest in efforts to improve community health through the formation of partnerships and networks. To achieve this goal, partnerships and their activities must be sustained over a long period (Shortell et al. 2002; Lasker and Weiss 2003). In this sense, sustainability is a key requirement for the success of collaborative partnerships and networks.

Alexander et al. (2003) developed a conceptual model of sustainability in community health partnerships and identified the potential determinants of sustainability using comparative case studies of four partnerships in the Community Care Network (CCN) Demonstration Program. Based on their qualitative analysis, the authors contend that there are five primary factors leading to sustainability of collaborative capacity: outcomes-based advocacy (the ability to effectively identify and communicate partnership achievements and unique contributions to internal and external stakeholders), vision-focus balance (the ability to reach agreements on a broad and long-term vision of community health), systems orientation (the ability to conceptualize community health problems and envision solutions in coordinated and cross-sectoral efforts), infrastructure development (the ability to deploy internal systems to support and sustain collaborative activities), and community linkage (the ability to create strong and working relationships with institutions and individuals in the community) (Alexander et al. 2003).

Willard and Creech (2006) define network sustainability as "a network continues to function until it achieves it goals, or until its members are no longer willing or able to continue, or until it becomes irrelevant" (pp. 3–4) and contend that there are four dimension of network sustainability: time (the life-cycles of networks), resources (secure financial and material support from a variety of sources), relationships (diverse and changing network memberships), and relevance (work of value to members and external stakeholders). They point out four general success factors (strategic management, internal management, external management, and financial management) and key success factors (recognizing the need for change and managing change) that are essential to achieve long-term network sustainability.

Lewis et al. (2008) explore network relationships and sustainability over the longer term based on an analysis of two government-funded primary care partnerships in Victoria, Australia. They assert that network partnerships require long-term, independent, and dedicated funding support and not just start-up funding. Scott et al. (2018) examine the sustainability of collaborative networks in higher education research projects through a complexity theoretic lens. They argue that complexity thinking is useful in examining the attributes of sustainable networks and point out that adaptability and flexibility are considered crucial for the sustainability of collaborative networks. In sum, our theoretical foundations draw together two different streams of theories that discuss short-term grants and network sustainability. Building upon these two theories, this research aims at addressing the questions related to the benefits and challenges to sustaining long-term partnerships in a short-term collaborative network supported by the CPPW grants.

METHODOLOGY

We used a qualitative research design to study the sustainability of the four nutrition initiatives funded by the CPPW grant in Douglas County, NE: Movin' After School, Farm to School, School Gardens, and Healthy Neighborhood Stores. To better understand the extent to which the activities have been sustained beyond the grant period, the factors affecting the continuation of the activities, and the role of the grant and/or other incentives in sustainability, we conducted interviews with program managers and administrators for the nutrition programs associated with the grant. We identified and contacted ten individuals that were involved in the administration and program management of the grant's nutrition activities. Six individuals agreed to interviews, two declined an interview citing that work on the program had not moved forward after the grant period, and two did not respond to our interview request. Interviews were conducted via Zoom and lasted approximately thirty minutes. To obtain candid responses, the interviewees were guaranteed anonymity.

We asked the interviewees questions about the key stakeholders, the short- and long-term effects of the programs, whether/how the grant was successful, which programs continued after the funding ended and changes over time, challenges facing the program, and whether the program is expected to continue over time. We chose to take notes rather than to record the interviews. Bucher, Fritz, and Quarantetli (1956) note that when interviews are not recorded, respondents are more willing to talk freely. Additionally, Lincoln and Guba (1985) argue that interviews are not as threatening when they are not recorded. After the interviews were completed, the interview notes were compiled and analyzed to distill common themes.

FINDINGS

Our interviews revealed three themes related to the sustainability of the CPPW grant-funded nutrition activities. These revolved around the importance of the grant, the extent to which these programs have continued since the grant ended, and the factors that relate to success and sustainability. Each of these themes is discussed in this section.

Importance of the CPPW Grant

Interviewees noted that receiving a grant of this magnitude was unusual for this community: "$5.2 million in 20 months is unbelievable. It kickstarted so many things." That generated excitement within the county and made a "splash" that would not have occurred with a more typical small, focused grant. Organizations that had not been willing to take action on nutrition were now interested. For example, one interviewee noted that

> the city planning department tolerated us but we couldn't get them to move on community gardens and water, couldn't get the Chamber of Commerce to move on healthy grocery stores, couldn't get anyone to pay attention to us. Suddenly we became the behemoth in the room. This time we could come into the room and say, now we have money, let's do something quickly. We might have gotten there without the grant, but it would have taken us 10 years of really slow growth.[1]

In the past, health-related grants were administered and operated by DCHD. CPPW allowed for greater involvement from other partner organizations who took the lead on activities. According to one interviewee: "Unlike many other communities, we spread 80 percent of the grant across the community, [and] let others do the work." This partnership approach was viewed as being important in making progress on reducing obesity, and, as one interviewee stated, "The grant allowed us to demonstrate how public health could be a coordinator and partner instead of always the doer."

This communitywide approach also helped in obtaining subsequent grant funding, for nutrition/obesity and other major issues. A follow-up, two-year $500,000 CDC Community Transformation Grant (CTG), and some funding from the state, allowed for some of the CPPW work to continue. Perhaps most importantly, though, as several interviewees noted, the CPPW work made an impact on the Omaha philanthropic community: "One of the things that happened was a demonstration that community effort could make a difference and giving large grants to communities. When we started this project, we brought community members together and let them decide the pathway we would follow." Furthermore, another interviewee stated that "All those planning processes showed that if you let the community make the decisions, things could happen. It was enough money to let us change the way we think about things." Since CPPW, that same process has since been used by local philanthropists for focusing on issues such as youth and poverty.

Continuation of Nutrition Activities

The nutrition activities related to the CPPW grant have had limited sustainability overall, with more success in some areas than others. Other than the initial build of seven gardens, the School Gardens program did not really get off the ground during the grant period, and no evidence was found of progress since then. This was seen as being largely due to timing: school is not in session in growing season. As one interviewee noted, "One thing that was fragile and never was in place was school gardens. I don't think they work in Nebraska in our climate. Where will produce go in summer? Who will manage it in summer?" However, a number of organizations have developed community gardens that were seen as being an outgrowth of the CPPW work, and this activity was viewed as being helpful to build the Farm to School concept.

The Farm to School program continues in at least a few local school districts, although it has been due to individual food services directors, rather than a coordinated activity. One interviewee, for example, uses local producers for cheese and chicken; she was in the process of working on purchasing local beef, but had to put it on hold when schools closed due to the pandemic. Farm to School is viewed as supporting local producers, using local products which have more nutritional value because they travel a shorter distance, and showing people how food is grown; "get kids to know that chocolate milk doesn't come from a cow." A toolkit for school districts was developed with the CPPW grant, which "helped people who really didn't know how to start to get going." The toolkit was seen as a "wonderful result from the partnership." School staff were also introduced to producers through the grant: "food service directors took trips to producers in the Lincoln/Omaha area, so you got to know what the producers were doing. You got to see on a smaller scale how they made it work."

Coordinated Farm to School efforts appear to have been dormant after the CPPW grant ended. Interviewees do not believe the toolkit has been updated, and meetings were rare. However, the state department of education now has an employee working on this topic, with renewed efforts in this area.

The Healthy Neighborhood Stores activity has had limited continued success. This was a partnership of DCHD, Nebraska Extension, and a local marketing firm. They worked with participating stores on food "price, promotion, placement and procurement." Customers were also incentivized to eat healthier: "We had staff on call to do food demonstrations, using healthy food with low cost using food available at the stores, and gave people free samples and recipes. Also, how to shop on a budget." The stores considered this beneficial, according to one interviewee: "A lot of store owners felt it was business development. It allowed them to do something that they wanted to do, but hadn't been able to do in a while. The grant was a quick influx of money and we could craft and build resources in a way that allowed stores to quickly pick them up." The grant was also used to prepare information that could be used on an ongoing basis: "We worked on building capacity with toolkits, with guides, so when the funding went away, at least we have resources to share with the community and store owners."

Only one store that participated under the CPPW grant is still considered to be a Healthy Neighborhood Store, although the Extension Service still has a connection with one other store. Grant funding continued to some extent until about eighteen months ago: "Healthy Neighborhood Stores has been pervasive in multiple follow-up grants . . . We had the benefit of 10–12 years of support." Several interviewees noted that it has been difficult to sustain this in existing stores because of changes in owners and name changes. In addition, loss of funding has reduced the ability of the Extension Service to focus on this area: "for a while I was able to hire 1–2 people to do those food demos, that was a good community connection," but it is no longer possible. Extension provides technical assistance as needed, though: "We are still giving stores opportunities to come in under this umbrella, for price promotion and placement of healthy options." In addition, they are currently implementing a "Double Up Food Bucks" program in the state where SNAP recipients can spend up to $20 and have it matched. The view of the interviewees was that "we made major differences in how small stores saw their role in having healthy food. Things didn't stay exactly as we thought they would but there are still good things happening. You can't go out and name them now as healthy neighborhood stores, they've morphed into something else."

Movin' After School also has had some continued success. This activity focused on physical exercise and healthier snacks for children. According to several interviewees, many afterschool programs no longer did as much physical activity, but still "have policies around what kinds of snacks they would have—Girls, Inc never put vending machines back in, and Completely Kids had moved towards a listing of healthy snacks." A toolkit was also created, and training conducted, for these programs within schools, which was seen as being a positive result. Overall, "We changed the image of afterschool programs on how to make these 2–3 hours really productive."

In addition to these specific activities, work in this community on improving nutrition has continued since the end of the CPPW grant in various ways. One interviewee stated:

> You see it all over the place, it's so surprising to me . . . It's a slow growth, incremental, but it's embraced all we were hoping for. Right after CPPW, in communities where public health owned everything and put all those employees in their own department, the activities just dissipated. In our city, the next grant was much smaller, but we were still sending the money to the organizations. They could keep things moving.

Local philanthropic organizations have also been influential: "So much of this work came out of public health, but now very similar work is being done around the auspices of basic needs coming out of the social services." For example, the United Way of the Midlands has become involved in food insecurity and nutrition, and their efforts led to the creation of Share Our Table, a collaborative effort focused on addressing food insecurity in the Omaha-Council Bluffs metro area. Other partnerships and organizations have also been created to focus on these areas.

Success and Sustainability Factors

The interviewees mentioned four common factors that affected the success and sustainability of the grant activities. The first is resources. For example, one school food service director noted that staffing challenges have reduced her ability to use Farm to School products: "Omaha had a 2.5 percent unemployment rate, we had a hard time hiring, so we're just trying to get the plate out. To be able to process fresh produce, cantaloupe chunks or peel sweet potatoes or snap beans, we just don't have the capacity." In addition, grant funding was critical to be able to pay staff to work on the programs and for other needs such as equipment. This was a significant issue for Healthy Neighborhood Stores: "You need someone managing it. You can train the stores but without the follow-up, you need someone, that's their job to help them and support that." Furthermore, one interviewee stated that "Right before the last grant ended other stores came online, but we didn't have enough capacity to help them."

Second, the importance of relationships was stressed. Healthy Neighborhood Stores depended on relationships between the Health Department, the Extension Service, the marketing firm that assisted with promotion, and storeowners. One interviewee stated that "One hundred percent of the success was due to the relationship between the store owner and DCHD," and this connection was broken when stores were sold. For Farm to School, one school food services director noted the need for "a good communication link" between this position and the food producers.

The third factor is leadership. The CPPW grant involved many partners, but DCHD was seen as the leader. Once the grant ended, DCHD was not able to keep staff to continue these efforts. For example, "Right now, there's not a person that's carrying the water for Healthy Neighborhood Stores at the Health Department." It then falls to other organizations to continue nutrition activities, which is difficult. One individual noted that "I have to piecemeal people to do this work. If it was housed somewhere else, we would get past this challenge of trying to braid twenty million things together." Two individuals were mentioned as being important leaders for these activities before they retired/changed jobs: "They were the champions and their focus changed." Some interest was noted for the idea of a regional health commission among several counties, which could potentially take on this leadership role.

Fourth, interviewees noted the difficulty of measuring the success of these activities. How do we know if nutrition is improving in a community? For kids who consume less sugar after school or become excited by eating fresh vegetables in school, or whose parents cook healthier meals through incentives and education at their neighborhood store, it may be decades before we see an impact on their health. Sustaining activities over a long period of time is challenging without evidence that they are making a difference. The Nutrition Environment Measures Survey (NEMS) addresses the nutrition environment in stores; these scores "show that we are increasing a teeny tiny bit. We aren't doing worse, and are trending in the right way." However, "the data around obesity is getting worse." Interviewees felt that the CPPW grant was helpful in being able to "go into health impact assessment. What's the impact of the work you do for housing, location of medical facilities, etc.? We started on that because we had the attention of others—that's really critical. You have to think about how health affects the long-term." However, measuring that long-term impact is not easy.

DISCUSSION

Our research sought to understand the degree to which grant-funded activities were sustained after the grant ends, the factors that affected the continuation of the activities, and the role the grant played in program sustainability. The "fly ball" theory uses a baseball analogy to suggest that some grants will result in home runs, and others in base hits, while some will be fly balls (or "outs"). The results have been mixed with the CPPW grant in Douglas County. None of the nutrition activities achieved a home run and none have continued in a way that they would be considered to be a sustained or growing program, since the grant ended in 2012.

However, several activities could be considered "base hits." There are still one or two Healthy Neighborhood Stores, and Nebraska Extension is working on expanding a consumer incentive program across the state. The Farm to School program is operating to some extent in at least a few school districts, and the Department of Education has recently appointed someone in a coordinating role. The Movin' After School program has also had some continued success with nutrition, although this does not appear to be a coordinated effort. The grant appeared to help these programs "get on base" to start working their way toward a score. We did find one "fly ball" result in the School Gardens program. This program barely begun during the grant period, and we saw no evidence of it since then (although community gardens have become popular). There are a variety of reasons for this, especially the misfit between the growing season and the school year.

The "fly ball" theory, then, seems to apply well to this grant. While none of the activities have been sustained in the same way, components have continued, and some resources still exist, such as toolkits. Interviewees also noted a strong focus on nutrition efforts more broadly in the Omaha community in recent years. They feel that the CPPW grant provided space and lessons for these other initiatives to take root.

The partnership approach used by Douglas County for the CPPW grant was viewed as being beneficial for those activities and succeeding projects. The community became integrated into the planning process which increased the buy-in to focus on addressing obesity. Relationships between the partners, and with other participants such as neighborhood storeowners, were seen as critical for success. Resources and leadership also appear to be necessary to sustain programs once grant funding ends. Networks have an advantage in organizing different actors working together to achieve a goal. However, sustainability is a key element for a successful collaboration in the theory of network governance. Our findings are consistent with the network governance literature. Theoretical factors affecting network sustainability such as independent, long-term resources, stable and diverse relationships with individuals, institutions, and communities, and strong network leaderships are critical success factors identified in our case study of CPPW nutrition activities (Alexander et al. 2003; Willard and Creech 2006; Lewis et al. 2008).

One significant challenge for grant funding is in understanding its effects. It is difficult to determine the impacts of nutrition programs, especially when they will not be evident in the short-run. Grants may also have consequences beyond the funded activities. Our interviewees noted the importance of this large grant to subsequent communitywide efforts, some directly related to nutrition and others dealing with other serious issues. How can/should these indirect effects be considered in evaluating grant success? Our study suggests that, as grants may be better implemented in stages, evaluation of grant programs may also be best conducted in stages. In the first stage, funders and evaluators could focus on feasibility of pilot programs. In the next stage, continuation of the pilot programs would be evaluated. Finally, the third stage would concentrate on long-term impacts of the grant programs.

CONCLUSION

Federal and state grant programs often focus on broad efforts and encourage extensive community partnerships to address major social issues. These grants are often short-term in nature, with large start-up costs, and the benefits may not be evident for years or even decades. What happens when short-term grant funds for collaborative efforts run out? Do the activities continue in the same or different forms? This study addresses these important questions through a case study of a short-term grant-funded collaborative effort in Douglas County, Nebraska to promote wellness and healthy eating. Building upon the "fly ball" and network governance theories, the study finds that (1) the CPPW short-term seed grant played an important role in engaging different partners in supporting healthy lifestyles in local communities; (2) none of the nutrition activities achieved a home run, several of the activities could be considered "base hits", and one was a "fly ball" result; and (3) four key factors contributed to the long-term sustainability of the collaborative network: resources, relationship, leadership, and the measurement of long-term benefits of short grant-funded activities.

This research has important theoretical and policy implications. First, although there is substantial literature related to fiscal federalism, especially the "flypaper effect" concept that grants tend to increase local spending in the short-run, there is very little research related to the longer-term effects of short-term grant funding. Douglas and Hartley's (2011) "fly ball" theory focused on drug courts. Our study contributes to the "fly ball" theory by examining the short-term grant in a different policy context. Second, this research also contributes to the network governance literature by expanding the discussion about network sustainability in a local community health partnership. Third, our findings suggest that grant funders should take sustainability into account and could provide grants in stages. Grant recipients are suggested to advance network sustainability by securing long-term funding support, developing strong working relationships and network leaderships, as well as showcasing the potential long-term benefits of partnerships.

The study also has limitations. Our research only concentrates on the nutrition-related CPPW activities. Future studies are encouraged to explore to what extent the physical activities funded by CPPW were sustained following the grant period. In addition, another avenue for future research would examine the long-term sustainability of CPPW grants in other communities. Comparative case studies can improve the generalizability of our research findings.

NOTE

1. This research has used pseudonyms to anonymizes all interviewees.

REFERENCES

Alexander, J. A., Weiner, B.J., Metzger, M. E., Shortell, S.M. et al. 2003. "Sustainability of collaborative capacity in community health partnerships." *Medical Care Research and Review*, *60*(4_suppl): 130S–160S.

Bucher, R., Fritz, C.E., and Quarantelli, E. L. "Tape recorded research: Some field and data processing problems." *Public Opinion Quarterly*, *20*(2): 426–439.

Bunnell, R., O'Neil, D., Soler, R., Payne, R., Giles, W. H. et al. 2012. "Fifty communities putting prevention to work: accelerating chronic disease prevention through policy, systems and environmental change." *Journal of Community Health*, *37*(5): 1081–1090.

Cheadle, A., Cromp, D., Krieger, J. W., Chan, N., McNees, M. et al. 2016. "Promoting policy, systems, and environment change to prevent chronic disease: lessons learned from the king county communities putting prevention to work initiative." *Journal of Public Health Management and Practice*, *22*(4): 348–359.

Douglas, J. W. and Hartley, R. E. 2011. "The fly ball effect: A theoretical framework for understanding the impacts of short-term seed grants." *Public Budgeting & Finance*, *31*(4): 74–92.

Fagen, M. C., Asada, Y., Welch, S., Dombrowski, R., Gilmet, K., Welter, C., and Mason, M. 2014. "Policy, systems, and environmentally oriented school-based obesity prevention: Opportunities and challenges." *Journal of Prevention & Intervention in the Community*, *42*(2): 95–111.

Hines, J. R. and Thaler, R. H. 1995. "The Flypaper Effect." *Journal of Economic Perspectives*, *9*(4): 217–226.

Hoflund, A. Bryce, Can Chen and Carol A. Ebdon. 2014. "Network management and leadership: Lessons learned from the Douglas County Communities putting prevention to work farm to school program." *Food Studies: An Interdisciplinary Journal, 3*(3): 45–56.

Kane, H., Hinnant, L., Day, K., Council, M., Tzeng, J. et al. 2017. "Pathways to program success: a qualitative comparative analysis (QCA) of communities putting prevention to work case study programs." *Journal of Public Health Management and Practice, 23*(2): 104–111.

Kuo, T., Robles, B., Trogdon, J. G., Ferencik, R., Simon, P. A., and Fielding, J. E. 2016. "Framing the local context and estimating the health impact of CPPW obesity prevention strategies in Los Angeles County, 2010–2012." *Journal of Public Health Management and Practice, 22*(4): 360–369.

Lasker, R. D. and Weiss, E. S. 2003. "Creating partnership synergy: The critical role of community stakeholders." *Journal of Health and Human Services Administration, 26*(1): 119–139.

Lewis, J. M., Baeza, J. I. and Alexander, D. 2008. "Partnerships in primary care in Australia: Network structure, dynamics and sustainability." *Social Science & Medicine, 67*(2): 280–291.

Lincoln, Y. S. and Guba, E. G. 1985. *Naturalist Inquiry.* Newbury Park, CA: Sage Publications.

Scott, A., Woolcott, G., Keast, R. and Chamberlain, D. 2018. "Sustainability of collaborative networks in higher education research projects: Why complexity? Why now?" *Public Management Review, 20*(7): 1068–1087.

Shortell, S. M. , A. P. Zukoski , J. A. Alexander , G. J. et al. 2002. "Evaluating partnerships for community health improvement: Tracking the footprints." *Journal of Health Politics, Policy and Law, 27*(1): 49–91.

Soler, R., Orenstein, D., Honeycutt, A. and Bradley, C. 2016. "Community-based interventions to decrease obesity and tobacco exposure and reduce health care costs: Outcome estimates from Communities Putting Prevention to Work for 2010–2020." *Preventing Chronic Disease, 13*(4): 101–108.

US General Accounting Office (GAO). 1979. "Federal seed money: More careful selection and application needed." Washington, DC.

Weiner, R. S., Woy, J. R., Sharfstein, S. S. and Bass, R. D. 1979. "Community mental health centers and the "seed money" concept: Effects of terminating federal funds." *Community Mental Health Journal, 15*(2): 129–138.

Willard, T. and Creech, H. 2006. "Sustainability of International Development Networks. *Review of IDRC Experience (1995–2005)."* Manitoba: International Institute for Sustainable Development.

Chapter 12

Framework for a Cost-Benefit Analysis of a Large-Scale Food Processing Plant in a Small Rural Community

The Case of Costco's Poultry Plant in Fremont, Nebraska

Sungho Park and Craig S. Maher

INTRODUCTION

Locating a large, industrial-scale food processing plant in a small community is often controversial. Proponents advocate for it mainly on the grounds of economic development, including expanded job opportunities, income growth, stability for farmers, and positive externalities within and across sectors. Opponents, however, maintain that these processing plants are different from other industrial facilities and often raise concerns about community food and agricultural security, environmental degradation (more specifically, waste runoff affecting water supplies), increasing welfare and K–12 costs, and safety. Hence, the return on government fiscal and administrative investment in a food processing plant as a means of economic development is unclear. To capture the breadth of these challenging policy conflicts, a robust cost-benefit analysis (CBA) that accounts for short-term and longer-term effects of an industrial food processing plant on a smaller community is valuable.

Whether public officials in practice conduct a thorough analysis of associated costs and benefits when making substantial fiscal and policy decisions is unclear. This may be attributable to a lack of literature. While several studies have examined its costs and benefits from a business standpoint (e.g., Parin and Zugarramurdi 1994), few studies offer a comprehensive CBA framework specifically applicable to an industrial-scale food processing plant and guide its application from a public or community perspective. This study aims to fill this research gap by developing a conceptual framework that identifies important costs and benefits associated with the establishment of an industrial-scale food processing plant in a community. To this end, we review and synthesize the existing literature of policy analysis and food policy.

The significance of this study is exacerbated by the fact that most of these plants include fiscal incentives—direct payments from state governments via grants and local incentives in the form of tax incremental financing. As public funds are finite, these resources should be expended in the most judicious manner. Unfortunately, many of the cost-benefit analyses conducted for these developments leave much to be desired. To solicit further implications for practice, we offer a framework utilizing the case of a new poultry plant in Fremont, Nebraska. The plant was officially proposed by Costco on May 2016. It was supported by the city, county, and state through a series of legislative approvals, including $18.3 million in tax incremental financing and various subsidy packages. The rationale behind the plant is found in the city's CBA results: "the benefits outweigh the costs of the proposed project" (City of Fremont, NE 2016, 19). This study offers a chance to revisit this conclusion based on a more comprehensive framework.

The next section is dedicated to developing a comprehensive CBA framework and guidelines based on a thorough review of the literature. It is followed by an introduction of the Costco poultry plant case, and a comparison between the city's CBA results of the plant and our conceptual framework. Such comparison leads to implications for practice, which are discussed in the conclusion.

CONCEPTUAL FRAMEWORK FOR A CBA OF A LOCAL FOOD PROCESSING PLANT

Consequences of Local Food Processing Plants

Large-scale food processing plants have garnered attention from local—especially rural—officials as an attractive option for economic development (Artz, Orazem, and Otto 2007). With the exception of a handful of studies, however, the literature lacks guidelines for CBA of food processing plants from a public or community standpoint. Abeles-Allison and Connor (1990) offered a simplified version of CBA for a local hog operation plant; the cost structure is measured as reduced property values around the plant and benefit factors only include local input purchases and hog producers' income increases. Schaffer, Koonnathamdee and Ray (n.d.) only focus on developing a descriptive economic formula of social costs per individual hog producer rather than offering specific CBA guidelines.

Fortunately, the current body of food policy literature on the social and economic consequences of industrial food processing plants is well developed, including studies on concentrated animal feeding operations (CAFOs). A systematic review of the literature can help in the development of a robust CBA framework. The most often mentioned positive consequence of food processing plants is local job growth (Broadway 2000). Food plants usually offer lower-paying jobs ($13 per hour on average; U.S. Bureau of Labor Statistics 2020a), and they tend to be filled by those who are new to the local labor force (Thornsbury, Kambhampaty, and Kenyon 1993). Workers' wages are often used to capture this employment effect of food processing plants (Schaffer et al. n.d.). Income growth or stability can also be the case for contract farmers as animal growers (Andrews and Kautza n.d.). MacDonald (2014), for example, documented that as of 2011, an individual contract broiler farmer earned 5.6 cents on average per live-weight pound delivered.

Studies also suggest that food processing plants could generate a negative impact on local income. The major reason is that the sustainability of jobs and income generated from a food processing plant are not always better than other local employment options. For example, Broadway and Stull (2006), in their study of two beef processing plants in Kansas, reported that the two plants had a yearly turnover rate exceeding 70–100 percent. This indicates that workers' job and income security could be lower than their expectations. In other words, they may experience a certain level of opportunity cost of working at a food processing plant, and such a cost could outweigh their income in the long run. A similar idea can be applied to contract farmers; Andrews and Kautza (n.d.) warn that contract farmers "can be cut out of the market when demand falls" (11). The issue could be more serious as farmers make significant capital investment to begin the production process.

Another potential consequence is associated with government finance. Locating an industrial plant, which usually involves large capital investment, can lead to increases in the plant site's property valuation, thereby contributing to government property tax income (Schaffer et al. n.d.). Its net benefit, however, often depends on what public financing mechanisms are employed. Tax incremental financing (TIF), for example, works in a manner in which the property tax base of TIF districts is frozen during a set period so a municipality can support a redevelopment project through debt financing based on the project's anticipated contribution to the future increment of property taxes (Maher, Park and Park 2019). Hence, it may have net negative impacts on government finance if actual property tax shifts due to TIF do not outweigh the sum of government debt, borrowing costs, and associated opportunity costs that span across TIF districts (Flora 1998).

Further, other government fiscal support including various subsidy packages offered to invite a plant could have immediate negative impacts on
government finances (Broadway and Stull 2006). Increased government fees
and charges could mitigate those impacts especially in the long term (Skees,
Black and Gramig 2003). Based on a survey of 25 food processing plants in
the United States, Boyd Company, Inc. (2018) finds that the annual electric
and natural gas power costs per food processing plant are $0.75 and $0.54
million, respectively. The use of water resources largely varies by animal
type according to Food Northwest (2020); the typical water consumption per
beef is 300 gallons whereas only 6.8 gallons are used, on average, per broiler
processing.

Locating a food processing plant may result in local population growth
because of its workforce demand (Huffman and Miranowski 1996). An
influx of population, including new immigrants, could generate positive
consequences given that it often leads to an expanded economic base for the
community. Along this line, some studies have argued that a food processing
plant may have a positive price impact on the real estate market primarily
due to new-comers' housing demand and subsequent construction demand
(Park, Lee and Seidl 1999). Taff, Tiffany and Weisberg (1996), for example,
focused on two Minnesota counties, and found that the property values of
houses within three miles of a feedlot were 6.6 percent higher than those
further from the feedlot.

More studies have been interested in the negative aspects of population
growth caused by food processing plants. Increased demand for public
services, including safety, education, transportation, and health and social
services, is an identified concern (Andrews and Kautza n.d.; Constance and
Tuinstra 2005). Quantifying public service costs is not an easy endeavor.
Research on government finance, however, may help given the interest
in estimating the unit cost of public service expenditures. The council of
state governments (2012), for example, reported that fifty states' average
public spending in 2010 was $5,150 per capita, including education and
public welfare costs of $1,849 and $1,494, respectively. Park (2018) finds
that the national average of municipal per capita public spending is $611,
including public works and police spending of $151 and $119, respectively.
Rector (2007) also found that total government expenditures would annually
increase by $30,160 per low-skill immigrant, including $14,270 for state and
local services and $15,890 for federal services. This may not capture the pre-
cise cost structure of public services, but could be a benchmark for estimating
the cost impact of a food processing plant on public services.

Processing plants' effects on the environment have also been studied by
researchers. There is a wide range of environmental externalities involved in
food processing plants (Halden and Schwab n.d.). More specifically, it has

been consistently reported that food processing plants generate serious odors and water pollution problems. Assuming that public and private efforts to mitigate environmental issues could be internalized into the quality of life in a community, prior studies often look at diminished property values around a processing plant to capture these environmental consequences. In a study of nine counties in North Carolina, Palmquist, Roka, and Vukina (1997) found that locating a swine-finishing plant led to a 4.8 percent average decrease in the value of residential properties within a one-half mile radius. Further, Herriges, Secchi and Babcock (2003), in their study of hog-processing operations, found a 10 percent price decrease in rural residential property values within three miles of a facility.

Industrial impacts of a food processing plant are also important. As positive consequences, a local food plant can contribute to the expansion of local or regional industrial activity, which is often described as multiplier (also known as ripple or second-round) effects (Broadway and Stull 2006). Though the precise multipliers for different food industries are hard to estimate, Park et al. (1999) suggested that swine and poultry facilities generally produce the multiplier ranging from 1 to 2 (i.e., $1 to $2 million extra income for each million dollars of production). Another group of studies, however, offer evidence that larger facilities generate significantly lower multiplier effects compared to smaller farms, so oftentimes their multipliers are close to zero (Gómez and Zhang 2000; Flora 1998).

Food processing plants may also produce negative consequences in terms of food security, at least in the short run. One of the major reasons for this concern is local farmers who would switch to contract animal growers (Janssen 2017); losing local farmers can lead to an immediate reduction in food supplies. To make up for the loss, consumers and retail sellers may need to rely on other local farmers enhancing their productivity or out-of-state food supplies. From an economic standpoint, this implies that there can be a partial loss of multiplier effects to local farming.

CBA of a Local Food Processing Plant: Framework

To construct the framework, we reorganize the consequences of a food processing plant discussed above based on the general CBA guidelines suggested by the policy analysis literature (Dunn 2018; Weimer and Vining 2017). Specifically, the positive and negative consequences of food processing plants are expected to represent benefits and costs (including opportunity costs as intangible elements). Each factor is classified into either the direct or indirect dimension, depending on the extent to which it is directly tied to a processing plant. The direct dimension includes two subcategories—job and income, and government finance. The indirect dimension consists of three subcategories—population growth, industrial consequences, and environmental consequences. Further, each factor should reflect both internal (i.e., within a local or community boundary) and external (i.e., third-party impacts and/or spillovers) elements.

We propose a framework for CBA of a local food processing plant in table 12.1. Note that we put the industrial consequences category—that is, multiplier effects—in parentheses. This is meant to highlight that policy analysts should consider this category with caution because including such multiplier effects can overestimate overall benefits and costs (Campbell and Brown 2003). For example, when one local company's annual production is worth $1 million with a multiplier of 2, the company's second-round industrial impacts, such as increased retail sales, can be $2 million. Adding this $2 million to the benefit side may be inappropriate as the (opportunity) costs of that

Table 12.1 Conceptual Framework for CBA of a Local Food Processing Plant

Category		Benefit	Cost
Direct	Job and income	• Job and income growth for workers • Contract farmers' income growth/stability	• Workers' opportunity costs • Contract farmers' opportunity costs, including capital investment
	Government finance	• Increased property tax income due to capital investment • Increased government fees and charges	• Costs of financing mechanisms, including opportunity costs • Other government fiscal support including subsidy packages
Indirect	Population growth	• Increased property values around the plant due to housing and construction demand	• Increased public service demand— safety, education, transportation, health and social services, among others.
	(Industrial consequences) Environmental consequences	(• Multiplier effects of the plant)	(• Disrupted food security) • Diminished property values around the plant

Note: There are some non-measurable (intangible) benefits and costs excluded from this framework such as cultural diversity and social conflict. It does not mean that they can be excluded from the CBA process. Rather, they should be considered in a qualitative manner.
Source: Created by the authors based on a review of the relevant literature.

$2 million, retail waste for example, cannot be easily captured. Hence, studies recommend that policy analysts should exclude those multiplier effects from their CBA. Instead, such ripple effects can be considered separately through an economic impact analysis (Taks et al. 2011).

CASE: COSTCO'S POULTRY PLANT
IN FREMONT, NEBRASKA

Fremont is a city in Dodge County, which is located in southeast Nebraska. As of 2018, the city has a population of 25,614 and a total of 10,963 housing units; the demographic feature of the city has been constant for the last decade (e.g., population increased by 0.8 percent; U.S. Census Bureau, 2018). Fremont's unemployment rate in June 2020 was 5.8 percent, which is higher than the same month in 2019 (3.3%) and 2018 (3.2%) (Nebraska Department of Labor 2020). The 2020 bump in unemployment is directly attributable to the COVID-19 pandemic that has affected all communities throughout the United States.

The demand for growth has been the underlying motivation behind several economic development projects and programs in Fremont and Dodge County. The Project No. 1 invited a Costco chicken plant including a hatchery (75,000 sq. ft.), a processing facility (250,000 sq. ft.), and feed mills to the Fremont area. The project was officially announced by Mayor Scott Getzschman in late March 2016, with the expectation that the "project through its job creation, capital investment and opportunity for rural agricultural producers would positively impact our region's (Fremont's) economic base and quality of life" (Liesveld March 29, 2016). The project was expected to create new jobs and attract $180 million capital investments to the region. The environmental and economic disadvantages of the project and the perceived inappropriateness of the use of public money (i.e., TIF) for the plant became subject to opponents' sharp criticism (Knapp May 17, 2016).

Despite this controversy, the Fremont City Council agreed to land rezoning (June 21 and July 7, 2016), a blight declaration (July 12, 2016) and the redevelopment plan recommended by the Fremont Planning Commission (July 19, 2016). The Project No. 1 was approved (8–0) on July 25, 2016. Costco later proposed a bigger plant including a 360,000 sq. ft. processing facility, a 85,000 sq. ft. hatchery, and feed mills (Granese December 27, 2016). The Fremont City Council approved (8–0) Costco's revised plan again on December 27, 2016. In the revised plan, the total estimated cost of the Project No. 1 was $275 million with $18.3 million in TIF. Construction began in early 2017 and production started in the fall of 2019.

City officials in Fremont, Nebraska conducted a CBA of the poultry plant as partial fulfillment of state TIF requirements (Nebraska Revised Statute Chapter 18 Section 2113). The results were made public during the City Council meeting on December 27, 2016 (City of Fremont, NE. 2016). Three different sets of costs and benefits for the plant were identified in the city's CBA Report.

First, the poultry plant was expected to create 800 to 1,000 jobs with no material adverse impact on employers and employees of firms within and around the plant because the jobs created would be filled over the course of several years. It was also documented in the CBA report that the plant will lead to approximately 125 contract farmers as chicken growers.

Second, the incremental improvement of the plant area's valuation was estimated to be \$93.3 million, up from \$2.2 million to \$95.5 million. The annual property tax shift was then projected to be \$1.8 million. The corresponding cost factor is the city's TIF use for utility extension, public streets, and site preparation purposes; it was expected to generate the city's indebtedness of \$18.3 million and additional administrative and interest costs of \$1.1 million for fourteen years. Some other impacts on local revenues other than property taxes were mentioned in the report, but they were not explicated in detail.

Lastly, the poultry plant was anticipated to generate multiplier effects on local business, including secondary effects on employment and business attraction, but those effects were not specifically estimated.

EVALUATING THE CITY'S CBA
THROUGH THE FRAMEWORK

To examine our framework through this case, we first rely on the framework and its guidelines discussed above to estimate the benefits and costs of the plant. We then use secondary data sources to supplement our estimation. At least short-term information is available through the city, county, and state given that the plant began operation a year ago. We also supplement the discussion with information collected from our communications with city officials and other community leaders.

The city's CBA results cover some of the costs and benefits presented in table 12.1, while other elements are missed. First, job and income growth for workers and farmers is the major benefit of the plant both in the city's report and in the framework. According to the city's CBA and multiple media sources, the plant's total annual income effect on workers and farmers could be approximately \$31.2 million and \$12.5 million, respectively, when assuming the full employment of 1,000 workers making a weekly wage of $600 each ($15*40 hours) and 125 contract farmers running 500 barns (Farrell September 27, 2018; Soderlin October 13, 2017).[1] In fact, the recent data shows that since the Costco plant went live in 2019, total employment in Fremont has grown. Between January 2019 and 2020, the net additional employment was 145 people. Perhaps more impressively, comparing May 2019 to May 2020, which is in the middle of the COVID-19 pandemic, the number of employed grew from 13,500 to 13,835.

Based on our framework, what is missing in the city's CBA is the opportunity cost of the plant regarding workers' and farmers' job security. Employment turnover has historically been problematic for these types of plants (as noted earlier from 70 to 100%). In this case, however, officials reported that Costco's turnover rate is in the 50–60 percent range and that rate reflects employees leaving out of concerns for COVID-19. Assuming a yearly turnover rate of 50–60 percent, the plant could annually lead to 500 to 600 workers who seek unemployment benefits. Since an average unemployed worker spends 7.7 weeks to find a new job while experiencing 50 percent wage replacement—about $300 per week in this case—through unemployment benefits (U.S. Bureau of Labor Statistics 2020b), it could annually cost a total of $1.2 million to $1.4 million.

An average farmer in Nebraska typically made an annual income of $61,130 in 2019 (U.S. Bureau of Labor Statistics 2020a). Focusing on the annual 10th or 25th percentile income where farmers may have stronger motivation to become contract growers, it is $33,880 or $52,180, respectively. Assuming those who make more than the average income have no motivation to contract with the plant, each farmer may annually experience an opportunity cost ranging from $33,880 to $61,130 when becoming a broiler grower. Therefore, the total amount of annual opportunity cost for 125 contract farmers could be from $4.2 million to $7.6 million when only considering their income replacement. In addition, Soderlin (October 13, 2017) reports that farmers should invest nearly $2 million in every four barns, totaling $250 million for 500 barns. Contract farmers may encounter a risk of losing this capital investment especially in the long run. To mitigate this potential cost problem, Costco has guaranteed that growers will be under contract for at least fifteen years (Farrell September 27, 2018).

The city's CBA, as suggested by our framework, identifies annual property tax shifts as a result of capital investment to be the key benefit of the plant. Specifically, the plant is expected to generate additional property taxes of $1.8 million annually for the local governments sharing the site (municipality, school district, county, etc.). This could be up to $2.4 million annually given that the site's valuation is currently estimated to be higher ($123 million) than the city's initial estimation ($95.5 million). On the other hand, the city's TIF use will give a total of $19.4 million back to the developer during the TIF period of fourteen years, which is equivalent to an annual expense of $1.4 million. The framework urges us to question whether the city's CBA captures the opportunity cost of TIF. Since the TIF project will freeze the site's valuation around the base level of $2.3 million, the overlying taxing entities will miss property value increases that would have been generated without TIF. The plant site's valuation has grown at an annual rate of two percent before the plant was located (Maher et al. 2019). As shown in table 12.2, therefore, the annual opportunity cost of TIF could be $7,535 on average (a total of $0.1 million for 14 years), considering that the county-wide levy is often around 20 mills (City of Fremont, NE. 2016). The annual opportunity cost of TIF could be much higher, up to $1.8 million, if assuming that the project would have happened without TIF.

City officials also expect the plant to contribute revenues other than property taxes to the local government. Assuming that the plant will follow the national food industry average (Boyd Company, Inc. 2018), its annual consumption of electric power ($0.75 million) and natural gas ($0.54 million) could generate $1.3 million in public revenues. City officials seem to have a similar estimation of gas ($0.35 million), but they expect higher electricity revenues of $4 million. Further, based on the findings of Food Northwest (2020), the plant is expected to annually consume 680 million gallons of water (6.8 gallons*100 million birds). Given the city's current industrial utility rates (City of Fremont, NE 2020b), the plant will pay annual water and sewer charges worth around $1.7 million. This is similar to the city's own estimation of $2 million. Some portion of these benefits may, however, be offset by other government fiscal support. For instance, the Fremont City

Table 12.2   Estimation of the Opportunity Cost of TIF Use

Year	The site's estimated valuation increase without TIF ($)	Estimated property tax increase without TIF ($)	Year	The site's estimated valuation increase without TIF ($)	Estimated property tax increase without TIF ($)
2018	46,000	920	2026	448,712	8,974
2019	92,920	1,858	2027	503,687	10,073
2020	140,778	2,815	2028	559,760	11,195
2021	189,594	3,791	2029	616,956	12,339
2022	239,385	4,787	2030	675,295	13,505
2023	290,173	5,803	2031	734,801	14,696
2024	341,977	6,839	Annual average	376,775	7,535
2025	394,816	7,896	fourteen-years total	5,274,854	105,491

Source: Estimated by the authors based on City of Fremont, NE (2016) and Maher et al. (2019).

Council offered $200,000 for engineering services in addition to the TIF funding (Starling May 31, 2016). The City Council also offered $1.35 million in incentives through the city's economic development fund to support the project (Soderlin October 13, 2017). Finally, the state decided to spend $62 million to construct a beltway around the plant, which will also cost the city an additional $20 million (Lamb June 2, 2020).

Costco announced that they will hire 1,000 Nebraskans to operate the plant (Welshans October 23, 2019). According to city officials, Costco currently hires 60 percent of its employees from Fremont and the other 40 percent are hired largely from surrounding communities such as Omaha, Schuyler, Columbus, Arlington, Blair, and Wahoo. This may lead to a marginal increase in the city's service spending. Based on Park's (2018) estimation, the city may need to spend $0.2 million more ($611*400 workers from surrounding communities) for public services. Nebraska Auditor of Public Accounts (2020) shows similar evidence that the city's protective service expenditures (police and fire), for example, grew only 1.3 percent ($0.1 million) when comparing governmental expenditures between 2019 and 2020.[2] Therefore, fears of the plant's opening resulting in service expenditure growth has not yet clearly materialized.

It is, however, still reasonable to expect that the plant may attract a number of new-comers, especially immigrants, in the future as has been found in prior studies (Broadway and Stull 2006; Constance and Tuinstra 2005). Based on Rector's (2007) estimation of the additional state and local service costs of $14,270 per immigrant, table 12.3 below shows three different cost scenarios where the plant hypothetically hires 200, 400, and 600 immigrants (considering a turnover rate up to 60%). The assumption here is that all immigrants come to the city from other states within the country. If we assume that all immigrants come from overseas, the cost estimation should generate greater values, including additional federal service costs, as also shown in table 12.3.

Table 12.3   Estimation of Additional Public Service Costs Per Immigrant

	200 immigrants	*400 immigrants*	*600 immigrants*
State and local services (unit cost: $14,270)	$2.9 million	$5.7 million	$8.6 million
Federal services (unit cost: $15,890)	$3.2 million	$6.4 million	$9.5 million
Total (unit cost: $30,160)	$6.1 million	$12.1 million	$18.1 million

Source: Estimated by the authors based on Rector (2007).

In the CBA report, city officials do not capture the impact of the plant on the property values around the site. The impact can be twofold, according to our framework: the plant could generate certain benefits due to population growth and subsequent increased housing and construction demand, whereas it could generate costs because of environmental degradation. In fact, Fremont has experienced new construction of 1,000 rental units over the past few years, with phase two in the planning stage. There are also 100 housing units under construction. On the other hand, concerns over the plant's potential environmental impacts continue to be expressed (Sangimino March 20, 2020).

The evidence documented by prior studies such Taff et al. (1996), Palmquist et al. (1997) and Herriges et al. (2003) suggest that the sum of those two-fold consequences may generate a net positive property value of 1.8 percent (6.6% increase vs. 4.8% decrease) or net negative property valuation of 3.4 percent (6.6% increase vs. 10% decrease) because the plant's potential positive consequences may outweigh its negative impacts, or vice versa. According to Dodge County Assessor's Office (2017), the assessed property valuation of the areas within three-miles of the plant is approximately $1,400 million, excluding the plant site's valuation. Applying a net increase rate of 2 percent presented above, the property valuation is estimated to be $1,428 million. In other words, residents who own properties around the plant may experience the annual benefit of approximately $25.2 million. In the opposite scenario, local residents may experience the annual cost of approximately $47.6 million.

Our CBA, based on the proposed framework, shows that the plant's total annual benefit can be $73.7 million to $77.7 million, while its total annual cost can be from $53.2 million to $76.5 million. The cost could be higher if considering non-recurring costs such as the potential risk of farmers' infrastructure investment and government fiscal support other than TIF. Though the total annual cost would be reduced by $1.8 million once the TIF district is retired, it would not significantly alter the overall cost-benefit structure. Overall, the plant is either cost-beneficial or it is not depending on assumptions.

As discussed, the plant's potential industrial multiplier effects should be separately and carefully considered. Thompson, Johnson and Giri (2012), for example, found that the poultry industry in Nebraska tends to produce an overall multiplier effect of 0.26, indicating that each $1 of poultry production value would yield $0.26. Simply applying this finding to the case, the total multiplier impact of the plant could be $78 million because the plant annually produces birds worth around $300 million (100 million birds*an average processing rate of $3 per bird). New or expanded business because of the new Costco plant should be part of this multiplier effect.[3] Further, the city's property taxes have grown 39 percent since 2017 according to Nebraska Auditor of Public Accounts (2020). Also, the city's option sales tax, which is the city's largest revenue source, have grown 24 percent since 2017 despite a recent decline due to COVID-19. These results can also be attributable to the plant's multiplier effects. However, this should not be viewed as net benefits because it does not include the costs of those multiplier effects.

In addition, the plant may have a negative economic impact in terms of food supply. Focusing on farms that produce lower than the state-wide average production level of $474,476 (U.S. Department of Agriculture 2017), each farm's annual average production in Nebraska is about $90,000. Based on Thompson et al. (2012) that reported 0.6 as the general multiplier impact of the agricultural industry in the state, each contract farmer is expected to lead to an annual reduction of $54,000 in multiplier effects of local farming, totaling $6.8 million for 125 contract farmers.

There are also immeasurable consequences associated with this development that are worthy of note. For example, immigration has been a difficult topic in Fremont for a number of years. Well before the Costco plant, Fremont passed a petition in 2010 stating that "all business entities doing business in the City of Fremont that employ one or more persons must register in the E-Verify program on or before May 4, 2012 . . . each adult occupant (age 18 or older) who lets, leases or rents a dwelling unit in the City of Fremont to obtain a residential occupancy license" (City of Fremont, NE 2020a). While Costco complies with the E-verification program, it casts a shadow over the city as a community unwelcoming to immigrants (Bishop September 30, 2016). The Costco development has forced the city of Fremont to recon with the issue of diversity and inclusivity in a way that that all communities, particularly smaller communities, will need to address if they hope to survive. More broadly, the plant has forced the community to reexamine its future. Local officials talk about the Costco facility forcing a discussion about community growth/economic development. Measuring the societal benefits of such social policy discussions is challenging but worthy of note.

CONCLUSION

This study aimed to address a gap in the literature by offering a conceptual framework and guidelines for CBA of a large-scale food processing plant. It is an important endeavor for policy and administration practice given that locating a food processing plant has been considered an attractive option for rural development. We reviewed and synthesized the policy analysis and food policy literature in order to develop a framework. Through the proposed framework, we suggested that policy analysts should strive to capture costs and benefits of a processing plant in at least five different dimensions—job and income, and government finance, population growth, industrial consequences, and environmental consequences. Prior food policy studies offer specific benchmarks for measuring each cost or benefit factor, but none have done so in a comprehensive manner.

The framework developed in this study was examined through the lens of a new Costco poultry processing plant in Fremont, Nebraska. The major finding of our case study is that our CBA framework can help practice by providing a comprehensive list of costs and benefits involved in an industrial food processing plant. Comparison of our framework and the city's CBA results confirms that city officials relied on an over-simplified cost-benefit structure to support the plant. While the city's CBA suggests overwhelming support for the project, our analysis suggests that the CBA could be net positive, or net negative depending on longer-term effects. Our CBA has a relatively narrow total annual benefit range ($73.7 million to $77.7 million), while total annual costs have a much wider range ($53.2 million to $76.5 million). The latter is largely a function of the plant's ability to retain local employees. The Costco plant has been successful in hiring local and retaining those employees at a greater rate than found in prior studies. Should this trend change—needing to attract more employees from outside the region and/or higher turnover rates—the community could experience a net cost associated with the plant. Furthermore, costs could be greater if non-recurring costs such as the potential risk of farmers' infrastructure investment and government fiscal support other than TIF are taken into account.

We were also able to confirm the validity of our framework and CBA guidelines by comparing our estimation with secondary data sources and information collected from city officials. This suggests that our framework has the potential to contribute to practice. The challenge, of course, is data collection and analysis. This is challenge exacerbated when the majority of these complicated projects are proposed in smaller communities that lack the personnel and/or resources to conduct more extensive CBAs. In such a case, state officials should have an obligation to step in and offer assistance. Unfortunately, in Nebraska, TIF laws are quite vague and CBA requirements are quite weak (Maher et al. 2019), which puts more pressure on local governments to get the analysis right since they bear the brunt of the policy decision.

Perhaps not too surprising, our CBA results do not provide a clear-cut answer. Our framework showed that the plant can be either efficient or inefficient depending on the assumptions employed by policy analysts. According to the policy analysis literature, this is a natural outcome. Policy analysts are expected to offer more information based on different assumptions rather than suggesting ones that support a single recommendation. Those assumptions can be about the directionality of policy impacts (i.e., negative vs. positive), their magnitude (i.e., small vs. large-scale), and/or their time span (i.e., short-term vs. long-term). Once various analysis results are offered, the final policy decision inherently becomes a political matter (Bickers and Williams 2001).

Finally, it is worthy of note that while a CBA can be a valuable tool, it should be considered one element of a richer discussion about committing to such a large endeavor. There are fiscal, environmental and societal implications; these facilities have the potential to transform small communities. How one perceives those changes, in most cases, lies in the eye of the beholder. Unfortunately, the degree to which the complexity surrounding these decisions often falls short as the fault lines typically pin those in favor of economic development against those opposed. At a minimum, our CBA approach offers an opportunity for framing some of these important discussions.

NOTES

1. Contrary to previous research, the Costco plant forced up wages in Fremont. Costco initially offered a starting wage of $13 per hour. By the 2019 opening, however, the starting pay was increased to $15. We learned from our interviews with city officials that this hourly rate, in turn, forced other processing plants in Fremont—WholeStone Farms and Fremont Beef Company—to also raise their wages. This wage impact should be part of the multiplier effects of the plant.

2. Public works spending went up 62.2 percent and culture and recreation expenditures spiked 78.2 percent. These expenditures more than likely have more to do with the City's recovery from major flooding in 2019 than anything else.

3. According to our email exchanges with city officials, the city estimated 15–20 businesses have either started business or expanded their business because of the new Costco plant.

REFERENCES

Abeles-Allison, Mark, and Larry J. Connor. 1990. "An analysis of local benefits and costs of Michigan hog operations experiencing environmental conflicts." Agricultural Economics Report #536, Department of Agricultural Economics, Michigan State University. Accessed June 15, 2020. Accessible at https://agecons earch.umn.edu/record/201396?ln=en.

Andrews, Brother D., and Timothy J. Kautza. n.d. "Impact of industrial farm animal production on rural communities" Pew Commission on Industrial Farm Animal Production. Accessed June 16, 2020. Accessible at http://www.pcifapia.org/_ images/212–8_PCIFAP_RuralCom_Finaltc.pdf.

Artz, Georgeanne M., Peter F. Orazem, and Daniel M. Otto. 2007. "Measuring the impact of meat packing and processing facilities in nonmetropolitan counties: A difference-in-differences approach." *American Journal of Agricultural Economics* 89(3): 557–570.

Bickers, Kenneth N., and John Taylor Williams. 2001. *Public policy analysis: A political economy approach.* Boston, MA: Houghton Mifflin Company.

Bishop, Marlon. September 30, 2016. The great immigration wars of Fremont, Nebraska. Latino USA. Accessed August 11, 2020. Accessible at https://www.lat inousa.org/2016/09/30/immigration-wars-of-fremont/.

Boyd Company, Inc. 2018. "Comparative food processing industry operating costs." Accessed July 10, 2020. Accessible at https://growgreatfallsmontana.org/wp-con tent/uploads/2019/08/Great-Falls-MT-Food-Processing-Operating-Cost-Comparat ive-Study-2018.pdf.

Broadway, Michael J. 2000. "Planning for change in small towns or trying to avoid the slaughterhouse blues." *Journal of Rural Studies* 16(1): 37–46.

Broadway, Michael J., and Donald D. Stull. 2006. "Meat processing and Garden City, KS: Boom and bust." *Journal of Rural Studies* 22(1): 55–66.

Campbell, Harry F., and Richard PC Brown. 2003. *Benefit-cost analysis: Financial and economic appraisal using spreadsheets.* Cambridge, UK: Cambridge University Press.

City of Fremont, NE. 2016. "Redevelopment plan amendment—South Fremont industrial redevelopment plan." Accessed June 25, 2020. Accessible at http://www .fremontne.gov/AgendaCenter/ViewFile/Agenda/_12272016-476.

City of Fremont, NE. 2020a. "Immigration ordinance news." Accessed August 11, 2020. Accessible at https://www.fremontne.gov/450/Immigration-Ordinance-News.

City of Fremont, NE. 2020b. "Utility rates." Accessed August 10, 2020. Accessible at https://fremontne.gov/164/Utility-Rates.

Constance, Douglas H., and Reny Tuinstra. 2005. "Corporate chickens and community conflict in east Texas: Growers' and neighbors' views on the impacts of industrial broiler production." *Culture and Agriculture*, 27(1): 45–60.

Dodge County Assessor's Office. 2017. "Property information search." Accessed August 11, 2020. Accessible at https://dodge.gworks.com/.

Dunn, William N. 2018. *Public policy analysis: An integrated approach.* New York, NY: Routledge.

Farrell, James. September 27, 2018. Raising a chicken plant, part 4: the barns. Fremont Tribune. Accessed July 16, 2020. Accessible at https://fremonttribune .com/news/local/raising-a-chicken-plant-part-4-the-barns/article_bd1b245b-4eb1 –5a26–99c5-b518143f8073.html.

Flora, Cornelia Butler. 1998. "Bringing home the bacon? The myth of the role of corporate hog farming in rural revitalization." The Kerr Center for Sustainable Agriculture. Accessed June 27, 2020. Accessible at https://files.eric.ed.gov/full text/ED462212.pdf.

Gómez, Miguel I., and Liying Zhang. 2000. "Impacts of concentration in hog production on economic growth in rural Illinois: An econometric analysis" Presented to the American Agricultural Economics Association Annual Meeting. Tampa, FL.

Government Accounting Standard Board (GASB). 2015. "Statement No. 77 of the Governmental Accounting Standards Board: Tax abatement disclosures." Accessed June 20, 2020. Accessible at https://www.gasb.org/jsp/GASB/Document _C/DocumentPage?cid=1176166283745&acceptedDisclaimer=true.

Granese, Don. December 27, 2016. Fremont City Council approves larger plant design for controversial Costco chicken plant. WOWT 6 News. Accessed August 4, 2020. Accessible at http://www.wowt.com/content/news/Fremont-Costco-ch icken-plant-a-growing-concern-to-some-considered-by-council—408440345.html.

Halden, Rolf U., and Kellogg J. Schwab. n.d. "Environmental impact of industrial farm animal production." Pew Commission on Industrial Farm Animal Production. Accessed June 16, 2020. Accessible at http://www.pcifapia.org/_images/212–4_En vImpact_tc_Final.pdf.

Herriges, Joseph A., Silvia Secchi, and Bruce A. Babcock. 2003 "Living with hogs in Iowa: The impact of livestock facilities on rural residential property values." Working Paper 03-WP 342. Center for Agricultural and Rural Development, Iowa State University. Accessed June 20, 2020. Accessible at https://www.card.iastate. edu/products/publications/pdf/03wp342.pdf.

Huffman, W. E. and J. A. Miranowski. 1996. "Immigration, meat packing, and trade: Implications for Iowa." Staff Paper #285. Iowa State University. Accessed June 20, 2020. Accessible at https://pdfs.semanticscholar.org/fa9a/18333bac0cb66c1e5 ed692d0ec507b3431d1.pdf.

Janssen, Brandi. 2017. *Making local food work: The challenges and opportunities of today's small farmers.* Iowa City, IA: University of Iowa Press.

Knapp, Fred. May 17, 2016. Fremont Chicken Proposal Brings Mixed Reactions. NET News. Accessed August 10, 2020. Accessible at http://netnebraska.org/article /news/1023793/fremont-chicken-proposal-brings-mixed-reactions.

Lamb, Eleanor. June 2, 2020. Nebraska DOT nears construction of Fremont beltway project. Accessed August 11, 2020. Accessible at https://www.ttnews.com/articles/ nebraska-dot-nears-construction-fremont-beltway-project.

Liesveld, John. March 29, 2016. Project Rawhide. Fremont Tribune. Accessed August 11, 2020. Accessible at http://fremonttribune.com/project-rawhide/article_ 39e2d17e-45fc-5901-a381–233b8dd500ef.html.

MacDonald, James. A. 2014. "Financial risks and incomes in contract broiler pro-duction." United States Department of Agriculture. Economic Research Service. Accessed July 20, 2020. Accessible at https://www.ers.usda.gov/amber-waves/201 4/august/financial-risks-and-incomes-in-contract-broiler-production/.

Maher, Craig S., Sungho Park, and Ji Hyung Park. 2019. "The (d)evolution of TIF use: Redevelopment to land development in Nebraska." In *Tax increment financing and economic development: Uses, structures, and impact*, Craig L. Johnson and Kenneth A. Kriz, eds. Albany, NY: SUNY Press, 173–198.

Nebraska Auditor of Public Accounts. 2020. "Basic budget data query." Accessed August 11, 2020. Accessible at https://www.nebraska.gov/auditor/reports/index .cgi?budget=1.

Nebraska Department of Labor. 2020. NEworks. Accessed August 17, 2020. https:// neworks.nebraska.gov/.

Palmquist, R. B., Fritz M. Roka, and Tomislav Vukina. 1997. "Hog Operations, environmental effects, and residential property values." *Land Economics* 73(1): 114–24.

Parin, Maria A., and Aurora Zugarramurdi. 1994. "Investment and production costs analysis in food processing plants." *International Journal of Production Economics* 34(1): 83–89.

Park, Dooho, Kyu-Hee Lee, and Andrew Seidl. 1999. "Rural Communities and Animal Feeding Operations: Economic and Environmental Considerations." Agricultural and Research Policy Report. Department of Agricultural and Resource Economics, Colorado State University.

Park, Sungho. 2018 "Game-theoretic thinking of state-imposed tax and expenditure limitations: Rule design, institutional diversity, and municipal fiscal outcomes." Doctoral dissertation, University of Nebraska at Omaha.

Rector, Robert. 2007. "The fiscal cost of low-skill immigrants to the U.S. taxpayer." Heritage Foundation. Accessed July 20, 2020. Accessible at https://www.aila.org/File/Related/07050260g.pdf.

Sangimino, Pat. March 20, 2020. Amid controversy, $4.99 Costco chickens translate to big boost for Nebraska economy. Lincoln Journal Star. Accessed August 15, 2020. Accessible at https://journalstar.com/special-section/new-directions/amid-controversy-4-99-costco-chickens-translate-to-big-boost-for-nebraska-economy/article_9e49fc5c-f639-52f8-ad2c-3e8a3e71f2ac.html.

Schaffer, Harwood D., Pracha Koonnathamdee, and Daryll E. Ray. n.d. "An economic analysis of the social costs of the industrialized production of pork in the United States." Pew Commission on Industrial Farm Animal Production. Accessed June 16, 2020. Accessible at http://www.pcifapia.org/_images/212-6_PCIFAP_Ecnmics_v5_tc.pdf.

Skees, Jerry R., J. Roy Black, and Benjamin M. Gramig. 2003. "Considering Market-based alternatives to improve the management of CAFOs. Presented to the American Agricultural Economics Association Annual Meeting. Montreal, Canada.

Snyder, Brian, and Mark J. Kaiser. 2009. "Ecological and economic cost-benefit analysis of offshore wind energy." *Renewable Energy* 34(6): 1567–1578.

Soderlin, Barbara. October 13, 2017. With Fremont processing plant on the way, Hooper farmer becomes first to invest in poultry, future. Omaha World-Herald. Accessed July 16, 2020. Accessible at https://omaha.com/money/with-fremont-processing-plant-on-the-way-hooper-farmer-becomes-first-to-invest-in-poultry/article_f5bbdc75-3c39-5f69-bb3b-b4175fe8602d.html.

Starling, Nick. May 31, 2016. Fremont City Council approves reimbursement cost for Costco plan. 3 News Now Omaha. Accessed August 10, 2020. Accessible at http://www.3newsnow.com/news/local-news/fremont-city-council-approves-reimbursement-cost-for-costco-plan.

Taff, Steven J., Douglas G. Tiffany, and Sanford Weisberg. 1996. "Measured effects of feedlots on residential property values in Minnesota: A report to the legislature." Staff Paper P96–12. University of Minnesota. Accessed July 12, 2020. Accessible at http://agebb.missouri.edu/commag/cafo/sources/Taff1996.pdf.

Taks, Marijke, Stefan Kesenne, Laurence Chalip, and Christine B. Green. 2011. "Economic impact analysis versus cost benefit analysis: The case of a medium-sized sport event." *International Journal of Sport Finance* 6(3): 187–203.

The council of state governments. 2012. "Where the money goes: State-by-state general expenditures by function." Accessed July 10, 2020. Accessible at https://kn owledgecenter.csg.org/kc/system/files/wherethemoneygoes.pdf.

Thompson, Eric, Bruce Johnson and Anil Giri. 2012. "The 2010 economic impact of the Nebraska agricultural production complex." Department of Agricultural Economics, the University of Nebraska–Lincoln. Accessed August 10, 2020. Accessible at https://agecon.unl.edu/research/nebraska-ag-economic-impact.pdf.

Thornsbury, Suzanne D., S. Murthy Kambhampaty, and David E. Kenyon. 1993. "Economic impact of a swine complex in Southside Virginia." Virginia's Rural Economic Analysis Program. Virginia Tech. Accessed July 10, 2020. Accessible at https://vtechworks.lib.vt.edu/bitstream/handle/10919/24665/VCE448_215_1993. pdf?sequence=1.

U.S. Bureau of Labor Statistics. 2020a. "Occupational employment and wage estimates" Accessed July 20, 2020. Accessible at https://www.bls.gov/oes/current/oes srci.htm.

U.S. Bureau of Labor Statistics. 2020b. "Unemployed persons by duration of unemployment." Accessed July 25, 2020. Accessible at https://www.bls.gov/news.relea se/empsit.t12.htm.

U.S. Census Bureau. 2018. American Community Survey. Accessed August 11, 2020. Accessible at https://www.census.gov/acs/www/data/data-tables-and-tools/ data-profiles/.

U.S. Department of Agriculture. 2017. "2017 Census of Agriculture." Accessed August 12, 2020. Accessible at https://www.nass.usda.gov/Publications/AgCensus /2017/Full_Report/Census_by_State/index.php.

Weimer, David L., and Aidan R. Vining. 2017. *Policy analysis: Concepts and practice.* New York, NY: Routledge.

Welshans, Krissa. October 23, 2019. Ribbon cutting held for Costco chicken plant. Supermarket News. Accessed August 11, 2020. Accessible at https://www.sup ermarketnews.com/meat/ribbon-cutting-held-costco-chicken-plant/.

Section V

EMERGENCY MANAGEMENT

Chapter 13

Addressing Nutrition During and After a Humanitarian Emergency

Sheila Fleischhacker

INTRODUCTION

This chapter focuses on the role of the administrative state in the United States (U.S.) food system in addressing food insecurity and promoting healthy eating during and after humanitarian emergencies. This essential role has roots dating back to our nation's earliest days and continues to persist as we tackle more frequent and intense emergencies, including the current pandemic, known as the Coronavirus Disease (COVID-19). The chapter begins with fundamental definitions and categories of humanitarian emergencies and then provides a rationale for why ensuring food and nutrition assistance during these emergencies are a critical ingredient to effective response and recovery, especially for vulnerable populations. Then, this chapter discusses key historical and contemporary policy and programmatic approaches relevant to food, nutrition, and health at the federal, tribal, territorial, state, and local levels in the United States that key stakeholders take during humanitarian emergencies and other emerging disruptions, including the current COVID-19 pandemic. This chapter concludes with synthesizing meaningful ways for public health and public administration professionals to shape relevant research, practice, and policy in the short- and long-term, particularly for addressing food insecurity.

WHAT IS A HUMANITARIAN EMERGENCY?

A humanitarian emergency is an event or a series of events that are threatening in terms of health, safety, or well-being of a community or large group of people, usually over a wide geographically area (HumanitarianCoalition

2020). These emergencies encompass natural disasters (biological, climato-logical, geophysical, hydrological, or meteorological), man-made emergen-cies, and complex emergencies. Since the 1970s, the incidence of natural disasters worldwide has steadily increased and the scale and complexity of disasters have also expanded (Rose and DeSmogBlog 2014). Contributing factors include climate change, poverty, urbanization, and underdevelopment. Man-made emergencies include armed conflicts (i.e., international armed conflicts, opposing two or more states, and noninternational armed conflicts, between government forces and nongovernmental armed groups, or between such groups only), plane and train crashes, fires, and industrial accidents, which are caused by industrial companies, either by accident, negligence, or incompetence (e.g., nuclear power plant exploring; oil spill) (ICRC 2008). Complex emergencies are often a combination of natural and man-made ele-ments and are usually characterized by extensive violence and loss of life, displacements of populations, widespread damage to societies and econom-ics, significant security risks for humanitarian relief workers in the affected areas, significant need for large-scale, multifaceted humanitarian assistance, and the hindrance or prevention of humanitarian assistance by political and military constraints. Examples include armed conflict, displaced populations, and food insecurity, which is the state of being without reliable access to a sufficient quantity of affordable, nutritious food. Or in more severe cases, examples of complex emergencies can include famine, which is defined as an extreme and general scarcity of food in a large geographical area caused by several factors including war, inflation, crop failure, population imbalance, or government policies. In the majority of these types of emergencies, survivors are left in urgent need of life-saving assistance including but not limited to shelter, food, water, and health care.

WHY ADDRESS NUTRITION DURING AND AFTER A HUMANITARIAN EMERGENCY?

Ensuring food and nutrition assistance during a humanitarian emergency is a critical ingredient to effective response and recovery (HumanitarianCoalition 2020; Tsuboyama-Kasaoka and Br Purba 2014; Moss et al. 2006). This is especially for vulnerable populations, which generally refer to individuals, households, or communities with reduced capacity to effectively resist or recover from life-threatening hazards by themselves. Their vulnerability is often associated with poverty (limited transportation, poor Internet, inadequate housing conditions), disability (e.g., wheelchair bound), life stage (e.g., children, women who are pregnant and/or lactating, or elders), or immigration status (e.g., migrants, refugees, or displaced people who were driven or expelled from their homeland by war, famine, tyranny, etc.). Vulnerable populations often live in areas whose geography also puts them at risk for flooding or disproportionate risks to facing a natural or man-made disaster. During humanitarian emergencies, affected populations face a variety of challenges to maintaining proper hydration, nutrition, hygiene, sanitation, and social/care situations. These challenges are even more difficult to overcome for vulnerable populations. Identifying and then addressing each of these challenges depends on the specific humanitarian emergency, along with the contextual and cultural needs of the affected populations, particularly the most vulnerable. The response must also factor in the safety and ability of humanitarian workers (e.g., mitigate COVID-19 transmission). Needs assessments using valid and reliable small-scale survey approaches are essential to identify, prioritize, and reach the most vulnerable populations; one tool is the Standardized Monitoring and Assessment of Relief and Transitions (SMART) methodology (Odjida and Hakizimana 2019).

Research demonstrates humanitarian emergencies are associated with increases in food insecurity, nutritional risks (e.g., stunting, disrupted infant, and young child feeding practices, inadequate micronutrient status such as iron deficiency), and often lead to an increase in acute malnutrition (Tsuboyama-Kasaoka and Br Purba 2014). As noted earlier, food insecurity exists when nutritionally adequate and safe foods are not available or the ability to acquire acceptable foods in socially acceptable ways is limited or uncertain (Coleman-Jensen et al. 2020). Malnutrition refers to deficiencies, excesses, or imbalances in a person's intake or energy and/or nutrients and often is caused by not having enough to eat, not eating enough of the right things, or being unable to use the food that one has access to (e.g., unable to cook due to power outrages or unable to use powered infant formula without access to safe water) (Odjida and Hakizimana 2019). A recent systematic review of health outcomes for children in Haiti between 2010–2018 following an earthquake found food insecurity and malnutrition persist eight years after the earthquake, among other health outcomes (Dube et al. 2018). The study authors recommended future health programs focus on the provision of clean water, sanitation, and other measures to prevent infectious diseases, promote mental health, and address food insecurity and malnutrition. Another review evaluated the effectiveness of nutrition interventions on defined health outcomes in children and adolescents (zero to eighteen years) within a disaster or complex emergency (Balhara et al. 2017). The review reported high- and medium-quality studies demonstrated positive impact of fortified spreads, ready-to-use therapeutic foods, micronutrient supplementation, and food and cash transfers, though based on limited meaningful data aggregation given the challenges of study design control under emergency conditions.

The U.S. Department of Agriculture (USDA) Economic Research Service (ERS) monitors national and state-level food insecurity (Coleman-Jensen et al. 2020). An estimated 10.5 percent of U.S. households were food insecure in 2019, which was a decline from a high of 14.9 in 2011. During the COVID-19 pandemic, food insecurity has increased, with one survey reporting up to 34.5 percent during April 2020 (Schanzenbach and Pitts 2020). Food insecurity has short- and long-term impacts including inadequate dietary intake, suboptimal development and function, increased hospitalizations, disrupted or underuse of prescribed medications, poorer management of chronic diseases, elevated and prolonged periods of stress, reduced academic achievement, decreased interpersonal skills, and fetal epigenetic changes (Seligman, Laraia, and Kushel 2010; Seligman and Schillinger 2010; Berkowitz et al. 2018).

Thus, delivering nutrition during humanitarian emergencies has increasingly demanded the delicate navigation between intersections of inadequate dietary intake, weight gain, and increased risk of certain chronic diseases. Providing sufficient calories with an emphasis on nutrient-dense foods and beverages, along with adequate protein and water-soluble vitamins is essential. There are a variety of additional food and nutrition considerations when preparing for, living through, and recovering from a humanitarian emergency, including but not limited to maintaining a few days' supply of shelf-stable foods and water, limiting opening refrigerators and freezers to keep the coldness in, and discarding perishable food that has been above 40°F for two hours or more. A cross-sectional study in New Jersey of food-secure families found adequate dietary-based emergency preparedness and low vulnerability to emergency-induced food insecurity (Golem and Byrd-Bredbenner 2015). But this is likely not the case for families who are food insecure nor, as seen with COVID-19, do individuals or families who face food insecurity challenges generally have the financial resources to stock up on even the suggested three-day food supply. Emerging efforts recognize the importance of using a health equity lens and considering the social determinants of health (i.e., conditions where people live, learn, work, and play that affect health risks and outcomes) when developing and executing humanitarian emergency response and recovery plans, policies, and resource allocations (Jacobs 2019).

WHAT IS THE FEDERAL FRAMEWORK
FOR DISASTER RESPONSE?

A variety of federal law, policy, and other guidance documents drive our nation's domestic disaster response and national emergency activities (GAO 2008; CRS 2020b). The U.S. Constitution provides a variety of explicit and implied emergency powers to the president if the nation is threatened by crisis, exigency, or emergency circumstances, with some limits and restraints. The Robert T. Stafford Disaster Relief and Emergency Assistance Act (P.L. 100–707) constitutes the statutory authority for most federal disaster response activities, especially as they pertain to the Federal Emergency Management Agency (FEMA). The National Preparedness System outlines how everyone in the whole community should move forward with their preparedness activities and achieve the National Preparedness Goal of "a secure and resilient nation with the capabilities required across the whole community to prevent, protect against, mitigate, respond to, and recover from the threats and hazards that pose the greatest risk." The whole community includes individuals and families, including those with access and functional needs; businesses; faith-based, and community organizations; nonprofit groups; school and academia; media out-lets; and all levels of government, including state, local, tribal, territorial, and federal partners. The National Preparedness System is made up of six parts: (1) identifying and assessing risk; (2) estimating capability requirements; (3) building and sustaining capabilities; (4) planning to deliver capabilities; (5) validating capabilities; and (6) reviewing and updating. The National Response Framework builds on more than twenty-five years of federal response guidance and details how the nation responds to all types of incidents, mobilizing the whole community (DHS 2019). This Framework is structured to help mem-bers of the whole community develop plans, integrate continuity plans, build capabilities to respond to cascading failures among businesses, supply chains, and infrastructure sectors, and collaborate to stabilize community lifelines and restore services. Community lifelines include safety and security; food, water, and shelter; health and medical; energy (power and fuel); communications; transportation; and hazardous materials. A new toolkit provides information and resources to help whole of community partners better coordinate to imple-ment the lifeline construct during incident response.

Table 13.1 summarizes selected roles and responsibilities relevant to humanitarian emergencies of key federal departments and agencies. Congress authorizes new funding or forgives debt obligations through disaster supple-mental appropriations or other appropriation mechanisms, for example, in 2018, $89.3 billion was appropriated (P.L. 115–123) and in 2019, $19.1 billion was appropriated (P.L. 116–20). Congress also provides critical over-sight to ensure all federal departments and agencies are effectively delivering on their mission and appropriately using allocated resources. Congress also has responsibilities to help connect their constituents to available resources through the government, nongovernment, and private sectors.

Tribal nations play an important role during humanitarian emergencies in or near tribal lands and have sovereign rights to seek and receive assistance and unique capabilities (e.g., Coast Guard's search and research) as needed, including requesting a presidential emergency or natural disaster declaration.

Table 13.1   Selected Roles and Responsibilities Relevant to Humanitarian Emergencies of Key Federal Departments and Agencies

U.S. Department of Agriculture (USDA)

Animal Plant Health Inspection Service (APHIS) and Agricultural Marketing Service (AMS)—Helps maintain the movement of America's food supply from farm to fork by working to maintain critical inspections, grading services, and reporting commodity prices.

Farm Production and Conservation (FPAC)—Helps mitigate the significant risks of farming through crop insurance services, technical assistance, lending, and disaster programs.

Food and Nutrition Service (FNS)—Ensures access to nutritious foods and beverages by working with states, tribes, and U.S. territories and other federal departments and agencies to support immediate and long-term recovery efforts.

Food Safety Inspection Service (FSIS)—Maintains meat, poultry, and processed egg inspection services, including monitoring and tracking employee absenteeism.

Foreign Agricultural Service—Works to create global trade opportunities for the producers and exporters of American farm and food products, including continued monitoring and reporting on U.S. agricultural exports, global agricultural trade, and trade policy priorities.

Natural Resources and the Environment—Suppresses wildfires and works to protect life, property, and natural resources.

Research, Education and Economics—Works to provide official statistics, timely translation of evidence to inform action, and conduct time-sensitive research as needed through the National Agricultural Statistics Service (NASS), the Economic Research Service (ERS), the Agricultural Research Service (ARS), and the National Institute of Food and Agriculture (NIFA).

Rural Development—Provides loans and grants to rural communities.

U.S. Department of Commerce (DoC)

National Oceanic and Atmospheric Administration—Provides scientific assessments on the conditions of the oceans, major waterways, and the atmosphere and works with FEMA to ensure the country is prepared for any hurricanes or other ocean and atmospheric related emergency.

U.S. Department of Defense (DoD)

Provides logistical support or generators; helps mobilize as needed large-scale and emergency contracts quickly; supports the National Interagency Fire Center including fire suppression activities.

U.S. Army Corps of Engineers—Helps plan, design, build, and operate locks and dams, among other projects that help with flood control and works on a variety of other public engineering services that help reduce risks from disasters.

Table 13.1   Selected Roles and Responsibilities Relevant to Humanitarian Emergencies of Key Federal Departments and Agencies (*Continued*)

U.S. Department of Health and Human Services (HHS)

Centers for Disease Control and Prevention (CDC)—Provides guidance and information to tribal, territorial, state, and local health departments to help prevent, respond to, and recover from humanitarian emergencies, including disease management.

Food and Drug Administration (FDA)—Helps maintain the movement of America's food supply by working to maintain critical inspections and provides resources to retailers and consumers about food safety and also helps with food and water safety during power outages and floods.

National Institutes of Health (NIH)—Supports research to help examine the health impacts of humanitarian emergencies.

Office of Human Services, Emergency Preparedness and Response—Leads the nation in preventing, preparing for, and responding to the adverse health effects of public health emergencies and disasters by providing expertise in human services policy, planning, operations, and partnerships.

Substance Abuse and Mental Health Services Administration—Provides 24/7 crisis counseling for anyone experiencing distress including food assistance referral resources.

US Public Health Service—The Commissioned Corps serve in agencies across the government and are called up to help address health-related aspects of disaster relief response and recovery.

U.S. Department of Homeland Security (DHS)

Principal federal official for domestic incident management provides the Executive Branch with an overall architecture for domestic incident management and coordinates the federal response; monitors activities, assesses risk, and activates specific response mechanisms to support other federal departments and agencies; ensures that overall federal actions are unified, complete, and synchronized.

Federal Emergency Management Agency—Principal advisor to the president, secretary of DHS, and the National Security Council regarding emergency management.

U.S. Customs and Border Protection—Helps keep terrorists and their weapons out of the United States while facilitating lawful international travel and trade and takes a comprehensive approach to border management and control, combining customs, immigration, border security, and agricultural protection into one coordinated and supportive activity.

U.S. Department of Housing and Urban Development (HUD)

Provides mortgage assistance, emergency preparedness guides for housing counseling agencies, as well as funding through community development and housing assistance.

(*Continued*)

Table 13.1   Selected Roles and Responsibilities Relevant to Humanitarian Emergencies of Key Federal Departments and Agencies (*Continued*)

U.S. Department of Justice (DoJ)

Attorney General—Leads criminal investigations of terrorist acts or terrorist threats by individuals or groups inside the United States or directed at U.S. citizens or institutions aboard, where such acts within the federal criminal jurisdiction of the United States.

U.S. Department of Labor (DoL)

Occupational Safety and Health Administration—Assures safe and healthful working conditions during and after humanitarian emergencies by setting and enforcing standards and providing training, outreach, education, and assistance.

U.S. Department of State (DoS)

Leads international and diplomatic implications that call for coordination and consultation with foreign governments and international organizations
U.S. Agency for International Development—Shares lessons learned from international humanitarian emergency responses.

U.S. Department of Transportation (DoT)

Leads efforts to repair roads and bridges damaged by storms, floods, and other unexpected events.

U.S. Environmental Protection Agency (EPA)

Helps build preparedness to mitigate future events and lessen the impacts of disasters by assisting federal, tribal, territorial, state, and local agencies and communities prior to disasters; promotes sustainable and resilient rebuilding; helps ensure safe drinking water and wastewater infrastructure, brownfields, air quality, or oil and hazardous materials clean-up; streamlines federal work to help permit or enforce requirements; and actively engages vulnerable and overburdened communities so they can meaningfully participate and have their issues addressed during recovery operations and planning.

U.S. Executive Office of the President

Has certain powers available that can be exercised in the event that the nation is threatened by crisis, exigency, or emergency circumstances.

U.S. Government Accountability Office (GAO)

Conducts studies relevant to humanitarian emergencies and responses.

Office of the Director of National Intelligence (DNI)

Leads the national intelligence community in intelligence integration.

Source: Created by Author

States have traditionally been a key figure in preparing for, responding to, and recovering from humanitarian emergencies (Sunshine et al. 2019). And as the frequency and intensity of disasters increased and while in the midst of the COVID-19 pandemic, states are being increasingly asked to step up to lead the response on the majority of smaller disaster events as federal resources are stretched. States help review and evaluate the local situation and determine if the situation is beyond the capability of the state. If so, the state can proclaim a state of emergency and request federal assistance. States can also ask other states for help. Local governments and U.S. territories usually provide the initial or "first provider" emergency response and help coordinate responses with public and private organizations. Most often local governments and U.S. territories lead response efforts with federal funding support, not necessarily FEMA physical presence. Local governments keep the state government abreast of the emergency and seek state and federal aid based on need and can proclaim a local state of emergency. At and between the national, tribal, territorial, state, and local levels, the authority and powers vary depending on the type of emergency declaration.

In addition, the private sector, nongovernment organizations including faith-based organizations and food banks, as well as citizens each play invaluable roles in our Nation's response to humanitarian emergencies. Community-based organizations are instrumental front-line workers that help prepare communities for humanitarian emergencies and help connect residents with resources, through Internet access, translation services, and other forms of technical assistance. Without question, a critical ingredient to our national response to humanitarian emergencies is emergency response and recovery workers. Whether professional staff or volunteers, efforts must be made before, during and after response and recovery efforts to ensure the safety of first responders and essential emergency response team members. The hazards they encounter include biological, behavioral health, chemical, ergonomic, physical, psychological, and radiological. And last but not least, individuals and families are the foundation to effective disaster response—in protecting themselves, their immediate and extended families, and their neighbors. Therefore, proper training and guidance is essential to ensuring all stakeholders are maximized before, during, and after response and recovery efforts.

HOW HAS NUTRITION BEEN ADDRESSED DURING AND AFTER A HUMANITARIAN EMERGENCY?

This section explains the key historical and contemporary policy and programmatic approaches relevant to food, nutrition, and health at the federal, tribal, territorial, state, and local levels that key stakeholders take during humanitarian emergencies and other emerging disruptions, including the current COVID-19 pandemic. This historical perspective helps demonstrate where and how changes have been made to not just provide food during emergencies but adequate nutritious foods and beverages for increasingly prolonged periods. In addition, this section examines the various past, present, and future logistical facilitators and barriers to effectively and efficiently ensuring food and nutrition assistance before, during, and after humanitarian crises and other emerging disruptions including the current COVID-19 pandemic.

ABOUT FEDERAL FOOD AND
NUTRITION ASSISTANCE

The U.S. Department of Agriculture (USDA) Food and Nutrition Service (FNS) administers a suite of fifteen programs; all of which have made adaptations to help Americans before, during, and after humanitarian emergencies (Fleischhacker, Parks, and Yaroch 2019). The key programs, which we will discuss now further in detail, include the Emergency Food Assistance Program (TEFAP) in conjunction with USDA Foods and the Supplemental Nutrition Assistance Program (SNAP), including Disaster SNAP (D-SNAP) and the Nutrition Assistance Program (NAP) (Abernathy 2015).

While not discussed in detail in this chapter, during disasters and especially during the COVID-19 pandemic, significant adaptations occurred within school and childcare based programs; specifically the USDA National School Lunch and Breakfast Programs (NSLP and SBP), Summer Food Service Program (SFSP)/Summer Seamless Option (SSO), and the Child and Adult Care Food Program (CACFP) (Dunn, Kenney, Fleischhacker et al. 2020; Kinsey et al. 2020). These adaptations have historically and contemporarily focused on easing administrative rules so that children and adolescents attending schools in affected areas can all receive free meals, despite traditional eligibility requirements, and also allow meal pattern flexibilities, recognizing fluctuations in a disrupted food supply and using USDA Foods at school sites may have been used in the immediate aftermath of the disaster. Within the USDA Special Supplemental Program for Women, Infant, and Children (WIC), administrative flexibilities are provided to participants and authorized retailers, with a particular emphasis on ensuring continued breastfeeding is supported and infant formula supplies are readily available (Dunn, Kenney, Bleich et al. 2020). During the COVID-19 pandemic, as one example, Congress appropriated $500 million for fiscal year 2020 to support anticipated increases in WIC enrollment, common and critical during economic depressions and also authorized the USDA to waive WIC regulatory requirements at a state's request, including the physical presence requirement and WIC Food Package substitutions. The CDC provides guidance regarding proper storage of breast milk and ready-to-use infant formula (CDC 2020). Within the U.S. Department of Health and Human Services, Meals on Wheels has made and is making significant adaptations during the COVID-19 pandemic to provide nutritious, safe meals to eligible, elder Americans.

THE EMERGENCY FOOD ASSISTANCE PROGRAM (TEFAP)

TEFAP has been instrumental in disaster relief efforts by providing commodities and administrative funds to states to operate this program (P.L. 98–8) (CRS 2018). The Hunger Prevention Act of 1988 (P.L. 100–435) authorized funds to be appropriated and formally named under the 1990 Farm Bill (P.L. 101–624). The Food and Nutrition Act of 2008 (P.L. 113–79) provides mandatory funding for the program's entitlement commodities and the 2018 Farm Bill 2018 (P.L. 115–334) reauthorized mandatory food purchases and reauthorizes discretionary storage and distribution grants. In the immediate aftermath of a presidentially declared disaster, affected states can request TEFAP and distribute USDA Foods from nonemergency programs such as the USDA National School Lunch and School Breakfast Programs (NSLP, SBP) to disaster relief agencies coordinating congregate, mass feeding sites free of charge, such the American Red Cross and the Salvation Army (USDA 2020b). These public or nonprofit organizations administer emergency feeding or other disaster relief programs, including food banks, food pantries, or soup kitchens. Under special circumstances, TEFAP and USDA Foods work with WIC Distribution Centers, among others, to ensure ample supplies of infant formula in disaster-affected areas, including forms that do not require water to be added. Household distribution can also be approved if the conditions allow for providing boxes directly to families. Usually, household distribution is approved until D-SNAP can be implemented (as detailed below). The USDA, among other federal departments and agencies, along with non-government organizational and academic partners are working to improve the nutrition quality of USDA Foods. These efforts complement ongoing efforts by Feeding America (a clearing house for national food donations since 1979 and the nation's largest domestic hunger-relief organization), among others, to improve the overall nutrition quality of foods at food banks, food pantries, and soup kitchens (Byker et al. 2019). There is also continued efforts to ensure food donations are not left rotting or in storage.

During the COVID-19 pandemic, TEFAP has been complemented by a USDA Agricultural Marketing Service program known as USDA Farmers to Families Food Box (USDA 2020a). This program has distributed more than 111 million food boxes since May 2020. The USDA is using its authority under the Families First Coronavirus Response Act (P.L. 116–127) to purchase and distribute agricultural products to those in need. AMS partners with national, regional, and local distributors to purchase fresh produce, dairy, and meat products from American producers of all sizes. The distributors pack family-sized boxes then transport them to food banks, community and faith-based organizations, and other nonprofit organizations serving Americans in need.

SUPPLEMENTAL NUTRITION ASSISTANCE PROGRAM (SNAP)

Formerly known as Food Stamps, SNAP is now an entitlement program and is the largest component of the Farm Bill and federal nutrition safety net, accounting for 68 percent of all federal food and nutrition assistance in fiscal year 2019 (Fleischhacker, Moran, and Bleich 2019). Close to forty million individuals and families, persons with disabilities, and elders participate in SNAP each month through electronic benefit transfer (EBT) accounts. Participants can use their EBT benefits at more than 240,000 authorized food retail outlets to purchase eligible foods and beverages. SNAP is structured in a way that allows for it to be used to provide the quick delivery of food and nutrition assistance to individuals and families affected by humanitarian emergencies. In addition, SNAP has increasingly become known as a recognized tool to stimulate the local economy. The USDA Economic Research Service (ERS) determined about $1 billion increase in SNAP benefits during an economic downturn increases the GDP by $1.54 billion, supports 13,560 new jobs, and creates $32 million in farm income. The USDA FNS also permits certain flexibilities to SNAP participants in disaster-affected areas. For example, FNS often approves a state request to allow for the purchase of hot foods with SNAP benefits as many participants are not able to store food or access cooking facilities during a disaster. The SNAP Restaurant Meals Program can be utilized in times of disaster or this current pandemic to help individuals and families who would benefit from prepared foods. During the COVID-19 pandemic, the Pandemic EBT (P-EBT) program is being used for the first time to distribute benefits to eligible SNAP families, along with eligible non-SNAP students to help families while students are not receiving school-based meals during school closures.

DISASTER SUPPLEMENTAL NUTRITION ASSISTANCE PROGRAM (D-SNAP)

Using SNAP or SNAP-like mechanisms, D-SNAP provides short-term federal food and nutrition assistance to income-eligible individuals and households with food loss or damage caused by natural disasters even if they would not normally qualify for SNAP (USDA 2020b). Congress granted the USDA this authority through section 5(f) of the Food and Nutrition Act of 2008 (P.L. 114–128), formerly the Food Stamp Act of 1977 (P.L. 95–113) and the Disaster Relief Act of 1974 (P.L. 93–288), as amended by the Stafford Disaster Relief and Assistance Act of 1988 (P.L. 100–707). D-SNAP is also used to help replace or supplement the SNAP benefits of persons who were receiving benefits when a disaster hit. That is, without a special act of Congress, FNS can approve automatic mass replacements of SNAP benefits to impacted households up to 50 percent of their monthly SNAP benefit. As one example, FNS approved California's request for certain counties and zip codes recently impacted by wildfires and power outrages that started on August 17, 2020. USDA can also approve state requests to change the distribution cycle for SNAP benefits. In addition, USDA can provide flexibilities for replacement benefits to help with reported food losses associated with a disaster. When seeking approval for D-SNAP, states and local administrators must demonstrate they have the administrative capacity in place to distribute these time-sensitive benefits. The timing and conditions of D-SNAP vary as each disaster is unique, but the program usually does not start until access to SNAP authorized retailers is restored and families are able to purchase and prepare foods at their own home. Usually, the benefits are for only one month but can be extended for an additional month depending on the circumstances. A recent lawsuit, *Miami Workers Center et al. v. Carroll, et al.* (1:17-cv-24047), helped secure the ability of SNAP participants with disabilities to enroll in D-SNAP via phone interviews instead of the required in-person interview.

NUTRITION ASSISTANCE PROGRAM (NAP)

Similar but significantly different, NAP provides federal food and nutrition assistance via capped, block grants—not through an entitlement program—to individuals and families living in certain U.S. territories, specifically, Puerto Rico, American Samoa, and the Commonwealth of the Northern Marian Islands (P.L. 97–35). NAP benefits generally provide less benefits than SNAP benefits. Another issue during disasters is D-SNAP is not an option under NAP, hindering the ability of these three U.S. territories in hurricane-prone areas to rapidly respond to address food insecurity during times of disaster. These two limitations were amplified during the recent lengthy power and water outages, along with Internet connectivity challenges experienced by Puerto Rico during Hurricanes Irma and Maria. NAP participants faced disrupted EBT operation, as well as inability to cook or store foods and beverages. Lack of safe water also hindered cooking and formula preparations.

The Food, Conservation, and Energy Act of 2008 (P.L. 110–246) required the Secretary of Agriculture to conduct a study of the feasibility and effects of including Puerto Rico as a "State" under Section 3 of the Food and Nutrition Act of 2008 (P.L. 110–246), instead of providing funding through the block grant. The 2010 feasibility study outlined a variety of policy decisions that would need to be made before implementing SNAP in Puerto Rico. The feasibility study also explained how SNAP would provide greater monthly food allotments to a wider net of eligible individuals and households and provide the flexibility necessary for Puerto Rico to be more responsive during natural disasters such as its regular and increasing hurricane seasons. Legislation (S.677) has been introduced in the 116th session (2019–2020) to enable Puerto Rico and other U.S. territories to participate in SNAP. There is also a legal battle underway regarding the lower federal benefits given to Puerto Rico compared to similarly situated and equally need U.S. citizens (*Martinez v. Azar, 376 F. Supp. 3d 191* (D.P.R. 2019)). Supplemental Congressional appropriations help but fail to provide the significant infrastructure investments nor SNAP change needed to better address food insecurity in Puerto Rico, among other U.S. territories. USDA implemented some temporary measures including a policy that allows displaced Puerto Ricans to apply for SNAP in areas they are currently residing and approved a waiver for NAP to temporarily allow purchase of ready-to-eat meals.

OTHER SOCIAL ASSISTANCE

Other critical resources available before, during, and after a humanitarian emergency including: FEMA benefits, Disaster Unemployment Assistance, Temporary Assistance for Needy Families (TANF), Medicaid, Fannie Mae and Freddie MAC, Community Development Block Grants for Disaster Recovery (CDBG-DR) and Mitigation (CDBG-MIT), tax relief, legal assistance, federal grants to help with transitioning educational learning to virtual options, among others (CRS 2020a).

KEY PRIORITIES FOR ADDRESSING NUTRITION DURING AND AFTER A HUMANITARIAN EMERGENCY

Public health and public administration professionals play integral roles in humanitarian response and recovery efforts, including preparing for, executing in real-time, and evaluating for lessons learned (TFAH 2020). Training for our next generation and current professionals how best to address nutrition during and after a humanitarian emergency is essential (Leaning and Guha-Sapri 2013).

First and foremost, public health and public administration professionals must understand the law and policy levers governing disaster response and recovery within and between national, tribal, territorial, state, and local levels and with nongovernment, academic, private, and community sectors. This includes understanding the role and intersections of the more than seventeen federal department and agencies involved in disaster response. Mastery of this information should hopefully inspire efforts to re-envision a more robust disaster relief system and instill the importance of advocating for more comprehensive, whole-of-community approaches at and between the federal, tribal, territorial, state, and local levels.

A critical piece of reconceptualizing our nation's disaster relief response is for public health and public administration professionals to help ensure more proactive, comprehensive planning occurs in coordination with key sectors using an equity lens (Jacobs 2019). A recent reflection piece on fifteen years post-Katrina New Orleans discussed how innovative but evolving approaches have been used to address food inequalities long documented within communities of Color (Rose and O'Malley 2020). We must better acknowledge and meaningfully act on the fact that proper nutrition during these times of crisis demand more prolonged approaches and necessitates more multidisciplinary treatment and prevention strategies to strengthen the resilience of our most vulnerable groups. Moreover, investing in monitoring and surveillance, along with real-time research and evaluation can help ensure we are developing and scaling up evidence-based disaster preparedness, response, and recovery approaches (Altare and Guha-Sapir 2014; NASEM 2019; Kishore et al. 2018).

Another component to addressing nutrition during and after humanitarian emergencies is better understanding how to effectively address climate change (TFAH 2019; Biehl et al. 2018). That is, public health and public administration professionals must help increase our nation's investments in developing and scaling up resilient food systems at the local, state, territorial, tribal, regional, national, and global levels. We also need better coordination across the food system and with disaster management systems to improve our short- and long-term response and recovery approaches. Existing disaster-related programs, flexibilities, and waivers have been successful, but there are also several, significant shortcomings. We quite frankly have too many recurring and systemic problems with our disaster responses with root causes in poverty. Our current disaster responses also lack the use of contextually and culturally relevant approaches to lift up our most vulnerable populations during these challenging conditions. We must recognize food and nutrition assistance approaches need to factor in that it takes weeks if not years to recover from a humanitarian emergency and most of our Americans are not currently healthy and are managing one if not multiple chronic diseases.

Efforts to streamline and improve coordination are critical. A recent paper put forth as one option a new Office of the National Director of Food and Nutrition (ODNFN) (Fleischhacker et al. 2020). Modeled after the Office of the Director of National Intelligence (ODNI) that was established after 9/11 terrorist attacks, the ODNFN would provide essential coordination and harmonization of the work of the more than ten U.S. departments and agencies comprising the federal nutrition community. This includes prioritizing translation and research needs for our federal nutrition assistance programs and better connecting our diet-related health disparities research needs with our food system investments. COVID-19 mortality disparities and food supply disruptions illustrated the importance of investing in our nation's food systems from farm to fork, particularly from our most vulnerable populations.

While the federal government plays a key role in humanitarian emergencies in this nation, the primary first responder is generally tribal, territorial, state, and local governments. Public health and public administration professionals must learn how best to work in and between these various governmental levels. The nongovernment and private sectors also have invaluable roles before, during, and after humanitarian emergencies. Better multisectoral coordination and joint trainings would help ensure effective mobilization and understanding of each sector's roles and responsibilities. And finally, individual and family roles are essential, along with communications that are effective at reaching *all* citizens (Checchi et al. 2017). Therefore, public health and public administration professionals must be trained and continually practice strategies to ensure collaboration, engagement, inclusion, and representation.

CONCLUSION

Humanitarian emergencies are happening and will continue to happen in the near- and long-term future with significant implications on food insecurity. Preparation is key. Public health and public administration professionals should seek to work on and *with* more proactive, interdepartmental, and multijurisdictional, community-engaged work to ensure future preparations and responses are better coordinated and more comprehensive, particularly for our most vulnerable populations. The *Administering and Managing the U.S. Food System: Revisiting Food Policy and Politics* volume provides a critical call for action to better address the intersections between food and public administration, with feasible recommendations to move forward in research, policy, and practice. A fundamental aspect of this call must include a specific emphasis on disaster response and recovery, along with food system resilience planning. More work remains by public administration scholars and practitioners to analyze historical and contemporary food systems intersections with public administration before, during and after humanitarian emergencies. Without question, we need a research agenda that includes public administration perspectives on how to better build the evidence base for contextually and culturally approach strategies to address food *and* nutrition insecurity before, during, and after humanitarian emergencies.

REFERENCES

Abernathy, T. 2015. "Responsibilities of the USDA-Food and Nutrition Service in Nutrition Assistance Response to Natural Disasters." *Journal of Nutritional Science and Vitaminology (Tokyo)* 61 (S14):doi: 10.3177/jnsv.61.S14.

Altare, C, and D Guha-Sapir. 2014. "The complex emergency database: A global repository of small-scale surveys on nutrition, health and mortality." *PLoS One* 9 (10):1–7.

Balhara, KS, DM Silvestri, WT Winders, A Selvam, SM Kivlehan, TK Becker, AC Levine, and Global Emergency Medicine Literature Review Group. 2017. "Impact of nutrition interventions on pediatric mortality and nutrition outcomes in humanitarian emergencies: A systematic review." *Tropical Medicine & International Health* 22 (12):1464–1492.

Berkowitz, SA, S Basu, JB Mejgs, and H Seligman. 2018. "Food insecurity and health care expenditures in the United States, 2011–2013." *Health Services Research* 53 (3):1600–1620.

Biehl, E, S Buzogany, K Baja, and RA Neff. 2018. "Planning for a resilient urban food system: A case study from Baltimore City, Maryland." *Journal of Agriculture, Food Systems, and Community Development* 8 (Suppl 2):39–53.

Bleich S, Dunn C, Fleischhacker S. "The Impact of Increasing SNAP Benefits on Stabilizing the Economy, Reducing Poverty and Food Insecurity amid COVID-19 Pandemic." Durham, NC: Healthy Eating Research; 2020. Available at: http://healthyeatingresearch.org (last visited September 18, 2020).

Byker, SC, E Weinmann, J Holder, M McCormick, CA Parks, K Vanderwood, C Coburn, N Johnson, and AL Yaroch. 2019. "The unprocessed pantry project framework to address nutrition in the emergency food system." *American Journal of Public Health* 109 (10):1368–1370.

Canning P & Stacy B. "The United States Department of Agriculture Economic Research Service. The Supplemental Nutrition Assistance Program (SNAP) and the Economy: New Estimates of the SNAP Multiplier." July 2019. Available at https://www.ers.usda.gov/webdocs/publications/93529/err265_summary.pdf?v=8010.7 (last visited September 17, 2020).

Checchi, F, A Warsame, V Treacy-Wong, J Polonsky, M van Ommeren, and C Prudhon. 2017. "Public health information in crisis-affected populations: a review of methods and their use for advocacy and action." *The Lancet* 390 (10109):2297–2313.

Coleman-Jensen A, et al. "U.S. Department of Agriculture Economic Research Service and Food and Nutrition Service." *Household Food Security in the United States in 2017*, ERR-256 (2018). Available at https://www.ers.usda.gov/webdocs/publications/90023/err-256.pdf?v=0 (last visited May 1, 2019).

Coleman-Jensen, A, MP Rabbitt, CA Gregory, and A Singh. 2020. "The United States Department of Agriculture Economic Research Service. Household Food Security in the United States in 2019. ERR-270." Available at https://www.ers.usda.gov/publications/pub-details/?pubid=99281 (last visited October 17, 2020).

CRS. 2018. "Congressional Research Service. The Emergency Food Assistance Program (TEFAP): Background and Funding." November 19. 2018. Available at https://fas.org/sgp/crs/misc/R45408.pdf (last visited October 17, 2020).

CRS. 2020a. "Congressional Research Service. 2020 Hurricane Season FAQ: Federal Disaster Assistance for Hurricanes During COVID-19 Pandemic." June 1, 2020. Available at https://crsreports.congress.gov/product/pdf/R/R46385 (last visited October 17, 2020).

CRS. 2020b. "Congressional Research Service. Emergency Authorities Under the National Emergencies Act, Stafford Act, and Public Health Service Act." Updated July 14, 2020. Available at https://crsreports.congress.gov/product/pdf/R/R46379 (last visited October 17, 2020).

DHS. 2019. "The United States Department of Homeland Security. National Response Framework." Fourth Edition. October 28, 2019. Available at https://www.fema.gov/emergency-managers/national-preparedness/frameworks/response (last visited October 17, 2020).

Dube, A, M Moffatt, C Davison, and S Bartels. 2018. "Health outcomes for children in Haiti since the 2010 earthquake: a systematic review." *Prehospital and Disaster Medicine* 33 (1):77–88.

Dunn, C, E Kenney, S Bleich, and S Fleischhacker. 2020. "Strengthening WIC's Impact During and After the COVID-19 Pandemic." Durham, NC: Healthy Eating Research; 2020. Available at: http://healthyeatingresearch.org (last visited September 17, 2020).

Dunn, CG, E Kenney, SE Fleischhacker, and SN Bleich. 2020. "Feeding low-income children during the Covid-19 pandemic." *The New England Journal of Medicine* DOI: 10.1056/NEJMp2005638.

"Federal Emergency Management Agency. National Preparedness Goal." Available at https://www.fema.gov/emergency-managers/national-preparedness/goal (last visited August 28, 2020).

"Federal Emergency Management Agency. National Preparedness System." Available at https://www.fema.gov/emergency-managers/national-preparedness/system (last visited August 28, 2020).

Fleischhacker, S, A Moran, and SN Bleich. 2019. "Legislative and executive branch developments affecting the United States Department of Agriculture Supplemental Nutrition Assistance Program." *Journal of Food Law & Policy* 15 (1):5.

Fleischhacker, S, CA Parks, and AL Yaroch. 2019. "Addressing food insecurity in the United States: The role of policy, systems changes, and environmental supports." *Translational Behavioral Medicine* 9 (5):827–836.

Fleischhacker, SE, CE Woteki, PM Coates, VS Hubbard, GE Flaherty, DR Glickman, TR Harkin, D Kessler, WW Li, J Loscalzo, A Parekh, S Rowe, PJ Stover, A Tagtow, A Joon Yun, and D Mozaffarian. 2020. "Strengthening national nutrition research: rationale and options for a new coordinated federal research effort and authority." *The American Journal of Clinical Nutrition* 112:721–769.

GAO. 2008. "The United States Government Accountability Office. Actions Taken to Implement the Post-Katrina Emergency Management Reform Act of 2006." November 21, 2008. Available at https://www.gao.gov/products/GAO-09-59R (last visited October 17, 2020).

Golem, DL, and C Byrd-Bredbenner. 2015. "Emergency Food Supplies in Food Secure Households." *Prehospital and Disaster Medicine* 30 (4):1–6.

HumanitarianCoalition. 2020. "What is a humanitarian emergency?"

ICRC. 2008. "International Committee of the Red Cross. How is the Term "Armed Conflict" Defined in International Humanitarian Law? Opinion Paper, March 2008. Available at https://www.icrc.org/en/doc/resources/documents/article/other/armed-conflict-article-170308.htm (last visited October 17, 2020).

"International Committee of the Red Cross. How is the term 'armed conflict' defined in international humanitarian law?" March 17, 2008. Available at https://www.icrc.org/en/doc/resources/documents/article/other/armed-conflict-article-170308.htm (last visited September 16, 2020).

Jacobs, F. 2019. "Black feminism and radical planning: New directions for disaster planning research." *Planning Theory* 18 (1):24–39.

Kinsey, EW, AA Hecht, CG Dunn, R Levi, MA Read, C Smith, P Niesen, HK Seligman, and ER Hager. 2020. "School closures during COVID-19: Opportunities for innovation in meal service." *American Journal of Public Health* 17:e1–e9.

Kishore, N, D Marques, A Mahmud, MV Kiang, I Rodriguez, A Fuller, P Ebner, C Sorensen, F Racy, J Lemery, L Maas, J Leaning, RA Irizarry, S Balsari, and CO Buckee. 2018. "Mortality in Puerto Rico after Hurricane Maria." *The New England Journal of Medicine* 379 (2):162–170.

Leaning, J, and D Guha-Sapri. 2013. "Natural disasters, armed conflict, and public health." *The New England Journal of Medicine* 369:1836–1842.

Moss, WJ, M Ramakrishnan, D Storms, AH Siegle, WM Weiss, I Lejnev, and L Muhe. 2006. "Child health in complex emergencies." *Bulletin of the World Health Organization* 84:58–64.

NASEM. 2019. "National Academies of Sciences, Engineering, and Medicine 2019. Methodologies for Evaluating and Grading Evidence: Considerations for Public Health Emergency Preparedness and Response: Proceedings of a Workshop in Brief." Washington, DC: The National Academies Press. Available

at https://www.nap.edu/catalog/25510/methodologies-for-evaluating-and-gra
ding-evidence-considerations-for-public-health (last visited October 17, 2020).

"National Response Framework." Fourth Edition. October 28, 2019. Available at
https://www.fema.gov/sites/default/files/2020–04/NRF_FINALApproved_2011
028.pdf (last visited September 1, 2020).

Odjida, EN, and S Hakizimana. 2019. "Data on acute malnutrition and mortality
among under-5 children of pastoralists in a humanitarian setting: a cross-sectional
Standardized Monitoring and Assessment of Relief and Transitions Study." *BMC
Research Notes* 12 (1):434.

Peterson, A, Johnson, B, Moulton, BE, Smith, EO, Suchman, A, Wilson, C,
Francisquini, S, Kauff, J, Ladinsky, J, & Castner, L. "Implementing SNAP in Puerto
Rico: A Feasibility Study." Prepared by Insight Policy Research under Contract
No. AG-3198-C-09–0001. 2010. Alexandria, VA: United States Department of
Agriculture, Food and Nutrition Service. Available at https://fns-prod.azureedge
.net/sites/default/files/PuertoRico.pdf (last visited September 17, 2020).

Rose, C, and DeSmogBlog. 2014. "Weather-related disasters rise five-fold from
1970s to 2000s." Ecologist. August 19, 2014. Available at https://theecologist
.org/2014/aug/19/weather-related-disasters-rise-five-fold-1970s-2000s (Last visited October 17, 2020).

Rose, D, and K O'Malley. 2020. "Food Access 3.0: Insights from post-Katrina New
Orleans on an evolving approach to food inequities." *American Journal of Public
Health* 110 (10):1495–1497.

Seligman, HK, BA Laraia, and MB Kushel. 2010. "Food insecurity is associated with
chronic disease among low-income NHANES participants." *Journal of Nutrition*
140 (2):304–310.

Seligman, HK, and D Schillinger. 2010. "Hunger and socioeconomic disparities in
chronic disease." *The New England Journal of Medicine* 363 (1):6–9.

Sunshine, G, K Thompson, AN Menon, N Anderson, M Penn, and LM Koonin. 2019.
"An assessment of state laws providing gubernatorial authority to remove legal
barriers to emergency response." *Health Security* 17 (2):156–161.

TFAH. 2019. "Trust for America's Health. Issue Report. Ready or Not: Protecting
the Public's Health from Diseases, Disasters, and Bioterrorism." February 2019.
Available at https://www.tfah.org/report-details/readyornot2020/ (last visited
October 17, 2020).

TFAH. 2020. "Trust for America's Health. Issue Report. A Blueprint for the 2021
Administration and Congress. The Promise of Good Health for All: Transforming
Public Health in America." October 2020. Available at https://www.tfah.org/repo
rt-details/blueprint2021/ (last visited October 17, 2020).

Tsuboyama-Kasaoka, N, and M Br Purba. 2014. "Nutrition and earthquakes:
experience and recommendations." *Asia-Pacific Journal of Public Health* 23
(4):505–513.

"United States Department of Agriculture Agricultural Marketing Service. USDA
Farmers to Families Fox Box." Available at https://www.ams.usda.gov/selling-fo
od-to-usda/farmers-to-families-food-box (last visited September 20, 2020).

"The United States Department of Health and Human Services. Press Release: HHS Announces Grants to Provide Meals for Older Adults." March 24, 2020. Available at https://www.hhs.gov/about/news/2020/03/24/hhs-announces-grants-to-provide-meals-for-older-adults.html (last visited September 20, 2020).

"United States Department of Homeland Security Federal Emergency Management Agency. Community Lifelines Implementation Toolkit." Available at https://www.fema.gov/emergency-managers/practitioners/lifelines-toolkit (last visited October 17, 2020).

"US Department of Homeland Security Federal Emergency Management Agency. The Stafford Act: Robert T. Stafford Disaster Relief and Emergency Assistance Act, as Amended." April 2013.

USDA. 2020a. "The United States Department of Agriculture Agricultural Marketing Service. USDA Farmers to Families Food Box." Available at https://www.ams.usda.gov/selling-food-to-usda/farmers-to-families-food-box (last visited October 17, 2020).

USDA. 2020b. "The United States Department of Agriculture Food and Nutrition Service. TEFAP Fact Sheet. What is The Emergency Food Assistance Program?" Available at https://www.fns.usda.gov/tefap/tefap-fact-sheet (last visited September 18, 2020).

"Wolkin A, CDC's Office of Public Health Preparedness and Response. Mission Possible: Preparing and Responding to Disasters through a Health Equity Lens." Available at https://blogs.cdc.gov/healthequity/2018/09/06/disasters/ (last visited September 19, 2020).

Chapter 14

Food Insecurity and an Economic Crisis

The Case of Omaha, Nebraska, during the Coronavirus Shutdowns

Emily MacNabb and B. J. Fletcher

INTRODUCTION

In March 2020, the United States began economic shutdowns in order to attempt to prevent, or at least slow the spread of the Coronavirus. This research looks not at the COVID-19 as the disaster under question, but at the closures. While the true tolls of these closures will not be fully understood for some time, at the time of this research the global pandemic is still raging, it is the intent to tell the story of the experiences of those in the Midwestern City of Omaha, Nebraska, and how these closures impacted the ability to access and obtain food. This research combines two lines of research, disaster research and food security in order to tell this story through a qualitative content analysis of fifty Omaha World Herald articles published between March and July 2020.

This research begins with brief reviews of the relevant disaster and food security literature, in which the two lines of research are examined. Next, the case itself and data collection methodology of qualitative content analysis is explored. The results section details findings from the qualitative content analysis, followed by the discussion and conclusion. Three main conclusions emerge from the findings in this research. First, the unique social dynamics of the economic closure in Omaha redefined the traditionally drawn parameters of what it means to be vulnerable to disaster or crisis. Second, there exists a substantial lack of preparedness on the part of organizations, spanning all sectors whose mission is to provide meals to food insecure individuals and families. In a short amount of time, in these organizations there was a large decrease in private donations and a spike in need of their services throughout the area. Lastly, the importance of the nonprofit and public sectors in address-ing the food insecurity caused by the closures cannot be understated. Due to the nature of the economic crisis, the private sector was crippled. Food insecurity in Omaha, Nebraska, was only managed by key alliances between organizations from all sectors, providing anecdotal evidence of the impor-tance of cross-sector collaborations in crisis response to food insecurity.

LITERATURE REVIEW

Defining Disasters and Crises: Finding a Place in the Literature for the Economic Disruption Caused by the Response to the Coronavirus

There are many ways to understand disaster events. While debates exist in defining what qualifies as an event to be studied in the discipline of Disaster Science and Emergency Management, there are some general points of con-sensus. These are "requirements" that must be present during an event to for the event to be considered a true disaster, and not an emergency (Quarantelli, 1985; Perry, 2007). First, the event itself must impact people, second, the must be a disruption of normal social activities of the community, and finally, the community itself and its leadership are overwhelmed, meaning that they cannot absorb and manage the event impacts, thus requiring outside aid to effectively respond and recover (Quarantelli, 2005).

It is important to note these three points do not specify a disaster caus-ing agents, only the social impacts. This leaves those that empirically study disaster events with a wide range of discretion. While some disaster and emergency management researchers concentrate on more traditionally exam-ined events such as flooding, other scholars have added nuance to the field by also including inquiry over political upheaval, this line of research is Crisis Research (Boin and Hart, 2007). Crisis Research was first published by European political scientists after the fall of the Soviet Union. Key findings from this body research acknowledge that a political crisis may also be con-sidered a disaster-like event according to the three main judging criteria, pre-fer the term "crisis" to describe these types of events (Boin and Hart, 2007). Specifically, a crisis is defined as when a community collectively perceives a threat to their values, institutions, and overall functionality, a crisis must-have elements of urgency, threat, and uncertainty (Boin and Hart, 2007). Events examined by crisis research scholars are typically those associated with political leadership and sporadic upheaval, including economic crises (Bont, Kofman-Bos, and Overdijk, 2004). While crises differ from true "disasters," one can argue that crises may cause the same social upheaval.

The economic fallout from the 2020 Coronavirus meets the three requirements of disasters: impact of people, a disruption of the normal social activities of the community, and the overwhelming of communities and their leadership, meaning that they cannot absorb and manage the event impacts, thus requiring outside aid to effectively respond and recover. Thus, while the disaster "agent" was not a traditionally examined type, the economic fallout from the closures, according to the standards set by both traditional disaster research and the newer politically and economically focused crisis research, the events beginning in March 2020 undertaken to slow the spread of COVID-19 belong in the greater disaster and emergency management literature.

Vulnerability Theory and Social Vulnerability

Vulnerability theory is the informing theory of the research into the impacts of the spring 2020 shutdowns on a local community's food security. This is a foundational theory in the study of disasters, crises, and emergencies. Vulnerability theory focuses on the societal dynamics within a community that produce disparities between social groups. It works from the assumption that disasters of all types are not merely "acts of god," that disasters are not leveling events that affect all people equally. Instead, "disasters" are events that manifest due to the actions, histories, and social dynamics within communities (Peek and Stough, 2006). According to vulnerability theory, due to the highly complicated dynamics that exist in all societies, some social groups are more likely to experience more severe impacts than others (Phillips et al., 2012). The social context of a community is key in predicting and understanding how various groups within that community will fare in the aftermath of an event. The way in which a society is socially constructed will make some more vulnerable to a disasters and crises than others, thus making them "socially vulnerable" (Peek and Stough, 2006; Phillips et al., 2012). The social marginalization within communities of certain populations impacts their socially constructed realities. These realities include higher rates of poverty, lack of affordable and safe housing, lack of access to high-quality employment, and more (Peek and Stough, 2006; Phillips et al., 2012; Phillips, 2015). Social vulnerability can thus be applied in diverse ways, with greater understanding emerging in the literature regarding food security concerns in the disaster science and emergency management literature (MacNabb and Fletcher, 2019). The everyday challenges of socially vulnerable peoples, such as the ability to access healthy foods, are now being understood in the context of disasters.

Food Security

Food security was first introduced in 1996 during the World Food Summit (McMichael, 2014). To achieve food security, "all people, at all times, have physical and economic access to sufficient safe and nutritious food that meets their dietary needs and food preferences for an active and healthy life" (Timmer, 2012, p. 12,315). Based on this goal, three dimensions exist to achieve food security. These include availability, access, and utilization. There needs to be "availability of sufficient quantities of food or appropriate quality, supplied through domestic production or imports; access by households and individuals to adequate resources to acquire appropriate food for a nutritious diet; and utilization of food through adequate diet, water, sanitation, and health care" (Timmer, 2012, p. 12,315).

Addressing the three dimensions of food security is vital to reducing food insecurity among vulnerable populations during a pandemic. These dimensions of food security fit into the field of the social determinants of health. Social determinants of health focus on aspects of individuals' living and working circumstances in relation to their lifestyles (Wilkinson and Marmont, 2003), a pandemic can impact an individuals' lifestyles. The social determinants of health are "factors that influence one's health status" (Shi, 2014, p. 9); typically, individuals' socioeconomic status, environment, behavior, heredity, and access to health care (Shi, 2014). Understanding the social determinants of health can help to provide a contextual understanding of the health implications of economic and social policies, during the time of a pandemic. Among the social determinants, nutrition plays a vital role in addressing an individual's overall health. Given this state, food insecurity is often associated with poor health and, to some degree, covertly exacerbates other health inequalities (McIntyre, 2003; Nolan et al., 2006; Wicks, Trevena, Quine, 2006) which, can be particularly challenging during a pandemic do to lose of employment and limited availability and access to needed resources.

Food security is often conceptualized as being structured on the three fundamental concepts of availability, access, and utilization. These three areas are foundationally hierarchical, availability is necessary, but not sufficient, to ensure access, access being necessary but not sufficient for utilization (Barrett, 2010). These areas can be thought of as the basic requirements for food security. Access can be associated with an individual or household well-being. Access accounts for a range of food choices individual(s) have based on income, prevailing prices, and both the formal and informal safety net arrangements to food. Access reflects the demand-side of food security (Barrett, 2010). In addition, access accounts for potential sociocultural limits on the foods that are consistently available based on the prevailing tastes and values within a community. Utilization reflects concerns about the extent to which individuals and households can make use of the food they are able to access (Barrett, 2010). These three concepts tie directly into the highly complicated dynamics that exist in all societies, which case some social groups to experience more severe impacts of disasters than others. All of which play an important role in addressing food security, a pandemic and exacerbate these dynamics and experiences of individuals in various social groups.

These concepts are important during a pandemic, which has had an effect at all levels of the food system. From a policy standpoint, food security, presents an interesting conundrum, especially during a pandemic. Steady progress has been made starting in the middle of the twentieth century in reducing the hundreds of millions of people experiencing poverty and hunger, measured by these aspects of food security however, the 2020 pandemic disrupted this progress and has shown to a large extent food security strategies and policies are in disorder. There seems to be a disconnect between what most countries say about their strategies and policies to address food security and the actions they take. There is a lack of coherent strategies for improving food security. It is unclear if strategies focus on income assistance programs, nutrition assistance programs, or a combination of these two aspects. A lack of coherent strategy often stems from a breakdown between the interconnected role markets and government policies play in providing sustainable food security measured by the fundamental aspects of food security (Timmer, 2012; Timmer, 2015). A pandemic can highlight a lack of coherent strategy.

METHODOLOGY

The Case: An Economic Crisis in a Local Community Caused by Response to a Global Pandemic

At the beginning of 2020, cases of the novel coronavirus (COVID-19) began emerging globally. Within weeks, cases began to spread throughout the world at rapid rates. As cases of this highly infectious virus continued to increase due to international travel and lack of knowledge pertaining to the nature of the virus itself, the World Health Organization moved to declare a pandemic. The pandemic quickly threatened the lives and livelihood of people throughout the world.

Facing these threats, countries were forced to weigh economic costs against the lives of their citizens. This dynamic put already vulnerable populations in even more precarious positions as shutdowns became inevitable to contain the spread. Vulnerable populations at the highest risk for serious illness from contracting COVID-19 include seniors, people with chronic illness, and people of color. However, as the economic closures of communities throughout the United States begin to take place in March 2020, the virus itself is no longer the only threat many would face. Businesses, schools, organizations, and more, would be forced to close down as people engaged in social distancing as widespread initiatives would be undertaken. Unemployment rates skyrocketed as many who had never faced such challenges found themselves out of work as the population of those in need grew. As a part of the economic challenges associated with the pandemic and closures, food insecurity among vulnerable populations increased along with populations not traditionally perceived as vulnerable or at risk of experiencing food insecurity.

Households experiencing food insecurity, lack access to adequate food for an active, healthy lifestyle for all individuals in the household. Prior to the COVID-19 pandemic, more than 37 million individuals, including more than 11 million children in the United States were considered food insecure (Hake et al., 2020). These rates indicate that food insecurity has reached lowest levels since before the Great Recession (Coleman-Jensen et al., 2019), the current pandemic is likely to lead to a decrease in the improvements made to food insecurity rates over the past decade. There has been a substantial increase in unemployment and a spike in the demand for assistance at local food banks and pantries across the United States during the pandemic (Hake et al., 2020). The entirety of the toll that the economic crisis caused by the coronavirus will likely not be known for some time.

The pandemic has increased the demand for assistance at local food banks across the country (Stewart(a), 2020). Based on projected impacts of the coronavirus on food insecurity by Feeding America, in the case of the state of Nebraska, approximately 333,760 individuals will live in a food-insecure household due to the pandemic, this is up from a total of 68,890 individuals from the 2018 calculations (Gundersen et al., 2020). This is roughly a 41 percent change in the overall food insecurity rate between 2018 and 2020, with the contributing factor being the COVID-19 pandemic (Gundersen et al., 2020). One contributing factor is the impact to the economy: in particular, to the increase in unemployment during the pandemic. In Nebraska, the pandemic has led to a projected adjusted annual unemployment rate of 0.071, accounting for approximately 39 percent of the overall percentage change to food insecurity in the state due to the pandemic (Gundersen et al., 2020). With these changes to the rate of food insecurity, food banks have seen an increased strain to meet the new demand for assistance. Food banks and pantries will continue to play a vital role in addressing food insecurity. Yet, the food banks and pantries face challenges of having adequate supplies to meet the needs of individuals due to a decrease in donations during the pandemic (Stewart(b), 2020).

The numerical data alone does not tell the full story of the experiences of those most impacted in the local community of the greater Omaha area. It is also important to emphasize the story of the economic crisis from closures in Spring–Summer 2020 is one that at the time of this writing has yet to end. The entirety of the toll that this event would have on those most vulnerable, and even those of moderate vulnerability, has yet to be fully evaluated. However, it is the purpose of this qualitative research to use a strategic content analysis of the largest newspaper in the area to tell this story as it took place, in real time. What was the food security-related experience of the greater Omaha, Nebraska, area during the economic crisis caused by COVID-19?

Content Analysis of Omaha World Herald Articles between March and July 2020

A qualitative content analysis of fifty articles from the Omaha World Herald tells the story of the impact on food insecurity in the locality of the Omaha area caused by the economic closures in the greater Omaha area. In order to conduct a content analysis on text having been produced in time with the crisis itself, a newspaper was deemed the best source. The Omaha World Herald was chosen because it is the largest newspaper in the area. The time period between March and July of 2020 was chosen because the economic closures around the United States began in mid-March, and July was the latest full month to have passed at the time of this research.

To gather the articles used in this research, several searches were conducted on the Omaha World Herald website including the following search terms: COVID-19, corona, coronavirus, pandemic, economic, recession, food insecurity, food bank, food pantry, and response. This search generated hundreds of articles published between March and July. Articles not directly relating to the experience of food insecurity or that of the food supply chain in general were excluded. In total, fifty articles meet the criteria for inclusion.

Qualitative content analysis is the systematic summary of key codes and categories from large bodies of text (Bengtsson, 2016; Erlingsson and Brysiewicz, 2017; Graneheim, Lindgren, and Lundman, 2017). This method of data analysis is effective in not only establishing patterns and themes within the body of text but also in linking the text itself to the social context in which it was generated. There are two main types of content analysis, including manifest, coding for what is being said and latent, coding for what is actually being talked about. There are also inductive and deductive methods for coding. Inductive is searching for patterns as they come up in the text and deductive being the testing of already existing theory or patterns (Graneheim, Lindgren, and Lundman, 2017).

Manifest coding was the best fit for this research, meaning that the articles were coded directly for what was being reported. In addition, abductive coding process paired well with the manifest coding approach, meaning that the process was a combination of inductive and deductive. This was done to more adequately tell the story of food insecurity caused or exacerbated by the economic fallout from the response to the coronavirus pandemic. This process what completed independently by each of us, to insure a higher level

of inter-rater reliability. Based on the related coding and resulting triangula-
tion a total of nine thematic categories were produced from the data. These
categories are general food insecurity, children and food insecurity, private
sector response to food insecurity, public sector response to food insecurity,
nonprofit sector response to food insecurity, food banks and pantries, fear,
food supply chain, and food industry impacts. The results from the coding
process will be discussed in the next section, placing the raw data within the
social contexts in which it was created.

RESULTS

The coding process produced results following the timeline of food insecurity
in relation to the economic impacts of the coronavirus shutdowns. In a short
amount of time, the unemployment numbers in the nation grew dramatically
and not only were previously vulnerable food insecure persons struggling to
gain access to food but also those who had suddenly lost their jobs. The numbers of articles per month are as follows: March 17, April 16, May 12, June
3, and July 2. The numbers of articles per month matches with the timeline
of the economic shutdowns to slow the spread of Coronavirus in the United
States.

General Food Insecurity

The theme of general food insecurity included articles specifically discussing the concerns of food insecurity and access in Omaha, Nebraska, but not
directly mentioning children. Articles discussing the impacts on children
were coded in the next thematic category, children/schools and food insecurity. In total, twenty-two of the fifty articles were coded for discussing general
food insecurity.

The timeline for this code shows the greatest number of articles in the
months of March, April, and May. The articles told the story of the growing
concerns over the rise in unemployment from the end of March going into
April (Hilgenkamp, 2020). The experience of families unable to heed official
recommendations to purchase two weeks of food at a time due to loss of work
or living paycheck to paycheck was also reported in the early months of the
economic shutdowns (Collins, 2020).

Children/Schools and Food Insecurity

The theme of children and schools was originally just that of children
and food insecurity; however, a heavy emphasis in the articles regarding

school systems closing emerged, schools were directly represented in the title of this theme. This theme was discussed in seventeen out of the fifty articles, showing concern for the ability of children to gain access to food due to rapid school closures. This is unsurprising, considering there already exists a concern for feeding at risk children during the summer months when they normally will not have access to school breakfasts and lunches. The majority of the articles discussing children and schools were published in March at the very beginning of the economic shutdowns. This would seem to indicate an immediate concern on the part of the Omaha community over the school closures and the ability to not only provide much needed meals for students but to also intervene in neglectful or abusive situations where children would be isolated (Stewart(a), 2020).

Private Sector Response to Food Insecurity

Due to the nature of the forced economic shutdowns, the results from coding for private sector response to the growing food insecurity during the months following were of great interest. Would the private sector be capable of providing support to philanthropic services in their communities during desolate times as they normally would? If not, what kind of gap would this leave? Articles were only included in this category that discussed responses directly related to food insecurity, not responses to worker safety or forced closures. Of the fifty articles, nine of the articles discussed some type of private sector response to the food insecurity issue during the economic shutdowns. There are many examples of private businesses taking part in responding to the growth of food insecurity in the data, including an Omaha McDonalds donating thousands of dollars of hamburger patties to local food banks (Stewart(b), 2020) and Nebraska Beef donating a variety of proteins to Food Bank of the Heartland (Karst, 2020).

Nonprofit Sector Response to Food Insecurity (Excluding Food Banks)

This theme included discussion of nonprofit organizations responding to food insecurity, not including food banks or food pantries. A total fourteen of fifty of the articles were found to discuss these responses. There were many examples of nonprofit organizations traditionally not with food-oriented missions teaming up with local food banks and pantries in order to address this sudden need, such as diaper banks teaming up with food banks to provide meals to children (McCann, 2020).

Public Sector Response to Food Insecurity

A total twenty-three of the fifty articles discussed some type of public sector response to the growth of food insecurity during the economic shutdown of 2020. A key finding related to public response was the collaborations that took place between all three sectors. In many of the articles in which the government response was discussed, it was done so in the context of cross-sector collaborations. In other words, the issue of food insecurity was handled by a variety of organizations across all three sectors working together, with the notable example of the Nebraska National Guard working with Food Bank of the Heartland to partake in drive-through food banks, dispersing food in a socially distanced manner. Due to the pandemic, there was a lack of volunteers and the Guard filled in this gap for several weeks (Hammel and Stodard, 2020; Liewer, 2020; Reed, 2020).

Food Bank/Pantry Response to Food Insecurity

Due to the high volume of food banks and pantries discussed in the articles, they were coded separately from other nonprofit organizations. This was also done because of the nature of their mission, meaning they were expected to have been a large part of the response in comparison to many other nonprofits adjusting their work to address the growing need. Unsurprisingly, this was the most common theme coded, with twenty-nine of the fifty articles discussing the response of food banks and pantries. A key food bank that was repeatedly discussed in the articles was Food Bank of the Heartland. Out of the total twenty-nine articles discussing food banks and pantries responding to the shutdowns, eighteen discussed response related actions of this food bank. Another important finding to note was the interconnectedness of this theme to that of the food supply chain and the changing dynamics of how these organizations would gain access to the food they provided to those who needed it. For example, private donations dropped drastically when the shutdowns began (Stewart(a), 2020; Lee, 2020).

Mention of Fear

Due to the nature of the 2020 economic shutdowns and spread of COVID-19, it was appropriate to account for the emotional reality of those experiencing these events in the Omaha area. This theme was only coded when fear was directly discussed, with eight out of the fifty total articles being included in this theme. An example of fear in the Omaha area directly mentioned was that of the food service workers and their fear of going to work as essential workers (La Monica, 2020). With the uncertainty gripping the world at the beginning of the pandemic, it is unsurprising that reporters could not abstain from remarking on the fear their community members and interviewees directly discussed. This theme assists in providing social context to the coded text.

Food Supply Chain

The food supply chain as a theme included articles that discussed the disruption of the greater food chain in the United States: how food grown and processed, and how it makes its way to grocery stores and restaurants in order to feed the nation. Out of the fifty articles, thirteen discussed impacts on the food supply chain from the economic shutdowns. There were a few major events that were present in these articles, including the spread of the virus in meat-packing plants that would impact the production and distribution of meat throughout the nation (Duffy and Stodard, 2020).

Food Industry Workers and Providers Impacts

The food industry impacts theme closely and relates to the food supply chain, yet with the distinction of specificity to the working conditions of food service workers and the impacts on the private businesses in this industry, such as restaurants and bars. While many of these articles were included in the food supply thematic category, it was decided that there needed to be a separate account for the experiences of the individual industry workers and their employing businesses. Key issues discussed under this theme in the articles included general safety of food service workers (restaurants, grocery stores, food production plants, etc.) and empty shelves at local grocery stores in the early months of the forced economic closures (Azizah, 2020). In total, eleven out of fifteen articles were coded under this theme.

DISCUSSION

As it has been reiterated, the implications of the economic shutdowns that took place due to the Coronavirus pandemic of 2020 have yet to be fully understood. This small qualitative case study and content analysis has only touched on a fraction of the larger story: the experience of food insecurity in Omaha, Nebraska, and nearby area between the months of March and July 2020. Lessons learned from this experience may, however, assist in preparing other communities for future quick onset economic crises. As we become more interconnected, we must understand that this is unlikely to be the last global pandemic, nor assume that the COVID-19 experience is the worst-case scenario possible for the global community.

There are three key points to draw from this research. The first relates to understanding of the term "vulnerable populations." Instead of viewing communities either vulnerable or not due to their demographics alone is not an effective way to conceptualize vulnerability (MacNabb and Fletcher, 2019). Groups that lie somewhere in between the "most" and "least" vulnerable, those who perhaps live paycheck to paycheck but live above the poverty line and typically make ends meet relatively well are an under looked demographic when planning for community crisis and disaster impacts. This dynamic was well outlined throughout the Omaha World Herald articles in this study. Panic buying taking place by those less economically impacted by the shutdowns and the greater effect of this behavior on the food supply chain made it difficult for individuals living paycheck to paycheck, but not necessarily meeting the requirements for government assistance, to access food. However, this work takes this concept of economic vulnerability much further, as it was found that those who were making high wages leading up the economic shutdowns found themselves without work and wages almost overnight, even those with high-level professional jobs. While there are positive impacts to having high-paying jobs in this scenario (e.g., they are likely to have more saved) this nuance to the previous understanding of what it means to be economically vulnerable to disasters and crises must be further investigated in future research, especially relating to economic closures. The shutdowns have changed the playing field for what it means to be economically vulnerable in the United States in a way that past, or more "traditional" disasters have not exacerbated.

A second key point is the lack of preparedness by food-related organizations across all sectors. The closest example to the type of response undertaken for the rapid growth of food insecurity was school lunch programs meant to provide food insecure children meals during the summer months. However, these programs and the organizations conducting them were not prepared with little notice to provide such services for extended periods and additional families. This hit to the food system was not something that the system was easily able to bear, nor was it prepared to carry. There were also issues encountered by the organizational response relating to the virus itself, such as providing services while maintaining social distancing. However, the organizations and programs were able to quickly adapt to these concerns, conducting drive through food banks. Finally, there were also concerns relating to the food supply chain. Not only were the typical streams of donations (private donors) less able to donate food (while demand was skyrocketing), but the food processing plants were also shutting down or operating at limited capacities due to the spread of the virus. Thus, even though the organizations attempting to obtain food to disperse to those who needed it had the funds to do so, there was less food available to purchase, and they were competing with other organizations and private businesses for it. The systems responding to the food security crisis experienced here need much more research to fully understand the true implications and lessons learned (or not learned).

The last point is the importance of the nonprofit and public sectors during the response to food insecurity caused by the economic shutdowns, especially during early months. Private-public partnerships play well-established roles in disaster response, but the dynamics in this case have proven much more complex than what previous research has pointed to. As previously mentioned, many of the private donors (including individuals and businesses) were unable to donate food to food banks and pantries. The private sector is an important part of the everyday response to food insecurity and disasters, and it was largely disabled in order to slow the spread of the virus. While there were examples of private entities donating and helping where they could, the bulk of the response landed largely on the shoulders of the public and even more so, on those of the nonprofit sector. However, even though the nonprofit sector pulled the most weight in tackling the food insecurity fallout from this crisis in this case study, the collaboration that took place between organizations and entities from all three sectors was key. This leads to one of the most important anecdotes this research provides: in an economic crisis brought on with little warning, where fear is perhaps one of the few things that all have in common, the response to help communities must consist of all three sectors in order to address the ever-changing reality of a global pandemic.

REFERENCES

Azizah, Mia. "Ricketts: Food supply chain is secure, suppliers and stores just need time to restock." Omaha World Herald. March 13, 2020.

Barrett, Christopher B. "Measuring food insecurity." *Science* 327, no. 5967 (2010): 825–828.

Bengtsson, Mariette. "How to plan and perform a qualitative study using content analysis." *Nursing Plus Open* 2 (2016): 8–14.

Boin, Arjen, Celesta Kofman-Bos, and Werner Overdijk. "Crisis simulations: Exploring tomorrow's vulnerabilities and threats." *Simulation & Gaming* 35, no. 3 (2004): 378–393.

Boin, Arjen, and Paul 't Hart. "The crisis approach." In *Handbook of disaster research*, pp. 42–54. Springer, New York, NY, 2007.

Coleman-Jensen, Alisha., Matthew P., Rabbitt, Christian, A., Gregory, and Anita, Singh. "Household Food Security in the United States in 2018." *USDA-ERS Economic Research Report* 270 (2019).

Collins, J. (2020, April 1). "April 1, rent's due: Many struggle to pay in virus outbreak." Omaha World Herald.

Duffy, Erin; Stodard, Martha. "'This is not good': COVID-19 cases surge in Grand Island area; 10 beef plant workers among the ill." Omaha World Herald. April 3, 2020.

Erlingsson, Christen, and Petra Brysiewicz. "A hands-on guide to doing content analysis." *African Journal of Emergency Medicine* 7, no. 3 (2017): 93–99.

Graneheim, Ulla H., Britt-Marie Lindgren, and Berit Lundman. "Methodological challenges in qualitative content analysis: A discussion paper." *Nurse education today* 56 (2017): 29–34.

Gundersen, Craig, Monica, Hake, Adam, Dewey, and Emily, Engelhard. "The Impact of the Coronavirus on Food Insecurity v1" [Data file and FAQ] (2020). Available from Feeding America: research@feedingamerica.org.

Hake, Monica, Emily, Engelhard, Adam, Dewey, and Craig, Gundersen. "The Impact of the Coronavirus on Food Insecurity" [Brief series] (2020). Available from Feeding America: https://www.feedingamerica.org/research/coronavirus-hunger-research.

Hammel, Paul; Stodard, Martha. "Nebraska National Guard's coronavirus response tops that of 2019 floods." Omaha World Herald. May 6, 2020.

Hilgenkamp, B. (2020, April 1). Financial fallout from coronavirus could hit hard in April, advocates say. Omaha World Herald.

Karst, Sierra. "Coronavirus updates: Change to marriage license process; Nebraska Beef gives products to food bank." Omaha World Herald. March 28, 2020.

La monica, Paul R. "The coronavirus economic 'disaster' scenario: Stagflation." Omaha World Herald. March 10, 2020.

Lee, Lauren. "With coronavirus closing schools, here's how you can help food insecure children." Omaha World Herald. March 19, 2020.

Liewer, Steve. "In Nebraska and Iowa, coronavirus is National Guard's biggest emergency response in years." Omaha World Herald. May 30, 2020.

MacNabb, Emily, and B. J. Fletcher. "Hurricanes, disasters, and food insecurity: The intersection of two social events." In *Emerging Voices in Natural Hazards Research*, pp. 121–144. Butterworth-Heinemann, 2019.

McCann, Dan. "The Life House is a dual force in critical time of need for diapers and food." Omaha World Herald. March 22, 2020.

McIntyre, Lynn. "Food security: more than a determinant of health." *Policy Options Montreal* 24, no. 3 (2003): 46–51.

McMichael, Philip. "Conclusion: The Food Sovereignty Lens" *Globalization and food sovereignty: Global and local change in new politics of food.* Toronto, Canada: University of Toronto Press, 2014.

Nolan, Michelle, Glenys Rikard-Bell, Mohammed Mohsin, and Mandy Williams. "Food insecurity in three socially disadvantaged localities in Sydney, Australia." *Health Promotion Journal of Australia* 17, no. 3 (2006): 247–253.

Peek, Lori, and Laura M. Stough. "Children with disabilities in the context of disaster: A social vulnerability perspective." *Child development* 81, no. 4 (2010): 1260–1270.

Perry, Marcia. "Natural disaster management planning." *International Journal of Physical Distribution & Logistics Management* (2007).

Phillips, Brenda D., Thomas A. Wikle, Angela Head Hakim, and Lynn Pike. "Establishing and operating shelters after Hurricane Katrina." *International Journal of Emergency Management* 8, no. 2 (2012): 153–167.

Phillips, Brenda D. *Disaster recovery.* CRC press, 2015.

Quarantelli, Enrico L. "What is disaster? The need for clarification in definition and conceptualization in research." *Disasters and Mental Health: Selected* 10 (1985): 41–73.

Quarantelli, Enrico L. "Catastrophes are different from disasters: Some implications for crisis planning and managing drawn from Katrina." In *Online forum and essays]–Social Science Research Council.* 2005.

Reed, Anna. "Editorial: Food insecurity burdens many Midlands households. These efforts are helping." Omaha World Herald. July 2, 2020.

Shi, Leiyu. *Introduction to health policy.* Chicago, IL: Health Administration Press (2014).

Stewart, Kelsey (a). "Food Bank for the Heartland Working to Help Struggling Families during Coronavirus Outbreak." Omaha World Herald. March 16, 2020.

Stewart, Kelsey (b). "Omaha-area McDonald's owner-operators donate more than 6,000 beef patties, other items to food bank." Omaha World Herald. April 21, 2020.

Timmer, C. Peter. "Behavioral dimensions of food security." *Proceedings of the National Academy of Sciences* 109, no. 31 (2012): 12315–12320.

Timmer, C. Peter. *Food security and scarcity: why ending hunger is so hard.* University of Pennsylvania Press, 2015.

Wicks, Rosemary, Lyndal J. Trevena, and Susan Quine. "Experiences of food insecurity among urban soup kitchen consumers: insights for improving nutrition and well-being." *Journal of the American Dietetic Association* 106, no. 6 (2006): 921–924.

Wilkinson, Richard G., and Michael Marmot, eds. *Social determinants of health: the solid facts.* World Health Organization, 2003.

Section VI

CONCLUSION

Conclusion

Connecting Food Systems and Public Administration: Key Takeaways and Future Research

A. Bryce Hoflund, John C. Jones, and Michelle C. Pautz

This volume represents one of the first attempts to compile research that focuses on food issues using a public administration lens. The studies included here are reflective not only of the methodological diversity inherent in public administration research but also the substantive areas within public administration that intersect with the study of food, such as budgeting, regulation, policy, and emergency management. Within each of those substantive areas, the chapters demonstrate a remarkable diversity in terms of topics and include research about SNAP calculations, crop insurance, the Farm Bill, taxes, food labelling, seed libraries, food insecurity, and so forth. In addition to the breadth of topics covered by the authors here, it is also worth pointing out the sheer number of chapters, often authored by groups of scholars and practitioners, demonstrating the interest in this subject across disciplinary lines. We offer this brief conclusion to highlight what these chapters demonstrate about the intersection of food policy and politics and public administration and explore some avenues for future research.

KEY TAKEAWAYS

These chapters highlight four important takeaways for public administration scholars and practitioners working in the realm of food policy and politics. The first takeaway is that since public administration as a field is inherently interdisciplinary and steeped in multidisciplinary perspectives, it offers a common language to talk about important issues related to food systems. The language of public administration can be used as a vehicle to connect those in different disciplines who are working on important food issues. In food systems research, there is often a disconnect between the scientific and technical aspects of food production, distribution, and consumption and the political and administrative underpinnings of the system. This disconnect is problematic because of the lack of acknowledgment of the multiple aspects—or even worse the treatment of the other aspects as a "black box"—hinders efforts to advance our understanding. Public administration provides a natural connection to analyze aspects as part of a larger system and allows scholars and practitioners to integrate all of those aspects to advance understanding. The chapters here demonstrate the ability to integrate the politics, the policy, and the technical and provide a more cohesive and comprehensive way to view, and perhaps advance, food studies.

The second takeaway from the chapters in this volume is that many of them highlight and consider the roles of a range of stakeholders involved in food policy. Food policy issues encompass so many dimensions and systems that the range of stakeholders involved is massive. Yet, too often, acknowledging and understanding myriad stakeholders, and their roles is difficult. These chapters help us acknowledge, integrate, and comprehend the stakeholders that are involved in food production, distribution, and consumption. Although it can be daunting to grasp the range of stakeholders and their roles, we must because of their effects on the policies that are developed and implemented in this area. Public administration provides opportunities to ensure that those stakeholders are incorporated into research and discussion.

The third takeaway is derived from and related to the previous two points. The chapters in this volume indicate that food systems and policy research is concerned with some of the same central questions that are at the heart of public administration, such as concerns about ensuring equity, allocating resources, addressing social justice issues, tackling inequality, helping vulnerable populations, among others. Over the last few decades, we have witnessed a changing role for public administration from one of working in silos to address pressing public problems to one that is more collaborative in nature. In particular, the chapters show that responses to the so-called "wicked problems" that plague the field and the development of solutions to these problems can come from different areas of the field collaborating with those working outside the field. This returns us to the point that we made earlier—that the range of roles stakeholders play in food policy is actually more profound than it might appear at first glance. For example, several of the chapters discuss and examine aspects of the historical development of the existing U.S. food system. These articles highlight the importance of creating a food system that is sustainable and equitable, nimble in terms of responding to governance and policy challenges, and representative of a diversity of perspectives in addressing challenges and creating solutions.

Finally, these chapters lend further evidence to dispel the politics/administration dichotomy that has often framed the discussion of topics in the field since its founding. These chapters demonstrate that the politics/administration dichotomy does not, and perhaps more importantly, should not, exist in the realm of food studies. Whether we are seeking to understand the development of nutrition labelling, incentives in crop insurance or the National School Lunch Program, or the creation of the farm bill each cycle, these chapters reinforce the necessity of a melding of politics and administration.

FUTURE RESEARCH

As we mentioned earlier, this work represents one of the first attempts to organize a volume that speaks to the intersection of public administration and food policy. This area is ripe for future exploration and, in this section, we present some ideas for future research. While this is by no means an exhaustive list, we tried to identify some substantive policy areas that need to be explored as well as theoretical questions that might be relevant to both scholars and practitioners.

Food issues cut across and impact a number of administration, management, and policy areas. The chapters in this volume highlight how food issues play out in terms of budgeting, policy, regulation, and emergency management and explore issues related to school lunches, food insecurity, labeling, among others. The chapters also demonstrate that there is no shortage of research to be done in any of these areas. Although this is a good start, it is only the tip of the iceberg. More work needs to be done that explores how food policy impacts issues such as climate change and the environment, food production, distribution, and consumption, individual and community health, zoning and planning, among others. Within these areas, there is also a need for comparative research, both domestically and internationally.

Beyond the chapters included in this volume, we see food systems and policy research as a viable vehicle for exploring important theoretical questions in the field of public administration. We see potential in at least five areas. First, there is a need to reconsider the role of the administrative state in this conversation. The chapters here illustrate a movement away from a top-down approach toward a more collaborative approach in which public administration is but one stakeholder. In a complex, global, multisectoral food system that cuts across so many areas of our lives from the environment to our health, this highlights the importance of understanding how collaboration works in such an environment. Simultaneously, food systems also can encompass hyper-local environments. Collaboration can take many forms, but we know from anecdotal experience that more research is needed that examines, for example, how health systems identify food insecure individuals and then connect those individuals to resources in their communities.

Second, we argue that there needs to be more research focused on the ethical questions and social justice concerns related to food systems in order to design policies and programs that are effective and equitable. This research could focus on, among other things, the discussion of food as a human right, as well as how race and ethnicity affect how individuals interface with different aspects of the food system. The normative foundations of public administration are well suited for this endeavor and public administration does not sidestep these essential ethical dimensions.

Third, there are also abundant opportunities to conduct policy advocacy research to determine how sharing stories and narratives around the nuance between hunger and food insecurity might change the stigma associated with each social problem and, ultimately, how public policies attempt to respond to those problems. Too often these conversations are marginalized and acknowledging these narratives is an important first step. Public policy research is the foundation for public policy advocacy, and again, public administration calls attention to these critical issues. For example, many higher education institutions around the United States are beginning to examine how hunger and food insecurity negatively impacts the achievement potential of their students. Colleges and universities are prime examples of larger public bureaucracies that can serve as test beds for outside of the box responses to these problems.

Fourth, additional research is needed that explores how different populations are affected by issues such as food insecurity. For example, while we have a good understanding of how food insecurity affects children, more research is needed to determine how different populations, such as the working poor, college students, LGBTQ communities, Hispanic communities, and Black communities, experience and are affected by this and other food-related issues.

Finally, the framework of the regulatory structure in the nation drives food policy and systems, yet the regulation surrounding food—its production, transportation, distribution, and consumption—is not heavily investigated, and where it is explored, it is often mired in disciplinary silos. As the pages of this volume reveal, the regulatory state helps explain some of the peculiarities of our food systems and more work remains. The labyrinth of regulations related to food is an area ripe for study, as well as in a comparative context.

We received more than twenty-five proposals in response to our original call for papers. While all of them were viable papers, we had to pare them down to the fourteen chapters contained in this volume. We argue that the sheer number of papers and topics demonstrates that food issues should no longer be a neglected area within public administration. In addition, in a field such as public administration in which the idea of "praxis"—being able to connect ideas with practice—lies at its very heart, there needs to be a conscious connection to practice in both the substantive and theoretical areas. As such, future work in this area needs to be accessible and approachable to a wide range of audiences. This is particularly important in terms of understanding what is happening on the front lines with regard to food systems and food policy work and using that to prepare the next generation of practitioners and activists who will be undertaking important food systems work in our communities. The chapters in this volume represent our initial call to action and demonstrate why using the language of public administration to discuss food issues is so important.

Index

About the Editors

A. Bryce Hoflund, PhD, is an associate professor and the Blue Cross Blue Shield of Nebraska Chair of Health Care Administration and Policy in the School of Public Administration at the University of Nebraska at Omaha. Her research focuses on food policy and food safety regulation, health policy and health care regulation, network organizations, and network management and leadership. She has published her work in *Regulation & Governance, Administration & Society,* the *Journal of Health and Human Services Administration, Public Organization Review, Political Science Quarterly,* and *Food Studies: An Interdisciplinary Journal.* In addition to serving as an editor for this volume, she served as a coeditor with Michelle C. Pautz and John C. Jones for *The Intersection of Food and Public Health: Current Policy Challenges and Solutions* which was published by Routledge in 2018. She holds a PhD in public administration from the Center for Public Administration and Policy at Virginia Tech, an MPA from Florida State University, and a BA in political science with a minor in public administration from American University.

John C. Jones, PhD, is an assistant professor in the Center for Environmental Studies and a funded faculty member of Institute of Inclusion, Inquiry, and Innovation (iCubed) at Virginia Commonwealth University in Richmond, Virginia. His main research interests surround the intersection of urban food system development, local governance, and the challenges facing America's postindustrial cities in a globalizing world. He draws upon his practitioner experience in government and politics at the local and state levels in Ohio and New Jersey to inform his work. His scholarship is available to the public through his website www.cultivatingcities.com. He holds a PhD in Urban

Systems from Rutgers University and the New Jersey Institute of Technology as well as a MPA and a BA in political science from the University of Dayton.

Michelle C. Pautz, PhD, is a professor of political science and assistant provost for the Common Academic Program at the University of Dayton. Her research largely focuses on two areas: the implementation of environmental regulation, particularly at the state level, and the portrayal of bureaucracy and bureaucrats in contemporary American cinema and its effects on audiences. She has published more than two dozen articles in journals ranging from *Administration & Society, Policy Studies Journal, and Review of Policy Research* to *Public Voices, PS: Political Science & Politics,* and *Journal of Political Science Education.* She has published seven books, including *Civil Servants on the Silver Screen: Hollywood's Depiction of Government and Bureaucrats, The Lilliputians of Environmental Regulation: The Perspective of State Regulators* (with Sara R. Rinfret), *US Environmental Policy in Action* (now in its second edition, also with Sara R. Rinfret), and *Public Policy: A Concise Introduction* (with Sara R. Rinfret and Denise Scheberle). She holds a PhD in public administration and a MPA from Virginia Tech and a BA in economics, political science, and public administration from Elon University.

About the Contributors

Nurcan Atalan-Helicke, PhD, is an associate professor of Environmental Studies and Sciences Program at Skidmore College in Saratoga Springs, NY. She works on food systems and sustainability particularly conservation of agricultural biodiversity, genetically modified food, and Islam. She has been working with small farmers and other stakeholders engaged in sustainable farming systems in Turkey and northeast United States. She teaches a civic engagement course, and works with community organizations in Saratoga Springs, NY. Her research has been published in interdisciplinary journals, including *Agriculture and Human Values, Gastronomica, Global Environmental Politics, Journal of Environmental Studies and Studies, and Sociology of Islam.*

Angela Babb, PhD, is an assistant research scientist in the Ostrom Workshop at Indiana University (IU). As a critical human geographer, Babb researches the political economy of food with a focus on food justice and nutrition assistance policy. She collaborates primarily with the IU Sustainable Food Systems Science working group on various projects, including an examination of the Supplemental Nutrition Assistance Program (SNAP) application process, and an investigation into food insecurity among older adults in rural Indiana. Babb is cofounder and current director of the Critical Food Studies Lab, a joint initiative of the IU Food Institute and the IU Department of Geography. Drawing on her background in mathematics and geography, Babb's primary research focus is the current calculation of SNAP benefits and the development of an alternative calculation that promotes food justice and health equity.

Jodi Benenson, PhD, is an assistant professor in the School of Public Administration at the University of Nebraska at Omaha. She conducts research at the intersection of nonprofit organizations and public policy, with a particular emphasis on youth civic engagement, voting, nonprofit advocacy, national service, service-learning, and social and economic mobility. She also serves as the Academic Director for the Young Southeast Asian Leaders Initiative (YSEALI) on Civic Engagement through the U.S. Department of State. Jodi received a BS and MPA from Indiana University and a PhD in social policy from the Heller School for Social Policy and Management at Brandeis University.

Brent Blevins, MPA, is a senior policy advisor for the U.S. House Committee on Science, Space, and Technology. He has more than a decade of experience on Capitol Hill, serving as subcommittee staff director and senior professional staff for the U.S. House Committee on Agriculture and senior professional staff for the U.S. House Committee on Natural Resources. Additionally, he served as a legislative assistant for U.S. Senate Majority Whip John Cornyn and U.S. Senator Luther Strange. While working on Capitol Hill, Brent had the opportunity to work on the 2014 and 2018 Farm Bills, among other pieces of legislation. Brent is a native of southwest Virginia and received a BA in history, a BA in political science, and a master of public administration from Virginia Tech.

Can Chen, PhD, is an assistant professor in the Department of Public Policy and Public Administration at Florida International University. His research areas include state and local infrastructure finance, fiscal transparency, and disaster finance. He has published widely in the leading public budgeting and finance and public management journals.

Carol Ebdon, PhD, is a professor in the School of Public Administration at the University of Nebraska at Omaha. Her research interests are primarily in the area of local government budgeting and financial management, such as public participation in the budgeting process, capital management, and alternative service delivery. She previously served as the Director of Finance for the City of Omaha, Nebraska, and the Director of Accounting for the City of Rochester, New York.

Rachel Emas, PhD, is an assistant teaching professor and MPA program director at the School of Public Affairs and Administration (SPAA) at Rutgers University-Newark. Dr. Emas has earned a National Certificate in Effective Teaching Practices from the American Council of University Educators and is currently completing a micro-credential in Creating an Inclusive Online

Learning Environment. In the Greater Newark community, she is heavily engaged in sustainability and urban local food systems. Dr. Emas works closely with the City of East Orange and the East Orange Sustainable Food Alliance in developing a framework for the creation of a local community food system. She also serves on the Food and Fitness Impact Team of Believe in a Healthy Newark, as well as several other sustainability and environmental advocacy committees in the City of Newark. From classroom and community, Dr. Emas works toward equity, accountability, and engagement.

Erin Feichtinger, PhD, is the director of Policy and Advocacy at Together, focusing on the policy areas of affordable housing, food security, and economic stability. She has worked on successful legislation at the state level including expanding tenant protections, and at the local level on Omaha's Rental Registration and Proactive Inspection Ordinance. Her work includes developing a broad coalition of advocacy partners and empowering community members to use their voice for positive change. Dr. Feichtinger received her bachelor's degree in Special Education and her PhD in Transnational Urban History from Loyola University Chicago.

Sheila Fleischhacker, PhD, J.D., R.D.N., is an adjunct professor of law at Georgetown University where she teaches a first-of-its-kind nutrition law and policy course and coteaches a unique course on the first 1,000 days of life. She is developing a course book that synthesizes key law and policy approaches from historical and contemporary perspectives across the globe to improving healthy eating and reducing nutrition-related noncommunicable diseases and food insecurity. As founder and president of Fly Health, LLC, she provides public health law research consulting services; a recent example is a report on the rationale and options to strengthen national nutrition research, which has secured support of 70+ organizations. She cofounded and cochairs a Healthy Eating Research (HER) and CDC-supported Nutrition and Obesity Policy Research and Evaluation Network (NOPREN) ad hoc COVID-19 working group that has grown to 400+ members, collaborates with more than forty organizations, and has published more than fifteen papers. Previously, she was the senior advisor of nutrition and food safety at the United States Department of Agriculture (USDA) Office of the Chief Scientist (2017–2018), on detail from the National Institutes of Health (2012–2018). During her federal service, she helped put forth the first-of-its kind National Nutrition Research Roadmap and chaired a USDA Inter-Departmental Nutrition Workshop Series. Dr. Fleischhacker received her bachelor's degree in 2000 and J.D. in 2007, with a Certificate in Health Law from Loyola University Chicago and PhD in Integrative Biosciences/Nutritional Sciences from The Pennsylvania State University in 2004.

B. J. Fletcher, PhD, received his PhD from the School of Public Administration at the University of Nebraska at Omaha. His research interests focus on public policy, food policy, and comparative policy, in particular, on food security and poverty in the United States and internationally. His research also focuses on socially vulnerable populations in the urban context around issues of social policy, public administration ethics, and emergency management and food security. He is also interested in research methodologies in public administration and public policy, focusing on phenomenology as an approach to understanding lived experiences and the role of social construction of identity in policy design.

Xaq Frohlich, PhD, is an assistant professor of history of technology at Auburn University. His research focuses on the intersection of science, law, and markets, and how the three have shaped our modern, everyday understanding of food, risk, and responsibility. He is currently completing a book, *From Label to Table: Regulating Food in the Information Age*, which explores the history of efforts by the U.S. Food and Drug Administration to manage food markets and health risk through the regulation of food standards and informative labels.

Clarivel Gonzalez, BA, is both a bilingual administrative assistant at a law firm and a tenant relations manager at a Property Management office. She is passionate about serving the Spanish speaking community and providing them with the best services possible. She is currently working on obtaining her master's degree in Christian Leadership. As wife and a soon-to-be mother she hopes to spread the Gospel of Jesus Christ to not only her children but the entire world.

Michael Haedicke. PhD, is an associate professor of sociology at the University of Maine. His scholarship examines how concerns about sustainability become institutionalized in markets and public policy arenas, with a particular interest in agrofood systems. He is the author of *Organizing Organic*, a book-length study of the U.S. organic foods industry and has also published his research in a variety of sociological journals and edited volumes. As a public sociologist, he has also authored op-eds and regularly participates in community meetings and interviews with the media.

Carina Isbell is a master's student in community development and applied economics at the University of Vermont. Her interests include the maintenance of natural resources critical to the long-term sustainability of agriculture and the values underlying farmers' decisions to engage in conservation. Her current research focuses on the social aspects of local seed systems in the northeastern

United States. Her past works includes a focus on crop diversity, conservation, and food access and justice for migrant farmworkers in Vermont.

Jake Jacobs, BS, is the Crop Insurance Education Coordinator for the Agricultural Risk Management and Crop Insurance Education Program at the University of Vermont. In this role she provides comprehensive information to producers about the risk management strategies available to them, with a focus on the federal risk management programs. Prior to working for the University of Vermont, Jake worked as a dairy nutrition and management consultant and spent many years working with high-needs children as an early childhood educator.

Kristal Jones, PhD, is a coowner and principal researcher at JG Research & Evaluation, an applied research firm focused on food systems, public health, and rural development. Her research focuses on the human drivers and impacts of agri-food system change, and utilizes mixed methodologies to gather, analyze, and interpret data. She previously spent several years as a research scientist at the National Socio-Environmental Synthesis Center (SESYNC) at the University of Maryland. There she focused on developing training programs for interdisciplinary data-drive team science, and developed research programs focused on the food-energy-water nexus and the environmental dynamics of food systems.

Carolyn Lois is currently a student in the Didactic Program in Dietetics at Simmons University in pursuit of becoming a licensed registered dietitian. She received her MS in food policy and applied nutrition from the Tufts Friedman School of Nutrition Science and Policy and a Bachelor of Arts in Environmental Studies from Skidmore College. She has witnessed the healing power of making and eating food as a way to connect with others and to oneself. Formerly, with dreams of becoming the next "Farmer Jane," she now looks forward to helping people heal their relationship with food in the clinical setting—and gardening on the weekends.

Craig S. Maher, PhD, is director of the School of Public Administration at the University of Nebraska at Omaha and the Nebraska State and Local Finance Lab. He teaches undergraduate and graduate-level courses in public budgeting, financial management, research methods, and Capstone. His primary research interests are in the areas of public financial management with emphases in revenue policy, fiscal federalism, and fiscal condition analysis. In 2017 and 2013, Dr. Maher was recipient of article of the awards from the *Journal of Public and Nonprofit Affairs* and Association of Government Accountants, respectively.

Emily MacNabb is a PhD candidate in public administration and emergency management in the School of Public Administration at the University of Nebraska at Omaha with experience in researching and teaching about hazards and disasters in a complicated social environment. Her mission is focused on reducing risks to those most vulnerable and to create more equitable disaster preparedness, response, recovery, and mitigation initiatives. She was born and raised in Omaha, Nebraska, and completed her bachelor's and master's degrees in political science and international relations at the University of Nebraska at Omaha. She completed a year and a half of her undergraduate degree at the University of Haifa in Israel studying middle east policy and counter terrorism. Emily is currently completing her PhD dissertation, researching the perceptions of different social groups regarding both their governments ability and willingness to respond to disaster scenarios. Emily also has experience in the nonprofit sector as well, working for both the Anti-Defamation League and the Omaha-based RESPECT program. Along with her background working in university and nonprofit environments, she has utilized her educational background in lobbying on Capitol Hill regarding a variety of U.S.-Middle East policy issues.

Helen Mebrate, PhD, currently works as a programme manager at Breaking Barriers, a London-based nonprofit helping refugees to acquire the knowledge, confidence, and experience to obtain stable and fulfilling employment. Prior to this, Helen worked in various nonprofit organizations in the United Kingdom. Helen holds a master's degree in environment, development, and politics from the School of Oriental and African Studies (SOAS) and a bachelor's degree in environmental studies from Skidmore College.

Sungho Park, PhD, is an assistant professor of Public Policy and Administration at the Department of Political Science, University of Alabama. His research interests are in public budgeting and financial management and include state and local fiscal condition, fiscal rules and institutions, government accounting and financial reporting, budget reform, and economic development financing. His research has appeared in the *American Review of Public Administration, Public Budgeting and Finance, Public Finance and Management, Journal of Public Budgeting, Accounting and Financial Management, State and Local Government Review, Public Administration Quarterly, Public Policy and Administration*, and other journals.

Laurie Ristino, Esq., is the founder and principal at Strategies for a Sustainable Future, which advises leading NGOs on policy and law strategies to improve food and agriculture systems to make them more resilient, sustainable, and equitable. She practiced law for twenty years, serving as a senior counsel at the USDA where she advised on an array of natural resource and environmental matters. More recently, she was appointed an associate law professor and the inaugural director of the Center for Agriculture and Food Systems at Vermont Law School. She is also a lecturer at Johns Hopkins University where she teaches a graduate course in environmental policy.

Amy Rosenthal received her PhD from the Edward J. Bloustein School of Planning and Public Policy at Rutgers University. Her contribution draws on her dissertation "'It should be healthy but it should be good': Student and Staff Perspectives on the National School Lunch Program." She is currently a social science research analyst with the U.S. Department of Agriculture Food and Nutrition Service. The findings and conclusions in this chapter are those of the author and should not be construed to represent any official USDA or U.S. government determination or policy.

Jennifer Geist Rutledge, PhD, is an associate professor of political science at John Jay College of Criminal Justice—CUNY. Her research generally focuses on food and agricultural policy and its overlap with welfare policy. Her book, *Feeding the Future: The Emergence of School Lunches as Global Social Policy* was published by Rutgers University Press in 2016 and presents a global history of school lunch programs. Her current research program is focused on food riots and their role in the development of the nation-state and welfare state, as well as the current implications of protest over food for state legitimacy and welfare. Her work is informed by theoretical approaches to public policy, as well as a commitment to the politics of rights and inequality.

Andrew J. Schneller, PhD, is an assistant professor of environmental studies and sciences program at Skidmore College in Saratoga Springs, NY. His research sites include Baja California Sur, Mexico, Uvita Costa Rica, and Upstate, NY, where he explores the outcomes of experiential environmental education, service learning, and volunteerism; civil society access to decision-making in developing nations and environmental justice communities; and innovative approaches to environmental communication to promote marine protection and public lands ecosystem restoration efforts. Selected publications include: For-profit environmental voluntourism in Costa Rica: Teen volunteer, host community, and environmental outcomes in the *Journal of Sustainable Tourism,* and Environmental Art in the Hudson River Watershed: Outcomes of Place-Based Experiential Environmental Education, in the journal *Applied Environmental Education and Communication.*

Danielle Smith, BA, is a research and evaluation specialist at Together, a social services provider in Omaha, Nebraska. Her research primarily deals with issues of housing quality and affordability and food insecurity, with the goal of understanding and promoting community needs in order to advance policy initiatives in the areas of housing justice and hunger. She obtained her Bachelor of Science in Community Health and Bachelor of Arts in Psychology from the State University of New York at Potsdam.

Daniel Tobin, PhD, is an assistant professor in the Department of Community Development and Applied Economics at the University of Vermont, where he is also affiliate faculty with the Food Systems Program and a Faculty Fellow in the Gund Institute for the Environment. His research focuses on sustainable production practices and risk management of small- and medium-farmers across the northeastern United States, the Andean region of South America, and East Africa. His teaching and outreach focus on issues of rural sustainable development and food system change.

Lightning Source UK Ltd.
Milton Keynes UK
UKHW022237020621
384823UK00002B/78